JAMES HALLIDAY'S
TOP 100
AUSTRALIAN
WINERIES

From vines to wines, histories to vintages

hardie grant books
MELBOURNE · LONDON

A short history

Wine has been continuously made in Australia for 190 years, and there are a number of family-owned companies with six generations directly involved in winemaking. It is often assumed that South Australia pioneered viticulture, but the first wine grapevines were planted in New South Wales in 1817–18, in Tasmania in 1823, then Western Australia in 1830, and finally in South Australia in 1837.

Australia's population in the first 60 years of the 19th century had many components. New South Wales and Tasmania received over 160 000 convicts from England; these were mainly people convicted of minor crimes, and sentenced to be deported to what was to become Australia, there to be used as slave (unpaid) labour for a period of years, some for the rest of their lives.

From the 1840s onwards South Australia received migrants from Silesia (part of modern-day Germany) who emigrated because of their religious beliefs, escaping persecution in their homeland. Many of these became grapegrowers and winemakers in the Barossa Valley, and their descendants still play a central role in winemaking and in the social life of the region.

The discovery of gold in Victoria in 1851 had a major impact on the economic and social fabric of the entire country, as the population rushed to the areas where gold was being mined. Here there was a large number of Chinese immigrants who helped dig the mines; when the gold ran out, many moved to Queensland to work in the sugarcane fields. Others established restaurants providing Chinese food in the capital cities, and continue in this role today.

Italians arrived in two waves, the first after World War I, the next after World War II. They have made a major contribution to the foundations of the 20th-century wine industry, as well as setting up almost as many Italian restaurants as there are Chinese.

Finally, the wine industry of the Swan Valley in Western Australia was built by immigrants from Dalmatia (part of modern-day Croatia), who arrived in Australia (and New Zealand) around the start of the 20th century.

The formation of the Commonwealth of Australia in 1901, the establishment of the vast irrigation systems on the Murray and Murrumbidgee rivers (Murray Darling and Riverina regions respectively), and World War I brought many changes in the economics of the wine industry.

While fortified wines were made alongside white and red table wines right from the outset of the 19th century, in the first half of the 20th century fortified wine accounted for over 90% of the total production. The Riverina and Murray Darling irrigation regions provided most of this wine, known as sherry (of which there are many types) and port (again, there are various types). Australia can no longer use those words for these wines, as a result of a bilateral wine agreement with the European Union, but – with a few notable exceptions – fortified wine now has little importance in Australia (it represents 1.6% of total production).

Over the second half of the 20th century the wine industry of today gradually took shape. Several milestones stand out. One was the creation in 1951 of Penfolds Grange (viewed by most as Australia's greatest wine, white or red). Another was the introduction, in 1953, of German technology in the making of white wines – temperature-controlled stainless steel tanks. Then there was a move to cooler regions from the traditional warm regions of the Hunter Valley in New South Wales, the Barossa Valley in South Australia, and the Swan Valley in Western Australia. Linked to this was the introduction of cool-climate grape varieties: chardonnay and sauvignon blanc (both white) and pinot noir and merlot (red). As at 2013, 144 grape varieties are grown in Australia on a commercial scale.

Up to the 1950s, semillon, riesling, shiraz and grenache had been the four most important grapes; cabernet sauvignon was known but only planted in small quantities. Shiraz and chardonnay are by far the most important varieties today, both planted in all regions, cool and hot, simply because they adapt so well to every type of climate and soil.

As at the 2012 vintage, the area and production of the most important red and white varieties were as follows:

White	Hectares	Tonnes	Red	Hectares	Tonnes
Chardonnay	25 491	374 249	Shiraz	42 012	379 925
Sauvignon Blanc	6927	86 711	Cabernet Sauvignon	25 879	220 954
Semillon	5632	80 224	Merlot	9286	127 201
Riesling	3893	30 349	Pinot Noir	4978	32 847

The other significant developments have been the world-famous and highly regarded Australian Wine Research Institute and numerous universities offering degrees in oenology and viticulture, headed by the University of Adelaide and Charles Sturt University.

Where did Australia's grapes come from?

While there have been importations of different grape varieties into Australia in the 19th, 20th and 21st centuries, by far the most important collection was that assembled by James Busby in 1831. A quite remarkable man, he was born in England in 1801, and had practical experience with agriculture in Ireland and Scotland. Intending to emigrate to New South Wales, he spent several months studying viticulture and winemaking in France in 1823-24. On arriving in New South Wales, he wrote and published two books on viticulture and winemaking, but then decided to return to Europe and systematically collect as many grape varieties as possible. He arrived in Cadiz, Spain, on 29 September 1831, and moved all the way north through Spain and France until he reached Champagne on 21 December 1831. He kept a daily diary in which he described precisely when and where he collected the key varieties – grenache from Rousillon, and shiraz/syrah from Hermitage, chardonnay and pinot noir from Clos Vougeot, and more chardonnay and pinot noir from Champagne. From the Luxembourg Garden in Paris he collected the Bordeaux varieties of cabernet sauvignon, petit verdot, malbec and carmenere (all red varieties) and sauvignon blanc and semillon.

He collected many other varieties from the Luxembourg Garden, from the Botanic Garden at Montpelier and elsewhere. In all, he collected 433 varieties, 362 of which survived the trip to Sydney. All of these vines were collected over 30 years before the arrival of phylloxera in France, which forced the replanting of all vineyards throughout Europe using grafted vines which were resistant to phylloxera. It is Australia's great good fortune that phylloxera has only ever attacked vineyards in parts of Victoria, leaving South Australia, New South Wales, Western Australia and Tasmania free of this parasite, which kills the vines by feeding on their roots.

The consequence is that Australia has the oldest shiraz vines (dating back to 1842 in the Barossa Valley and 1867 in the Hunter Valley) in the world, the oldest mourvedre (1853), the oldest pinot noir and pinot meunier (1866), the oldest cabernet sauvignon (1880), and possibly the oldest semillon and chardonnay (1908).

Location of regions

With the exception of two regions in Queensland, all Australian wine regions lie in a band 30°–40° south. Those of Western Australia occupy a tiny corner of the south-west of the state, and there is also a tiny corner in the south-east of South Australia. In New South Wales the regions run north–south along either side of the Great Dividing Range or are adjacent to the Murray River, which marks the southern border of the state with Victoria. The latter state breaks the pattern of all other states, with regions occupying over 80% of the surface area. Even Tasmania has viticulture restricted to its south, east and north coasts.

Australia has a land area of about 769 202 400ha, and its vineyard plantings are 148 509ha, 0.019% of the total area.

There are large areas with soils that are suitable for viticulture, but that are unlikely to be planted because there is insufficient rainfall, or inadequate access to surface water (lakes or rivers) or subterranean water.

Australia's Wine Regions – Geographical Indications

State/Zone	Region	Subregion
South Eastern Australia[1]		
South Australia		
Adelaide (Super Zone, includes Mount Lofty Ranges, Fleurieu and Barossa)		
Barossa	Barossa Valley	
	Eden Valley	High Eden
Far North	Southern Flinders Ranges	
Fleurieu	Currency Creek	
	Kangaroo Island	
	Langhorne Creek	
	McLaren Vale	
	Southern Fleurieu	
Limestone Coast	Coonawarra	
	Mount Benson	
	Mount Gambier	
	Padthaway	
	Robe	
	Wrattonbully	
Lower Murray	Riverland	
Mount Lofty Ranges	Adelaide Hills	Lenswood
		Piccadilly Valley
	Adelaide Plains	
	Clare Valley	
The Peninsulas		

New South Wales		
Big Rivers	Murray Darling[2]	
	Perricoota	
	Riverina	
	Swan Hill[2]	
Central Ranges	Cowra	
	Mudgee	
	Orange	
Hunter Valley	Hunter	Broke Fordwich
		Pokolbin
		Upper Hunter Valley
Northern Rivers	Hastings River	
Northern Slopes	New England Australia	
South Coast	Shoalhaven Coast	
	Southern Highlands	
Southern New South Wales	Canberra District	
	Gundagai	
	Hilltops	
	Tumbarumba	
Western Plains		
Western Australia		
Central Western Australia		
Eastern Plains – Inland and North of Western Australia		
Greater Perth	Peel	
	Perth Hills	
	Swan District	Swan Valley
South West Australia	Blackwood Valley	
	Geographe	
	Great Southern	Albany
		Denmark
		Frankland River
		Mount Barker
		Porongurup
	Manjimup	
	Margaret River	
	Pemberton	
West Australian South East Coastal		

Queensland		
	Granite Belt	
	South Burnett	
Victoria		
Central Victoria	Bendigo	
	Goulburn Valley	Nagambie Lakes
	Heathcote	
	Strathbogie Ranges	
	Upper Goulburn	
Gippsland		
North East Victoria	Alpine Valleys	
	Beechworth	
	Glenrowan	
	King Valley	
	Rutherglen	
North West Victoria	Murray Darling[2]	
	Swan Hill[2]	
Port Phillip	Geelong	
	Macedon Ranges	
	Mornington Peninsula	
	Sunbury	
	Yarra Valley	
Western Victoria	Grampians	Great Western
	Henty	
	Pyrenees	
Tasmania		
Northern Australia		
Australian Capital Territory		

1. The zone South Eastern Australia incorporates the whole of the states of NSW, Vic. and Tas. and only part of Qld and SA.
2. Murray Darling and Swan Hill are contained within the zones of Big Rivers (NSW) and North West Victoria (Vic.).

Terroir

Terroir is a French word which cannot be adequately translated into any single English word, simply because it covers a multitude of factors. Bruno Prats, the former proprietor of Chateau Cos d'Estournel in the Medoc, explained it thus:

> The very French notion of terroir looks at all the natural conditions which influence the biology of the vines and thus the composition of the grape itself. The terroir is the coming together of the climate, the soil, and the landscape. It is the combination of an infinite number of factors: temperatures by night and by day, rainfall distribution, hours of sunlight, slope and drainage, to name but a few. All these factors react with each other to form, in each part of the vineyard, what French wine growers call a terroir.

The late Peter Sichel, former president of the Grand Crus de Bordeaux, put it even more succinctly when he said, 'Terroir determines the character of a wine, man its quality.'

It lies at the heart of the French appellation system, itself built up by 1000 years of practical experience and observation. This system has led to a most precise and detailed delineation of quality, to the identification of a limited number of grape varieties considered to be especially suited to the terroir (and the climate) in a particular area, and to the exclusion by force of law of all others. It has led also to the prescription of pruning methods, and to the specification of maximum yields and of minimum alcoholic strengths (solved by the use of chaptalisation).

History shows that the vineyards of France were originally planted by default, in terroir which was too deficient to support other forms of horticulture or farming. In Bordeaux there is a saying: 'If these soils were not the best in the world, they would be the worst.' But that in no way diminishes the validity of the subsequent matching of grape and soil, nor of the identification of those microscopic dots on the face of the earth which produce wines of the ineffable majesty of Chateau Petrus (Bordeaux), Romanée-Conti and Le Montrachet (Burgundy) and their ilk.

Australian vignerons may be denied the extraordinary prestige and marketing power of the top French producers, but there are compensations: they are free of the rigidity and constraints of the appellation system, and can (and do) prove that fine wine can be made in a far wider range of circumstances than the French would ever admit.

It may well be that ignorance was bliss, but the average Australian vigneron of the recent past made little attempt to correlate specific soil types with particular grape varieties and, outside certain broad parameters, made almost no attempt to link soil type and quality. (Such linkage as did occur was between climate, variety and quality.) Those broad parameters define an ideal soil as a sandy loam, preferably interspersed with gravel or small, fragmented rock. It should be deep, free-draining and of low to moderate fertility. There should be no mineral element deficiencies and it should have sufficient water-holding capacity to supply enough moisture to the vines to prevent premature defoliation.

Correct moisture supply to the vine is all-important and, apart from anchorage and nutrients, is the principal function of soil in determining growth. During early shoot growth until flowering (early November to late December, depending on region and variety) vines should be well supplied with moisture. By the time the fruit starts to ripen (January to February) available water should tail off, causing vegetative growth to stabilise, and the vine to focus its attention on ripening the grapes by sugar accumulation. (The photosynthetic activity of the vine's leaves causes carbohydrates stored in the system to be converted to sugar in the grapes.)

All observers are agreed that the future of Australian winemaking lies in the vineyard, and, as a consequence, attitudes and practices are changing significantly. Cutting-edge technology is being used: airborne sensing via electromagnetic radiation (EMR) directed at the soil, the EMR device measuring the amount of energy reflected back. Together the radio wave emissions, radar and laser-imaging radar and near-infrared radiation data collected by the EMR device can provide detailed images of the soil structure (and vine growth and cropping levels) on areas as small as 100 square metres.

Airborne digital elevation mapping surveys have recently established that Coonawarra's famous terra rossa soils all occur at an elevation of 54–61 metres above sea level, the adjacent unsuitable black soils at an elevation of 50–53 metres. So, within 5 or 10 metres, and at an elevation (say) 2 metres lower, you can move from some of the greatest soils in Australia to some of the worst. While this is a near-unique example of terroir at work, the unhappy truth is that the boundaries of the Coonawarra GI, drawn by a court order after a long-running legal battle, are straight lines with no relationship to the red and black soil patterns.

The changes in attitude are also epitomised by the 'distinguished site' concept devised and promoted by Brian Croser. This can be applied both to existing vineyards and (equally importantly) to sites and soil being evaluated for their suitability for plantings. The soil may be physically examined by excavation on a grid pattern as small as 5 square metres. Overnight, a large company can acquire intimate knowledge of its plantings; Wynns Coonawarra Estate is one example of a large producer using these techniques to selectively harvest the crop and make replanting decisions.

To summarise, the supply of moisture – neither too much nor too little, and made available at the right times – is crucial for quality grapes. If the correct supply can be achieved naturally through the soil's moisture retention, so much the better. In France, for example, it is provided by the alluvial gravel and clay mix of Bordeaux, and the limestone marl (a mix of limestone and clay) of Burgundy. But in both Australia and France, identification of the best terroir (in the broadest sense of that term) is (or was) of paramount importance. In France, the search concluded centuries ago; in Australia, it has only just begun.

Climate

It will be obvious from the foregoing that French vignerons regard much of the impact of climate is inextricably involved in terroir. Their Australian and Californian counterparts turn the approach upside down: they argue that climate is the most important influence on the quality of grapes, without denying that in some instances the soil, subsoil and rock components of terroir are of equal importance (Coonawarra being a prime example).

The first concept to grasp is the difference between macro-climate (regional climate), meso-climate (site climate) and micro-climate (the immediate climate among rows and within a grapevine canopy), the last a much-misused word. So much depends on the topography of the region; if it is laser flat, the data may well be accepted at face value. But even there, the French notion of terroir comes into play: this encompasses both terrestrial and aerial factors. Thus Coonawarra has a largely homogenous climate (up to two weeks' difference in picking dates from north to south), but vines growing on the terra rossa (red soil) produce vastly superior cabernet sauvignon and shiraz to those on the sandy grey or (worse still) heavy black soils which, right or wrong, also fall within the official Coonawarra Geographic Indication (GI).

It is also important to understand what an important factor wind is in determining the ability of a region, an individual site and/or a particular vintage to produce grapes of a predictable quality or style. The easiest example to comprehend (if one has visited it) is California's Salinas Valley, followed closely by California's Carneros. Both of these are relatively flat (Salinas particularly) and the winds blow virtually every day through the growing season for a predictable period each day and in an absolutely inevitable direction. They effectively turn what would be warm growing conditions in the absence of wind into cool conditions.

Now take an area like the Yarra Valley in Victoria, with multiple hills of differing heights and sub-valleys facing variously every point of the compass. South-facing slopes are in principle the coolest, north-facing the warmest. The dominant wind, particularly when wind speed increases, is north or north-west. In some circumstances a sheltered south-west-facing slope may creep up on an exposed northeast-facing slope in terms of ripening capacity.

Nonetheless, for Australia climate is the most significant factor (outside vignerons' control) impinging on grape quality and wine style. As I have observed earlier, for the winemakers of France, soil is of greater importance.

Indeed, if one looks at Bordeaux and Burgundy, France's two greatest wine districts, and then focuses the microscope on their principal subregions, there is detailed discussion on the physical/terrestrial elements of terroir; by this I mean the soil profile from the surface to the subsoil. But in none of the books or atlases (including Hugh Johnson's great *The World Atlas of Wine*, first published in 1971, the 7th edition by Mitchell Beazley, 2013) is there any attempt to dissect or measure climate in the way Australian academics have so done.

It is true that spring frosts and summer hailstorms may hit one spot and miss another, and no less true that one château or grower may be more successful than his neighbour in one year but not the next. Even more so is it true that climatic swings from one vintage to the next are of crucial importance in shaping the quality (and to a lesser degree the character) of the wines of each vintage.

There is thus a fundamental distinction between climate and weather, and by their very nature these swings or changes cannot usefully be individually recorded; one inevitably has to take long-term averages in ascribing temperature, rainfall, humidity, wind, frost and whatever other data one wishes to use in presenting an overall picture of the macro-climate of a region. So it is understandable that the French tend to take macro-climate for granted, and to look to the soil and topographic components of terroir to explain and characterise their wines.

All of this in turn proceeds on patterns of classification and constraint which have been built up over many centuries, even if formal French codification did not start until the middle of the 19th century and only gained the force of law in the 20th century.

How different the position of the New World. There are effectively no constraints on which grape varieties you can plant, how you prune them or how you use and blend the wine you make from the grapes. Almost every one of the regions discussed in this book is of much larger scale and of more diverse topography than most of the regions of France: as well as Coonawarra, Padthaway, the Riverland in South Australia and the Riverina in New South Wales are topographic exceptions on the Australian front.

If this were not enough, Australia's experience in matching terroir, climate and grape varieties is, in some instances, and mainly in the cooler regions of Australia, less than 30 years old. Examples include (but are not limited to) Yarra Valley and Tasmanian Pinot Noir; Great Southern Riesling; Adelaide Hills Sauvignon Blanc; Heathcote (and other Central Victorian regions) Shiraz; Margaret River and Yarra Valley Chardonnay; and Tasmanian sparkling wine. The symbiotic link between Hunter Valley Semillon, Coonawarra Cabernet Sauvignon, Clare and Eden Valley Riesling and Barossa Valley Shiraz go back 100 years or more, but have only been brought into focus over the last 30–40 years. Moreover, each of these regions produces a multiplicity of other varieties, and none has exclusivity on its core variety.

So with such a complex matrix of grape variety, soil, aspect and topography within each Australian region (and each subregion) we have had little option but to come back to climate as the primary factor in determining wine character. In doing so the experts in Australasia and the United States have encountered great difficulties in providing climatic indices which are on the one hand sufficiently succinct to be understood and of practical use, and on the other meaningful and reasonably accurate.

Nonetheless, most attention has focused on temperature as being the most important aspect of climate in determining wine style. In 1944 the distinguished American oenologists Amerine and Winkler introduced a classification system which traces its roots back to 1735, and thence to the mid-19th-century observation by de Candolle that there is little vegetative growth in the vine at temperatures below 10°C (50°F). Their system has been refined (and criticised) by various commentators with a special interest in climate, but all agree that temperatures below 10°C should be disregarded in assessing what Amerine and Winkler called heat degree days (HDD).

The foremost Australian research academic, Dr John Gladstones, writes, 'Temperature is central to all aspects of viticulture ... it alone controls vine phenology, i.e. the vine's rate of physiological development through budbreak to flowering, setting, veraison, and finally fruit ripeness.' He goes on to provide a more accurate measure of climate with his concept (and calculation of) E° days, or biologically effective degree days at page 11 of his masterwork *Wine, Terroir and Climate Change* (Wakefield Press, 2011).

In his book, Gladstones provides a far more detailed analysis of his approach to all aspects of measuring climate, in part referenced by a series of tables of 18 regions from around the world, and separate site adjustments and notes for the extremely detailed figures in the tables proper. Thus, the E° figures have been adjusted as far as possible by Gladstones to incorporate latitude, altitude, diurnal temperature range, vineyard slopes, inclination to midday sun, soil type, proximity to/distance from water bodies and exposure to/protection from prevailing winds. No one has previously attempted this, and it is a major advance.

But Gladstones would be the first to point out that exceptions will prove the rule: any vigneron will know that even a 100-metre separation of vineyard blocks may result in very different outcomes for the same variety grown and tended in the same way.

He also validly draws attention to seasonal variability, which in various parts of eastern Australia has been grossly affected by drought (from 1996 to 2010), extreme prolonged heat in 1998, bushfires in Victoria in 2009, continuous rain in a cool 2011 spring and summer. There is no way these aberrations can or should be incorporated into the statistics or regional guidelines, beyond noting that some regions may be more liable to them than others.

Australian wine styles compared to those of France/Germany/Spain

It is important to understand that Australia has no areas of terroir and climate that are precisely similar to those of France (or any other country), and that the reverse is equally true. This can lead to the statement that even if an Australian winemaker tried to exactly copy a similar French wine it could not do so (true), and that it follows that any comparison between French and Australian wine is either futile or invalid (untrue).

Why is it untrue? First, because wine is a truly global commodity, and in restaurants and retail wine shops around the world the customer is confronted with choosing between wines from different countries and regions. This will be impossible if the customer has no idea whatsoever how two wines made from the same variety and similar age will differ from each other.

The importance of a measure for evaluation of style and quality

Even more importantly, there has to be a yardstick, a point of comparison: it is true of the Olympic 100-metre sprint record; of Tiger Woods' golf skill; of a luxury sports car; chess; the list is endless. So it is that most agree that Bordeaux makes the greatest cabernet sauvignon and/or merlot red wines, Burgundy the greatest pinot noir wines (Red Burgundies) and the greatest chardonnay wines (White Burgundies/Chablis), the northern Rhône Valley the greatest shiraz wines, the southern Rhône Valley the greatest grenache wines, the Loire Valley the greatest sauvignon blanc and chenin blanc wines, Alsace and Germany the greatest riesling wines, dry or sweet, Bordeaux the greatest sweet and dry sauvignon blanc semillon blends (Sauternes), and Champagne the greatest sparkling wines.

But in each case they are not the only examples; similar wines are made elsewhere in the northern and southern hemispheres, which gives them a universal currency, like the euro or the US dollar, and increases consumers' interest – and their ability to make outright quality comparisons (regardless of cost) or value-for-money comparisons (factoring in both quality and price).

Breed or pedigree

There is also a less easily measured value: pedigree. The English wine trade has an expression, 'One glimpse of the label is worth 20 years' experience in the business.' If you see the label is Château Lafite or Domaine de la Romanée-Conti or Dom Pérignon you will automatically rate the wine more favourably; if it is a wine you have never heard of, or know is not expensive, your bias will be against it.

Blind tasting

Thus, in seeking to learn more about the world of wine, when tasting and comparing wines of a similar style or varietal composition, place a cover over the labels (preferably the whole bottles) and write a reference (e.g. 1, 2, 3, etc) on each of the covers after the bottles have been moved randomly.

You then taste, compare and rank the wines. If you are part of a group (say 6–10 people), sharing the cost of the bottles (with as large a range in price as you can afford), with at least some French wines which are well known, this is a very good teaching method. The covers are then removed, and you will see your own preference rating; if there is no issue of embarrassment, everyone calls out their ranking, and you thereby come up with a group preference ranking.

Comparisons between Australian and French wines

Red wines

Bordeaux

The majority of these are cabernet sauvignon–dominant, with lesser amounts of merlot, cabernet franc and petit verdot – but always some; these are informally called Left Bank, meaning they come from the left (or western) bank of the Gironde River, and merlot/cabernet franc–dominant if they come from Saint-Émilion or Pomerol, the right (eastern) bank. None of the Bordeaux wines is 100% cabernet sauvignon, which is made extensively in Australia and California's Napa Valley. But if you compare an Australian cabernet sauvignon with a Haut Médoc or Graves wine of similar age, the Australian wine will be smoother, less tannic, and have more obvious berry fruit flavours. On the other side, the French (Bordeaux) wine will have more complexity and structure conferred by the terroir and climate, and expressed through the tannins (and new oak) in the wine.

Burgundy

Red Burgundy is 100% pinot noir, and its Australian counterparts are likewise 100% pinot noir. The colour of Burgundy is always far lighter in depth than that of Bordeaux and the hue has more red than purple. It also changes more quickly, with red/brown notes appearing, but this does not mean the wine is past its best; often the contrary is the case.

The most simple rule is to regard the colour of Burgundy as unimportant and no guide to its quality. Australian pinot noir from its cool regions (particularly southern Victoria and Tasmania) has similar characteristics. For both Burgundy and Australian pinot noir the aroma – the perfume – of the bouquet is of extreme importance. The Burgundians say, 'Get the bouquet right, and the palate will look after itself'; Bordeaux winemakers take precisely the opposite view – 'Get the palate right, and the bouquet will look after itself.'

This does not mean the palate as a whole is irrelevant for Burgundy. The finish and aftertaste are as important as the bouquet. While pinot noir has far less tannin in its skins than cabernet sauvignon, and is lighter-bodied, the palate is long, and the flavours expand on the finish and aftertaste. The expression often used is 'opening like a peacock's tail'.

All these characteristics are as true of high-quality Australian pinot noir as they are of Burgundy.

Rhône Valley

Syrah (or shiraz, the same grape) is chiefly grown in the northern end of the Rhône Valley; in the south it is either not used at all or blended with up to 12 other varieties. The greatest examples of syrah are grown on the Hill of Hermitage, and although the number of producers is relatively small, their fame is great. The wine is multi-layered, deep in colour and full of black fruit flavours, allied with touches of spice and pepper, and (in the case of the famous house of Guigal) high-quality new oak. The style has a lot of similarities with Australia's best known shiraz, Penfolds Grange. Throughout much of the 20th century, syrah received little attention outside of the northern Rhône Valley and South Australia (the Barossa Valley in particular), but in the wake of Robert Parker Jr's discovery of the great wines of the Rhône Valley, and of the many Barossa Valley shirazs made from vines up to or over 100 years old, there has been a rapid increase in plantings around the world. However, the

Barossa Valley, the Clare Valley, McLaren Vale, Coonawarra, Central Victoria and the Hunter Valley all have 100-year-old shiraz vines, some up to 150 years old. It is impossible for any other country or region to catch up.

White wines

Burgundy

White Burgundy (always 100% chardonnay) is generally accepted as the greatest white wine in the world, especially its Grand Crus, headed by Le Montrachet. These Grand Crus have a power, depth and length equal to or greater than that of Red Burgundy Grand Crus (pinot noir). Moreover, they have the complexity more frequently found in red wine; while 100% new French oak plays some role in this, it is the terroir of the communes of Puligny-Montrachet and Chassagne-Montrachet that invests these wines with so much character.

However, the story is somewhat complicated by the fact that the communes of Corton-Charlemagne (further north) and Chablis (far further north, but technically still part of Burgundy) also produce Grand Crus (likewise 100% chardonnay). These are less powerful and rich than those of Puligny and Chassagne, but do have great length and a minerally purity to their make-up. Especially in Chablis, new oak is used sparingly.

The best cool-region chardonnays of Australia can be surprisingly similar to the style and quality of Burgundy. Margaret River can emulate the Montrachet family, the Yarra Valley Corton-Charlemagne and Chablis. It is with this grape that the greatest changes (and improvements) in Australia's wines have taken place over the past decade.

Alsace

Riesling grown and made in Alsace is usually fermented to dryness, and can have considerable alcohol and body. Dry Australian rieslings are finer, lighter-bodied and more precise, and when young are less complex than those of Alsace. But with 10–15 years' bottle age (especially under screwcap) the Australian wines from the Clare and Eden valleys change dramatically, with far greater mouthfeel and richness than they had in their youth, closing the gap with Alsace.

The other face of riesling is that provided by Germany. While there are dry rieslings from the Rheingau and other regions, many place the rieslings of the Mosel Valley at the top of the quality tree. These may be Kabinett, where the sweetness of a low level of unfermented sugar is so well balanced by acidity you barely taste the sweetness. As the level of unfermented sugar increases, with Spätlese and Auslese the most commonly encountered wines, the sweetness is increasingly obvious, but the acidity always leaves the mouth fresh.

Australia is making more rieslings in these styles, with the Mosel Kabinett model most frequently encountered. The style is different, and it would be foolish to pretend that Australia can equal the wines of the Mosel Valley in terms of quality, but they are nonetheless very good. On the other hand, Tasmania is producing some exceptional botrytis rieslings with levels up to and beyond the sweetness of Auslese.

Sauternes

The semillon sauvignon blanc botrytis wines of Sauternes (Bordeaux) is made world famous by Château d'Yquem. There are, of course, many other outstanding producers of the Sauternes style in Bordeaux. But for over 30 years, one Australian maker in particular has produced exceptional botrytis semillon wines. This is De Bortoli, its wine known as Noble One. It may not have the final complexity of great Sauternes, but it is certainly every bit as luscious and rich.

Hunter Valley Semillon

There really is no equivalent to semillon from the Hunter Valley from any other wine-producing country or region in the world. The wine typically is 10–10.5% alc/vol, is fermented dry, and bottled within three months or so of vintage. At this point in its life it is virtually colourless, and only experts can assess the quality, so discreet is the aroma and flavour. But over the next 5–10 years, the colour turns to a glowing yellow-green, the aroma and flavour to honey and butter on lightly browned toast, all the while kept fresh and bracing by its acidity.

Champagne

The climate and terroir of Champagne is, of course, unique, as is the 200+ years of experience in making the wine. It may be blanc de blanc (100% chardonnay), blanc de noir (100% pinot noir), a blend of chardonnay and pinot noir (usually for vintage champagne) or a blend of chardonnay, pinot noir and pinot meunier (usually for non-vintage). The Champenoise have invested more time in visiting all the markets of the world than any other region of France has, and their hospitality in receiving visitors to Champagne is legendary. All of this puts this great wine on a throne all of its own, one that will last to the end of time.

Australia has been making sparkling wine for over 150 years, using the traditional method (*méthode champenoise*) for its best wines. At the 1855 International Paris Exhibition, which directly gave rise to the classification of Bordeaux wines into five growths, Hunter Valley winemaker James King entered various wines, including a sparkling wine which the judges said, 'Has a bouquet, body and flavour equal to the finest champagnes'. This wine was chosen to be served to Napoleon III during the closing ceremony of the exhibition.

Attention swung to Victoria in the later part of the century, and remained there until the 1990s, when Tasmania proved beyond doubt that it is the finest Australian region for the production of *méthode champenoise* sparkling wines. These are kept for up to 12 years on lees, and are every bit as complex as vintage champagne. Blanc de blanc, rose, non-vintage and vintage wines respectively made from chardonnay, pinot noir and pinot meunier are all produced.

Sherry and Port

These are fortified wines. Australia's most famous is the 100-year-old Seppeltsfield Para Liqueur, only sold when it is (at least) 100 years old; it has no equal elsewhere in the world. One-hundred-year-old Madeira is superb, with incredible length and intensity, but not the same richness and body as the Para Liqueur. Likewise, the old muscats and muscadelles/topaques from North East Victoria have no corresponding styles in either Spain or Portugal. Malaga (from Spain) is the closest to these wines in terms of richness, but cannot equal their complexity.

Overview of Australian wine

All of the major wine-producing countries of the world, including Australia, produce very small quantities (seldom more than 5% of the total vintage production each year) of fine wines, often described as ultra premium. These succeed because of their quality. The other 95% – and, to emphasise the point, this is as true of France, Italy, Spain and California, to name but a few, as it is of Australia – are technically well-made wines which sell on the basis of their price, which is far lower than that of ultra-premium wines. With the exception of Penfolds Grange, Henschke Hill of Grace, and some of the Penfolds Special Bin wines, the advantage Australian ultra-premium wines have compared to those of France and elsewhere is their combination of quality and price. In other words, they are significantly less expensive than those of France.

Australia has a unique range of climate and soil, greater than any other single wine-producing country in the world. It produces high-quality sparkling wines from Tasmania and southern Victoria which are world class. The notoriously difficult pinot noir flourishes in Tasmania and southern Victoria, but also in the Adelaide Hills (South Australia) and Porongurup (Western Australia). Australia produces an exceptional range of chardonnay and shiraz, both varieties grown throughout all of the 63 official regions. This results in fine, cool-climate styles; richer wines from moderately warm regions; and (especially in the case of shiraz) exceptional wines from the warmest regions.

It has a range of climate and terroir ideally suited to riesling, again ranging from very cool to moderate climates, the latter with cold overnight temperatures.

At the other end of the scale, Australia produces some of the world's greatest (and unique) fortified wines in North East Victoria, centred on Rutherglen. These are made from either muscadelle (now called topaque, formerly tokay) or muscat (muscat à petit grains). Aged in old oak in a hot part of the winery, they achieve exceptional intensity and complexity.

Geographic Indications – Australia's Appellation (AOC) system

Geographic Indication (GI) is the term for the officially recognised super zones, zones, regions and subregions of Australia which have been entered in the Register of Protected Names pursuant to the *Australian Wine and Brandy Corporation Act 1980* (Cth). At its most general, registration is based on state boundaries or an aggregation of states or parts thereof. The broadest is South Eastern Australia, which takes in the whole of New South Wales, Victoria and Tasmania and those sectors of Queensland and South Australia in which grapes are (or may conceivably be in the future) grown. Next come individual states, designations which need no explanation. Each state is then divided into zones; securing agreement on the names and boundaries of the zones was completed in 1996. The regulations provide that a zone is simply an area of land, without any particular qualifying attributes. The one super zone is Adelaide, which includes the Mount Lofty Ranges, Fleurieu and Barossa zones.

Each zone can then be subdivided into regions (the vast majority are), and each region into subregions (of which there are only a few). A region must be a single parcel (or piece) of land, comprising at least five independently owned wine grape vineyards of at least 5ha each, and usually producing a total of at least 500 tonnes of wine grapes a year. A region is required to be *measurably* different from adjoining regions, and have *measurable* homogeneity in grapegrowing attributes over its area. A subregion must also be a single parcel of land, comprising at least five independently owned wine grape vineyards of at least 5ha each, and usually producing at least 500 tonnes of wine grapes annually. However, a subregion is required to be *substantially* different from other parts of the region, and have *substantial* homogeneity in grapegrowing attributes over the area. As is obvious, the legislation is vague, and the difference between a region and a subregion is extremely subtle. Once registered, however, it is the end of the matter; the relevant decision is written in unalterable stone (see below).

The procedures for registration were and are inevitably tortuous and slow. First, the application for registration (and the detailed supporting material) must come from the region's vignerons. There is no payment for the work involved, which may be made more difficult by internal disagreements on the name or precise boundaries to be adopted. Moreover, if regional boundaries abut, there has to be inter-regional agreement, as there cannot be regional overlap of the kind one finds under comparable legislation in the US.

The six-year battle over the boundaries of Coonawarra, costing many millions of dollars in legal and experts' fees, showed just how drawn-out the process can be. Moreover, the boundaries ultimately decided were wider than anyone imagined, and still having illogical sections at various points along the way.

As the number of Australian wineries continues to increase, and their geographic spread likewise, more regions and/or subregions will be created, albeit at a slower rate than hitherto.

Label laws

There are a series of controls on the form and content of wine labels that coexist with the Geographic Indications regulations. The most important is what is commonly called truth-in-labelling, guaranteed by the Label Integrity Program (LIP). This is a control system self-imposed on Australian winemakers, the cost of compliance likewise funded by Australian wineries (by a levy charged on each tonne of grapes crushed). It requires winemakers to keep the most scrupulous and detailed records; this enables an audit to be made at any stage. The records must account for every tonne of grapes processed, whether estate-grown or contract-grown, and track the wine from those grapes, whether it is estate-bottled and sold, bottled, or sold without a label, or sold as bulk wine. Each year there is a parallel audit of a given variety within a given region, which charts how much of that variety is made from grapes grown in the region, how much is made from grapes grown elsewhere, and how the wine made from those grapes is disposed of. There are also annual random audits of winemakers large and small, and specific audits where the Australian Wine and Brandy Corporation is put on notice of possible irregularities.

The minimum amount of information required for the label on every bottle of wine sold in Australia is the producer's name and address, the alcohol level, the number of standard drinks the bottle contains, the statement 'Contains sulfites' (unless no SO_2 has been added at any time prior to the wine being bottled) and either 'Wine of Australia' or 'Product of Australia'. Additionally, there must be a declaration if any of a number of prescribed allergenic substances have been used during the making of the wine. The relevant substances are milk and casein, egg whites, nuts and isinglass. The legal requirement is that the statement must say either that the substance is in the wine or that it has been used in its manufacture. The most common form of compliance is 'Produced with the aid of milk products and traces may remain', using 'egg', 'fish' or 'milk' as appropriate, these all being fining agents.

There is no requirement that the vintage, the variety or varieties, or the region or regions be stated. In the vast majority of instances, of course, they are stated, in which case the following principles apply. If a single variety is stated, the wine must contain at least 85% of that variety. If two or more varieties are stated, they must be arranged in descending order of volumetric importance. If only two varieties are shown, the second cannot be less than 5%. (Thus a shiraz viognier with less than 5% viognier has to state shiraz on the front label, but the incorporation of viognier can be disclosed on the back label.)

If the vintage is specified, the wine must be at least 85% from that vintage, and if a single region is specified, the wine must likewise be 85% from that region. If more than one region is displayed, the regions must be shown in descending order of volumetric importance. All of these 'label claims' must be substantiated by records kept at the winery under the LIP.

Wine bottle closures

The use of cork (crafted from the bark of a specific type of oak tree, *Quercus suber*) placed inside the neck of the wine bottle is a 350-year-old technology. This alone should be a reason to question whether there may be a better way of keeping the wine safe. Next, as the Portuguese makers of cork are happy to point out, cork is a natural product. There are two issues here: first, the composition of cork is one of nature's marvels – it is incredibly complex, with 40 million hexagonal gas-filled cells in every cubic centimetre. This inevitably means that no two corks are exactly the same: the difference may be so small that only a super computer could tell it, or it may be obvious to the naked eye.

Next, the bottle is most definitely not a natural product, so why should its union with cork have the magical quality assumed by those who prefer or defend the choice of cork? But even more to the point, while the exterior of the bottle neck can be guaranteed to a thousandth of a millimetre, the same is not true of the interior of a bottle neck. The cumulative effect of cork and bottle neck variability means that no two bottles of the same wine bottled on the same day and stored in the same conditions will be precisely the same; the differences may not be obvious when the wine is young, but they will become ever more obvious as the wine ages over the years.

The opposite is the case with a screwcap. It is manufactured to extremely fine specifications, as is the external neck of the bottle. It is possible for an inexperienced user of the equipment which places the screwcap on the bottle to set up the process incorrectly, but this rarely happens. Thus, every bottle of the same wine under screwcap is, and always will be, identical to every other bottle kept under similar storage conditions. Moreover, screwcapped bottles are better able than cork-closed wines to withstand poor conditions, particularly heat during transport and storage. Bottles with screwcaps do not leak as heat increases the pressure inside the bottle, whereas corks will leak, leaving a tell-tale dribble of wine on the bottom of the capsule and down the label. Over time, a sufficient volume of wine will be displaced to lower the level of the wine in the bottle by 6cm or more, and ultimately will fail altogether to keep the contents in the bottle.

As at 2013, 99% of all white table wines (irrespective of price) sold in Australia had screwcap closures, as did 98.8% of red wines with a price of $20 or less. It is only with red wines over $20 that one-piece cork still has a meaningful presence, at 12.2% (but declining). I have used the term 'sold in Australia' because I am aware that some exporters bow to the demands of the US and Chinese markets (among others) for corks. Slowly, but inevitably, those markets will realise that screwcaps are far superior to corks. It is already a constantly changing situation, and the impact of cork-bottled export sales on these statistics is impossible to accurately analyse.

The development of wine under screwcap

The development of wine does not require oxygen; technically, it is anaerobic. But if there is an ongoing supply of oxygen through or past the cork, it will accelerate that development. The greatest wine scientist, Louis Pasteur (1822–95) said, 'Oxygen is the enemy of wine.'

Thus development of wine does occur under a screwcap, albeit more slowly than under cork. More importantly, the rate of development will be identical for all bottles of any given wine. Under cork, the development of any two or more bottles of a given wine will be different. For three reasons that difference will be more obvious with white than with red wines. First, the comparative colour change between two or more bottles will become increasingly obvious as the wine ages, with some bottles lighter in colour, others deeper, reflecting the different rates of oxygen intake into the bottle, and hence the wine. The second reason is that white wines do not have tannins, and red wines do. These tannins provide protection by interacting with oxygen, and falling out of solution in the form of sediment (or crust) in the bottom of the bottle.

The third reason is the density of the colour of red wines. It is true that regardless of the closure, the colour will become lighter over time, but a differential rate of loss of density is far more difficult to detect than (paradoxically) the rate of increase in white wine colour.

Alkoomi

Est 1971
Wingebellup Road, Frankland River, WA 6396
Open 7 days 10–5
Getting there 4 hours' drive from Perth CBD
Contact (08) 9855 2229; info@alkoomiwines.com.au; www.alkoomiwines.com.au
Region Frankland River
Lat 34°22'S
Elev 200–300m
E° Days 1574
Harvest 28 February–14 April

Estate vineyards 104.6ha
Varieties planted Sauvignon blanc (25.6), shiraz (19.7), cabernet sauvignon (16.8), semillon (13.2), chardonnay (9.5), riesling (8.8), merlot (3.4), malbec (2), cabernet franc (1.2), viognier (1.1), petit verdot (1), carnelian (0.8), tempranillo (0.8), verdelho (0.7)
Dozens produced 60 000 No increase planned.
Exports To China and Hong Kong through Wine Culture Limited (ph) +86 21 6326 8899; info@ wineculture.com.cn. Also to all major markets.
Winemaker Andrew Cherry

Key wines

Blackbutt (Cabernet blend)
How it is made: A blend of cabernet sauvignon, malbec, cabernet franc, merlot and petit verdot, the majority of the grapes coming from the original 1971 plantings. Each variety is separately fermented in small open fermenters, with hand-plunging. The components are taken to French oak (50% new) and matured for 18 months. At this point all of the barrels are tasted and the final blend determined, with the wine thereafter taken back to oak for a further 6 months. It is not fined, and is filtered just prior to bottling. 600 dozen made.

How it tastes: The 40-year-old vines provide effortless power to the array of red and black fruits that drive the bouquet and medium-bodied palate alike; cedary oak and slippery/silky tannins add lustre to a high-quality wine. Cellar to 20 years from vintage.

Best vintages: 2008, 2007, 2005, 2002, 1999

Jarrah Frankland River Shiraz
How it is made: The grapes come from the oldest block of shiraz, planted in 1971, and are fermented in 2 small open fermenters, hand-plunged 3 times a day, then pressed and taken to French oak (50% new). The final selection is decided after a barrel selection process throughout the 18–24 months' maturation (vintage dependent). Filtered just prior to bottling. 600 dozen made.

How it tastes: Crimson-purple in its youth, it has a fragrant spice, red berry and briar bouquet leading into a medium-bodied palate introducing black fruits to go along with the red berry of the bouquet; spice, licorice, powdery tannins and quality oak result in a high-quality shiraz. Cellar to 15+ years from vintage.

Best vintages: 2009, 2007, 2002, 2000, 1999

Alkoomi

The memory of my first visit to Alkoomi in 1981 is written large, joined at the hip with the memory of the Rocky Gully Hotel – which is unfair, because the Alkoomi wines were very good, the hotel decidedly not. There was a single bulb in the centre of the room, the on/off switch a piece of frayed cord which could only be reached by a life-threatening stand on a rickety table.

Mervyn (known as Merv) and Judi Lange had a 1200ha wool and grain farm, and were the first farmers in the Frankland River region to plant a few hectares of vines. It was intended to eventually increase the plantings to around 8ha, and on Department of Agriculture advice, 75% was to be shiraz and cabernet sauvignon, 25% white varieties.

By the time I visited there were 13ha planted, the posts hand-hewn on the property, the rows wide enough to accommodate the large farm tractor, and a do-it-all-yourself business model established – it continues to this day. From vineyard birth to fully packaged wine is the proud boast, and I'll wager the bank has never advanced a dollar to the business.

This should not be taken as a suggestion that there has been any farmer bumpkin mentality on the part of the Langes. In 2010 they handed over ownership of the business to daughter Sandy Hallett and husband Rod, who had been an integral part of the business for many years, and, with their three daughters Laura, Emily and Molly, they now represent the second and third generations.

Without any fanfare of trumpets, Rod has planted selected clover and rye grasses in the middle of each row, helping conserve soil moisture and strangling weed growth, thus eliminating the use of herbicides. Added soil microbes and kelp (seaweed) applications have led to a more healthy soil profile. Nor does it stop there. In the wetter winter months he used a GPS device to map the natural contours of the land (many of the blocks are on slopes), and diverted water run-off to storage dams without the use of pumps, reducing the carbon footprint, and securing better quality irrigation water.

On the other side of the business, a second cellar door has been opened in Albany, a recognition of an unalterable fact: the vineyard is still off the beaten track, especially on weekdays. Another outcome of the basic business model is that the wines represent exceptional value for money, with 10 of the 15 wines available at the bricks and mortar cellar doors, and the electronic alternative for home delivery, all at competitive prices.

Even the six-year-old red wine flagbearers, the Blackbutt (a Bordeaux-style blend) and the Jarrah Shiraz, are far less expensive than most of their eastern states' counterparts, with the ridiculously cheap Frankland River Riesling winning gold medals when young or old. Wine show success is always welcome, but I can't see any likelihood that Sandy or Rod will let it go to their heads.

All Saints Estate

Est 1864
All Saints Road, Wahgunyah, Vic 3687
Open Mon–Sat 9–5.30, Sun 10–5.30
Getting there 3 hours' drive from
Melbourne CBD
Contact 1800 021 621;
customerservice@allsaintswine.com.au;
www.allsaintswine.com.au
Region Rutherglen
Lat 36°03′S
Elev 170m
E° Days 1591
Harvest 17 February–27 March

Estate vineyards 33.46 ha
Varieties planted Shiraz (12.89),
muscat (4.92), marsanne (2.68),
durif (1.45), plus smaller plantings
of cabernet sauvignon, merlot, ruby
cabernet, riesling and chardonnay
Dozens produced 18 000 No increase
planned.
Exports To the UK, the US and
Singapore.
Winemaker Dan Crane, Nick Brown

Key wines

Family Cellar Shiraz

How it is made: Wild yeast fermentation takes place in open concrete, wax-lined fermenters, hand-plunged 3 times daily, then spending an additional 2–3 weeks on skins before transfer to an 1883 hand-cranked wooden basket press. The wine spends 14 months in French oak barriques (25% new). 1000 dozen made.

How it tastes: Generously proportioned black cherry, plum and blackberry fruit is the first-up flavour before the quality oak becomes apparent, with well-balanced tannins on the finish. Cellar to 15 years from vintage.

Best vintages: 2013, 2010, 2008, 2006, 2003

Family Cellar Durif

How it is made: The only differences between this and the Shiraz are that this is left up to a month on skins prior to being pressed, and then aged in French oak puncheons (25% new). 1100 dozen made.

How it tastes: Full of sweet black fruits, layers of spice, and soft but important tannins; all fill the mouth. Cellar to 20 years from vintage.

Best vintages: 2013, 2010, 2008, 2006, 2003

All Saints Estate

A first-time visitor to All Saints Estate might well wonder how a turreted castle, erected around an internal quadrangle, came to be built at a place like Wahgunyah. The first George Sutherland Smith arrived in Australia in the 1850s. His family had worked for generations as carpenters and joiners at the castle of Mey at Caithness, Scotland, in the parish of All Saints. He and his brother-in-law, John Banks, had trained as engineers at the Edinburgh Railway Institute and, after their arrival in Australia in 1852, constructed bridges and large institutional buildings.

John Banks had profitably plied the river trade on the Murray in the 1860s, and in 1864 Sutherland Smith and Banks purchased a large river-front block at Wahgunyah on which they planted the vines, and on which George Sutherland Smith would want to build his own castle. This he literally did: a clay pit was dug on the riverbank, and the kiln that he used to fire the bricks still stands today.

The vineyards flourished on the sandy loam of the Murray, and George Sutherland Smith and John Banks quickly learnt the art of winemaking. In the manner of the day they were active exhibitors in overseas competitions and, while not challenging Morris at Fairfield, had many successes.

The sandy soils of the vineyard did not stop phylloxera (even though other similar vineyards across the region were spared for some years), and in the 1890s David Banks Smith, George's son, had to replant all the vineyards with grafted phylloxera-resistant rootstocks. Notwithstanding the cost and disruption involved, the turn of the century was a time of expansion for the Sutherland Smith business. The winery capacity was extended on several occasions to feed the growing market, which had been served by the establishment of a Melbourne warehouse and bottling facilities.

The business continued in the ownership of the Sutherland Smith family for well over 100 years, before being acquired by an investment syndicate in the late 1980s. The sudden death of the CEO of that syndicate led to the appointment of a receiver, and the sale of considerable quantities of the large stocks of old fortified wines, leading to the (incorrect) belief at the time that all the best aged wines had been sold. In 1991 Brown Brothers acquired All Saints, and set about restoring all aspects of the business.

A few years later, and as part of an amicable rearrangement of the Brown Brothers family interests, Peter R. Brown sold his share in Brown Brothers and acquired All Saints Estate (and St Leonards Vineyard) from the family. In November 2005 Peter Brown was killed in a road accident, and his three children (the fourth generation of the Brown family) – Eliza, Angela and Nicholas – took over management. Eliza became a youthful but energetic CEO, with Angela taking responsibility for brand development and export markets, and Nicholas going down the viticulture and winemaking path. All Saints is an outstanding tourist destination, and has a wide range of venues for everything from weddings to one-on-one visits.

The quality of the fortified wines is equal to the best of Rutherglen, and the increasing range of table wines are also very good. The enthusiasm (and skill) of Peter Brown's children has restored All Saints to its former glory, honouring the vision of their father.

Ashton Hills

Est 1982
Tregarthen Road, Ashton, SA 5137
Open W'ends & most public hols 11–5.30
Getting there 25 minutes' drive from
Adelaide CBD
Contact (08) 8390 1243;
A.H.V@bigpond.net.au
Region Adelaide Hills
Lat 34°00'S
Elev 496m
E° Days 1359
Harvest 12 March–30 April

Estate vineyards 3ha
Varieties planted Pinot noir (2.64),
riesling (0.36)
Dozens produced 1500 No increase
planned.
Exports Wines are not currently
exported.
Winemaker Stephen George

Key wines

Reserve Pinot Noir
How it is made: Both 100% whole bunch and 100% whole berry ferments are employed, more of the former in warmer years. The two components are blended prior to maturation in French oak barriques (one-third new, the remainder 2–3 years old), spending 10 months in barrel. Never fined, and usually not filtered.

How it tastes: A quite beautiful wine that takes the best characters of the Estate and the Piccadilly Valley versions, and then multiplies those characters many times. It is awash with cherry and plum fruit, and has superb mouthfeel, allowing harmonious access to every nuance of the flavours. Cellar to 10 years from vintage.

Best vintages: 2012, 2010, 2009, 2008, 2005

Salmon Brut
How it is made: This is a 100% bottle-fermented, whole bunch-pressed pinot noir held on primary lees in tank before tirage for the second fermentation, and, with red pinot noir table wine added for colour as is the case with most Champagne roses, disgorged after a minimum of 2 years.

How it tastes: Pink, with just the slightest touch of salmon; strawberry and cherry fruit flavours are crystal clear, augmented by the percentage of pinot noir table wine added, but without diminishing the haunting delicacy of the wine. Cellar to 7 years from release.

Best vintages: 2011, 2010, 2009, 2005, 2003

Ashton Hills

This is an ultimate example of beauty coming in a small package, but achieved without sentimentality. The tall, spare figure of owner and winemaker Stephen George has spent over 30 years working with a single, 3ha estate vineyard, acquiring an intimate knowledge of every metre of the terroir, and making the wines on a similar micro-scale. So it came as a major surprise to find that in the spring of 2011 he had grafted the chardonnay, pinot gris and gewurztraminer to pinot noir, leaving the vineyard with only two grape varieties: pinot noir and riesling. It is true that the wine he simply called Three was an odd blend of pinot gris, riesling and gewurztraminer, which I once described as succeeding in spite of itself, but the chardonnay was used to make an elegant bottle-fermented blanc de blancs sparkling wine to accompany the similarly made Salmon Brut.

The move also left him with riesling, the most noble of the German varieties, idolised by a majority of Australian wine professionals, but ignored by the thundering herd of consumers of sauvignon blanc, pinot grigio, pinot gris and – of course – chardonnay.

The very considerable upside is the increase in the area of pinot noir, and the increased scope he has to make four pinot-based wines when the weather gods have smiled: the Salmon Brut sparkling wine, then (in rising quality and price) Piccadilly Valley, Estate and Reserve Pinot Noir.

It was not until the pinot noir vines were over 20 years old that Stephen George made the first Reserve version; he declined to do so in 2004, '06, '07 and '11. It adds a level of intensity to the unfailing elegance and fragrance of all his pinot noirs, characters that make them the best examples from the Adelaide Hills. There is no doubt the elevated vineyard site and the average age of the vines are important, but so is the utterly remarkable collection of 18 clones of pinot noir planted on this very small vineyard. I know of no other Australian producer to have more than 10 clones; most have between one (called MV6) and three or four more.

Over the years he had much to do with the making of the majestically powerful Wendouree wines, had a second (quasi-negociant) business, Galah Wines, and also made a shiraz from his father's small vineyard at Burra, northeast of the Clare Valley.

He is now content with his Ashton Hills wines, almost entirely sold through his mail list, even eschewing a website, does not export, and does not sell to more than a few restaurants and independent retailers.

Baileys of Glenrowan

Est 1870
779 Taminick Gap Road, Glenrowan, Vic 3675
Open 7 days 10–5
Getting there 2.5 hours' drive from Melbourne CBD
Contact (03) 5766 1600; cellardoor@baileysofglenrowan.com.au; www.baileysofglenrowan.com.au
Region Glenrowan
Lat 36°27′S
Elev 190m
E° Days 1647
Harvest 14 March–30 April

Estate vineyards 144.3 ha
Varieties planted Shiraz (58.2), cabernet sauvignon (39.2), durif (15.8), merlot (13.3), muscat (10.2), muscadelle (3.9), nero d'Avola (3.2), small plantings of Portuguese varieties (0.5)
Dozens produced 15 000 Some increase expected.
Exports Wines are not currently exported.
Winemaker Paul Dahlenburg

Key wines

1920s Block Shiraz

How it is made: Due to the natural high tannin levels in the small berries, the aim is to treat the grapes as gently as possible. They are destemmed, not crushed, cold-soaked for at least 5 days, the must is only pumped over early in the fermentation, with minimal plunging thereafter, then matured in large vats and puncheons (100% French) for 14 to 18 months. Not fined, but is crossflow-filtered.

How it tastes: Deep crimson-purple; wonderfully rich, yet supple, with multiple layers of black fruits, licorice and perfectly controlled ripe tannins. Cellar to 25 years from vintage.

Best vintages: 2013, 2010, 2006, 2005, 2002

Muscat and Topaque

How it is made: The juice is not fermented; instead, neutral high-strength spirit is added once the juice has come from the press. While it has a normal fortified level of 17.5% alc/vol, it all comes from the spirit. This approach provides highly aromatic and fresh characters that remain throughout the many years the wines spend in a combination of large old vats and smaller oak barrels; they are made using a solera system. Another unusual aspect is that Baileys only makes two of the four levels – Classic and Rare – and does not make the base level or Grand.

How it tastes: The colour is mahogany, grading to olive on the rim, the aromatic bouquet and palate redolent of highly spiced Christmas pudding. The most remarkable achievement is the freshness of the wines, which border on delicate, and incite the desire to scoff it down – a vinous crime worthy of capital punishment.

Best vintages: NA

Baileys of Glenrowan

One of the most enduring stories of Australian folklore is that of the bushranger Ned Kelly and his homemade bulletproof headpiece and chest protector. Some saw him as a modern-day Robin Hood, stealing from the rich and giving to the poor. That did not prevent his ultimate capture in Glenrowan in 1880, and his sentence of death which followed.

It is relatively wild, sparsely populated country today; it was even more so back then. But this did not deter Richard Bailey (with his young family) from establishing a store in Glenrowan in the 1860s to supply miners with food and provisions. When the gold ran out and the miners moved on, the family bought a nearby property, which they called Bundarra.

As well as farming, they planted vines, and in 1870 produced their first small amount of fortified wine. Phylloxera arrived in the 1890s, and son Varley Bailey replanted part of the vineyard with shiraz (in 1904); further plantings of shiraz, muscat and muscadelle (known as tokay) followed in the 1920s.

In 1964 I wrote to Baileys enclosing a cheque for three dozen bottles of 1953 Hermitage (as shiraz was then called) at 45 cents a bottle, and two dozen bottles of 1958 Hermitage at 35 cents a bottle. It was sent by rail, and I had to go to Darling Harbour Railway Station (in Sydney) to collect it, and share the order with a close friend. The '53 was mainly consumed at barbeques, the '58 often used in cooking a Greek dish I was fond of at the time called *stifado*. Four years later I visited Baileys for the first time, meeting an aged Alan Bailey (great-grandson of Richard Bailey).

Four years later again, Harry Tinson (with a Masters degree in Physical Engineering) was part of the corporate planning department of Davis Consolidated Industries (mainly known for its Davis gelatine). The Board decided the company should diversify its activities, and Tinson was charged with the responsibility of finding an appropriate winery.

He chose Baileys, and the Board instructed him to negotiate an agreement to buy a 50% share. Bailey said all or nothing, and the next moment Tinson found himself acting general manager/winemaker of a wholly owned subsidiary of Davis Consolidated. (He eventually retired 14 years later.)

Subsequent corporate mergers and acquisitions saw waxing and waning fortunes of Baileys. The vineyards increased to 143ha by the end of the 1990s, and extensive new winemaking equipment was installed in 1998. A 100-year-old basket press was brought back into use, and in 2000 the cellar door was extensively renovated.

In 2007 bushfires meant that no red wine was made, and in the interim much of the winemaking equipment had been moved to sister company Yarra Ridge. In 2009 Foster's (then the owner) put the winery on the market, but the property was withdrawn from sale, and when Treasury Wine Estates was created, it agreed with winemaker Paul Dahlenburg's request that all the casks and winemaking equipment be returned to the winery. Dahlenburg is fiercely committed to the heritage of Baileys and to the quality of its wines.

Balnaves of Coonawarra

Est 1975
Main Road, Coonawarra, SA 5263
Open Mon–Fri 9–5, w'ends 12–5
Getting there 4 hours' drive from Adelaide CBD
Contact (08) 8737 2946; kirsty.balnaves@balnaves.com.au; www.balnaves.com.au
Region Coonawarra
Lat 37°18′S
Elev 59m
E° Days 1379
Harvest 11 March–7 May

Estate vineyards 57.1 ha
Varieties planted Cabernet sauvignon (42.4), shiraz (5.3), merlot (5), chardonnay (2.4), viognier (1), cabernet franc (1)
Dozens produced 10 000 No increase planned.
Exports To China through Vinous Australis (ph) +61 409 963 223; pflew@mac.com, and to Hong Kong through Boutique Wines (ph) 852 2525 3031; sales@boutiquewines.com.hk. Also to the UK, Canada, Denmark, Japan, Indonesia and Singapore.
Winemaker Pete Bissell

Key wines

The Tally Reserve Cabernet Sauvignon
How it is made: The grapes come from 3 blocks, hand-picked at the rate of 2 fermenters per day, crushed into open fermenters with specially selected cultured yeasts, and pumped over twice a day. The temperature is taken up to 28–30°C, then cooled to 26–28°C. After 7–10 days, and completion of fermentation, wines with the potential to become part of The Tally will be kept on skins for a further 20–25 days to modify the tannins and lengthen the structure of the palate. The parcels are blended after 12 months in oak and then returned for a further 6 months prior to egg white fining and bottling. The oak is French, 50–100% new depending on the vintage.

How it tastes: This is one of the richest Coonawarra cabernet sauvignons, much in the opulent, full-bodied mould of Wynns Coonawarra Estate John Riddoch; it needs 5+ years for all the oak to come into balance, and will develop well for a minimum of 25 years from vintage.

Best vintages: 2010, 2009, 2005, 2004, 2001

Cabernet Sauvignon
How it is made: This comes from the best blocks not required for The Tally, and is made in the same way, except that the prolonged skin contact is only a minor part, and less new oak is used.

How it tastes: Strong purple-crimson in its youth, the rich bouquet and medium to full-bodied palate is bursting with intense, perfectly ripened blackcurrant fruit, the oak evident, but not over the top. Cellar to 20 years from vintage.

Best vintages: 2010, 2008, 2005, 2004, 2001

Balnaves of Coonawarra

The Balnaves family, Coonawarra and cabernet sauvignon are concentric circles, indivisible from each other, albeit with the only winemaker ever employed, Peter Bissell, adding another important dimension to the story. Founder Doug Balnaves was born in Penola (the small but most important town in Coonawarra) and worked in the local sheep industry, having married nursing sister Annette in 1967, until 1971. In that year he was made development manager for the planned vineyard of Hungerford Hill, and he spent the next 17 years learning everything there was to know about grapegrowing in the region.

In 1988 Doug Balnaves left Hungerford Hill, and he (with Annette) set up a vineyard management and development company as well as expanding the small cabernet vineyard he had planted in 1976 (1.2ha) and 1982 (4.12ha). The first Balnaves wines were contract-made in 1990, as were the next four vintages, but the continuing vineyard plantings in 1990, 1992, 1994 (and thereafter) led to the decision to build a 600-tonne estate winery in 1995.

It was here that Pete Bissell came on board to design and run the winery. He came with an exceptionally impressive career already behind him, although you would not guess that from his softly spoken voice and gentle demeanour. It began with a First Class Honours degree in Biochemistry in 1982, his thesis on colour extraction from pinot noir in Canterbury, New Zealand. He then worked in Bordeaux until the end of 1984, before obtaining a Graduate Diploma in Oenology from Roseworthy College (now University of Adelaide) in 1988, working with four legendary winemakers during his studies.

In 1989 he joined Wynns Coonawarra Estate, working northern hemisphere vintages in 1993 (Russia) and 1994 (south of France). The skill set he had accumulated over the years made him the ideal person to work with the architectural team charged with designing a winery to be in harmony with the landscape, yet embodying a belltower with a panoramic view of the laser-flat vineyards of Coonawarra as a local beacon for visitors.

Annette Balnaves, a committed photographer whose work illuminates the winery's website, was long in charge of the cellar door, but in 1998 became chair of the Limestone Coast Tourism Association. Daughter Kirsty Balnaves worked in places as utterly different as the hot, dry mining town of Broken Hill and Cradle Mountain, Tasmania, before returning to the University of Adelaide to study marketing and management, then joining the company as director of marketing and finance.

Balnaves only makes one white wine, a chardonnay that is one of the best to come from the region, but Coonawarra's *raison d'être* is cabernet sauvignon, or blends with cabernet as a component. Indeed, The Blend (as it is prosaically called) of merlot, cabernet sauvignon and cabernet franc is one of the best value red wines to come from Coonawarra. The cabernet merlot is also meritorious.

It is with the cabernet sauvignon, and its icon version, The Tally Reserve, that all the pieces of the jigsaw puzzle come together. First, only a portion (the best, of course) of the crop is used for these wines, with that not needed sold as grapes/wine. Second, even with this embarrassment of riches, the company purchased the high-quality 4ha Lear Vineyard in 2012, and will buy other high-quality vineyards if they suit the wine matrix. Balnaves has also planted the two most recent clones of cabernet sauvignon ex France to evaluate their performance on the limestone soils of Coonawarra.

The fat lady hasn't sung, it would seem.

Bannockburn Vineyards

Est 1974
Midland Highway, Bannockburn,
Vic 3331 (postal)
Open By appt
Getting there 1 hour's drive from
Melbourne CBD
Contact (03) 5281 1363;
sales@bannockburnvineyards.com;
www.bannockburnvineyards.com
Region Geelong
Lat 38°09'S
Elev 25–150m
E° Days 1377
Harvest 8 March–21 May

Estate vineyards 24 ha
Varieties planted Pinot noir (7.6),
chardonnay (5.1), shiraz (4.8), cabernet
sauvignon (3), sauvignon blanc (1.8),
merlot (0.8), riesling (0.5), malbec (0.4)
Dozens produced 10 000 No increase
planned.
Exports To China and Hong Kong
through Beijing Ao Hua Yang Guang Jiu
Ye Gong Si (Australia Sunshine Creek
Beijing) (ph) 8610 8521 1888;
www.sunshinecreek.com. Also to
Canada and Singapore.
Winemaker Michael Glover

Key wines

Geelong Pinot Noir
How it is made: Usually a blend of 4 parcels from the estate Olive Tree Hill, Anne's,
Stuart and de la Terre vineyards; hand-picked and 100% whole-bunch, wild yeast-
fermented in good vintages with 21 days on skins; spends 18 months in French
oak barriques (33% new). Not fined, and only coarse-filtered. 900 dozen made in
good vintages.

How it tastes: A complex bouquet, with sustained exotic spices, black cherry
and plum fruits; the palate is powerful and long, with strong savoury/stemmy
undercurrents to the fruit. Cellar to 15 years from vintage.

Best vintages: 2012, 2010, 2006, 2004, 2001

Geelong Chardonnay
How it is made: Hand-picked, whole-bunch-pressed to a mix of French oak
barriques, puncheons (one-third new) and stainless steel, wild yeast-fermented,
then natural 100% mlf (malolactic fermentation) and left on lees for 2 years to gain
natural stability. Not fined, but sterile-filtered. 1000 dozen made.

How it tastes: An exceptionally textured wine, powerful and rich, but so seamless,
the stone fruit, oak and acidity so perfectly balanced, that there is no semblance of
weight. Cellar to 10+ years from vintage.

Best vintages: 2011, 2010, 2008, 2004, 2001

Bannockburn Vineyards

Geelong had the dubious distinction of being the first region in Australia to have its vineyards destroyed by phylloxera. Moreover, when phylloxera arrived, Geelong was one of the most important producers in the state; Ebenezer Ward, who had made a career writing in great detail about the vineyards and wineries of South Australia (his articles were collated in a book published in 1862), turned his attention to Victoria in 1864. He describes more than 50 vineyards in Geelong in that year, many with wineries, but the region continued to grow rapidly, reaching a peak in 1875. It was either in that year, or 1877, that phylloxera was discovered, little more than a decade after it had taken hold in France.

After intense political wrangling, the government ordered the eradication of 80 vineyards totalling over 250ha, with another 100ha initially escaping the eradication order, but ultimately falling prey to phylloxera. It was not until 1966 that vines (grafted onto American rootstock) reappeared in the Sefton's Idyll Vineyard, followed by Anakie in 1968, Tarcoola in 1972 (all three having since disappeared), and Stuart Hooper's Bannockburn in 1973, making it now the region's senior (winery) citizen.

He was a wealthy Melbourne businessman who had the money, the patience and the desire to make wine of high quality. The early years were full of trial and error: error in endeavouring to grow young vines without some water to keep them alive. A dam was created, the vines then grew (slowly), a showpiece winery was built and appropriately equipped, and Gary Farr was installed as winemaker at the end of the 1970s.

In 1983 both of us (Gary and me) arrived at Domaine Dujac (in Burgundy's Morey-St-Denis) to work the vintage, neither of us knowing of the other's plans. We both enjoyed the experience enormously, but only Gary Farr returned every year for a considerable time thereafter (ultimately followed by son Nick). Gary freely admits his trailblazing success with Bannockburn pinot noir (and chardonnay) was inspired by his multi-vintage experience at the highly rated Domaine Dujac.

The Bannockburn vineyards are established on four separate sites, the soil varying from black-brown volcanic loam to dense clay on a limestone base. The first vines were planted in 1974 and through the 1980s (some of the oldest in the region), the most recent in 2007 – an ultra-high-density 2ha planting of pinot noir and shiraz. The low rainfall, strong prevailing winds, and low soil fertility lead to naturally low yields, reinforced by only using irrigation on young vines or in periods of heat and drought-induced stress.

In 2005 Gary Farr left to concentrate on his own vineyards and winery (joined by son Nick) and was replaced by Michael Glover. He continues the four special wines: S.R.H., a chardonnay from the oldest vines named in honour of Stuart Reginald Hooper; Serre, pinot noir from the first close-planted, low-trellised vines, naturally yielding 0.5kg a vine; Range, from the 1974 plantings of shiraz, yielding 1kg a vine; and Stuart, a pinot noir from the oldest pinot noir vineyard, planted in 1978.

Bass Phillip

Est 1979
Tosch's Road, Leongatha South, Vic 3953
Open By appt
Getting there 1.75 hours' drive from Melbourne CBD
Contact (03) 5664 3341; bpwines@tpg.com.au; www.bassphillip.com
Region Gippsland
Lat 38°38'S
Elev 83m
E° Days 1288
Harvest 14 March–1 May

Estate vineyards 17ha
Varieties planted Pinot noir (12.9), chardonnay (3.2), gamay (0.7), gewurztraminer (0.2)
Dozens produced 3500 No increase planned.
Exports To China and Hong Kong through Bass Phillip (www.bassphillip.com). Also to Japan, Singapore and Thailand.
Winemaker Phillip Jones

Key wines

Reserve Pinot Noir
How it is made: The wine is made from the same tiny block each year it carries the label, with only 25–60 dozen produced. 'There are no rules,' says Jones: destemmed more than crushed; natural yeast-fermented; plunged 2–3 times per day; pressed when dry to 100% new light toast oak ex François Freres tonnellerie; and 18 months in barrel, not racked until after next vintage.

How it tastes: A perfumed bouquet of cherries and forest strawberries, the palate of astonishing purity, elegant harmony and almost surreal length. At its best it is Australia's greatest pinot noir. Cellar to 20 years from vintage.

Best vintages: 2012, 2010, 2009, 2007, 2003

Premium Pinot Noir
How it is made: The same winemaking practices are used for this as for the Reserve, the differences coming from the vineyards. 250 dozen made.

How it tastes: There are those who argue that comparisons at this level are invidious: does it really matter if Romanée-Conti is (by its price, scarcity and quality) better than La Tache? If Romanée-Conti did not exist, La Tache would be widely regarded as the greatest Burgundy. So it is with Bass Phillip Premium. It has superb length, balance and harmony, red fruits, spices, fine tannins and oak (you know it has to be there) all in a seamless weaving of silk and satin. Cellar to 15 years from vintage.

Best vintages: 2012, 2010, 2009, 2007, 2004

Bass Phillip

The winery – and wine – name was not inspired by the name of the founder and winemaker Phillip Jones, but by the early explorers of the West Gippsland region and its surrounding waters, George Bass and Arthur Phillip. It is strange that Jones has been the pioneer of viticulture in the region, yet unsurprising that when he first established his vineyard in 1979 he planted the Bordeaux varieties, headed by cabernet sauvignon. He soon realised that the climate was too cool for cabernet, and by the mid-1980s the vineyard was entirely replanted to pinot noir and chardonnay.

Even then, Jones had to come to grips with an environment that posed unique challenges; its annual rainfall of 1000 mm, and its mineral-rich, silty loam soils were ideal for dairy and beef cattle. The humidity is high throughout the growing season, and while day/night summer temperatures can vary by 20°C, this is due to cool nights, not high daytime heat.

Pinot noir and chardonnay enjoy a humid climate, and the challenge confronting Jones was to control vine vigour and high yield. He has achieved this by segmentation of very small plots, constant attention to detail in the vineyards with vine-by-vine management, ultra close planting of vines (9000 per hectare, only slightly more than Burgundy, and over three times the norm for Australian vineyards), with a base of strict organic protocols extending to the use of biodynamic composts and sprays.

The ultimate paradox then emerges. In 1991 he ended a battle with bureaucracy which allowed him to release his wines from the 1984 to 1989 vintages; I attended the first official tasting of those wines, and immediately knew that I was in the presence of greatness. As the next 20 years have gone by, Jones has painstakingly refined his understanding of the vineyard, and the responses he makes to the vines in terms of the all-important picking dates, and fermentation and maturation techniques and nuances.

Today he has to be regarded as the greatest maker of pinot noir in Australia, his best wines losing nothing in comparison with Grand Cru Burgundies. The paradox? The few other vineyards and even fewer wineries that have put down roots anywhere nearby have failed to come close to Phillip Jones' mastery of vine and wine.

Before I return to his superb pinot noirs, I should add that he makes some exceptionally good and distinctive chardonnays, and an utterly eclectic, left-field gewurztraminer. The pinots have a multi-tiered structure, starting with the Crown Prince and Four Vineyards at the bottom, then Estate, followed by Issan, next Premium, and ultimately the Reserve, the last only made in the best vintages.

These wines are indissolubly linked by their sense of place, to this unique vineyard oasis, their intensity, their length on the palate and, above all else, their ability to develop in bottle – develop in the sense of adding complexity and fragrance over several decades. The only qualification is that West Gippsland hovers on the same razor's edge as Burgundy: some Bass Phillip vintages will be truly magnificent (such as 2010 and 2012), others testing the commitment and skill of the winemaker (2011).

Bay of Fires/House of Arras

Est 2001
40 Baxters Road, Pipers River, Tas 7252
Open 7 days 10–5
Getting there 45 minutes' drive from
Launceston CBD
Contact (03) 6382 7622;
cellardoor@bayoffireswines.com.au;
www.bayoffireswines.com.au
Region Northern Tasmania
Lat 41°27′S
Elev 81m
E° Days 1208
Harvest 11 March–10 May

Estate vineyards NFP
Varieties planted As with other
wineries that are part of a much larger
wine business under single ownership,
vineyard resources are shared across all
brands in the group.
Dozens produced NFP
Exports Wines are not currently
exported.
Winemaker Peter Dredge, Ed Carr

Key wines

Bay of Fires Pinot Noir

How it is made: The grapes are fermented as separate parcels in small open-top stainless steel fermenters, some with between 10% and 30% whole-bunch inclusion, vintage dependent. The balance of the fruit is destemmed into bins, and tipped into the fermenters, thus not breaking the whole berries, and avoiding bitter tannins. Near the end of fermentation, the wine is basket-pressed and taken to top-quality French oak barriques (around 30% new, the remainder 1- and 2-year-old), where it finishes its primary fermentation and undergoes mlf.

How it tastes: Intensely coloured, it has gained recognition as one of Australia's greatest pinot noirs, with multiple layers of red and black cherry, spice and plum fruit running through an exceptionally long and pure palate; fine and supple tannins provide texture and structure, oak also making a positive contribution. Cellar to 10 years from vintage.

Best vintages: 2012, 2010, 2009, 2005, 2002

House of Arras Blanc de Blanc

How it is made: The grapes come from the Pipers River and Upper Derwent districts, hand-picked chardonnay is whole-bunch-pressed and fermented in stainless steel with prix de mousse yeast. A small amount of oak is used to add to texture, not flavour. 100% of the wine undergoes mlf. It is then taken to bottle for the secondary fermentation, using the traditional method, where it spends a minimum of 8 years on lees prior to disgorgement.

How it tastes: Pale quartz-green; white flower and brioche aromas; very intense and very long; lovely citrus/white peach fruit; dazzling purity. A prolific winner of wine show gold medals and trophies. Cellar to 5 years from disgorgement.

Best vintages: 2004, 2001

Bay of Fires/House of Arras

Bay of Fires' pre-history dates back to 1985, when the first vines were planted at what was called Rochecombe by Swiss-born Bernard and Brigitte Roche. A succession of devastating spring frosts (and no frost sprinkler protection) led to its sale to the JAC Group, led by beef magnate Josef Chromy. JAC in turn was compelled to sell the vineyard and winery to Pipers Brook, which changed its name to Ninth Island. In 2001, BRL Hardy acquired the winery and its modest 20ha surrounding vineyard, renaming it Bay of Fires, and thereafter appending House of Arras.

Its website gives no details of its somewhat turbulent past, preferring to concentrate on the present and future. First up is the network of contract grapegrowers assembled by the infinitely experienced cool-climate viticulturist Ray Guerin (who cut his teeth at the large Hoddles Creek Vineyard owned by Hardys in the Upper Yarra Valley for 20 years) and compatriot Steve Kirby.

These two monitor growers in the Tamar Valley providing full-flavoured pinot noir and chardonnay for table wine: Pipers River (the home district), one of the coolest and wettest regions, particularly suited to producing fine sparkling base wine; the Coal River Valley in the south, distinguished by its ability to produce high-quality, slow-maturing wine of all varieties and styles, noted for their softness and perfume; the East Coast, able to provide chardonnay and pinot noir with a robust depth; Huon Valley, the wettest, coolest and most southerly subregion, producing the best grapes for sparkling wine; and the Derwent River Valley, itself split into two distinct viticultural sections, the warm and sheltered lower portion growing grapes with richness and ripeness, none more so than pinot noir, and the Upper Derwent, the second source of exceptional chardonnay and pinot noir for sparkling wines.

It is obvious from this that the idea Tasmania is a single source of these two grapes is entirely wrong, and any visitor who traces a path through the areas pinpointed above will immediately see the very different landforms and vegetation of each district.

It also explains why there is ever-increasing demand from winemakers on the mainland for pinot noir and chardonnay for both sparkling and table wine, and why Treasury Wine Estates was very happy to purchase the 83ha White Hills Vineyard from Brown Brothers, which had come as part of the $31 million Tamar Ridge Winery and vineyards (the largest wine business in the state) purchased by Brown Brothers from the star-crossed Gunns Limited forestry company.

There are two winemakers behind Bay of Fires. The first is long-serving Ed Carr, making what are without a doubt Australia's greatest traditional method sparkling wines, with a depth and complexity as profound as those of any Grand Marque Champagne producers, especially with 8 to more than 10 years on yeast lees (tirage).

The second is the former globe-trotting Peter Dredge, who was appointed in 2010, the year in which he was one of the 12 Len Evans Tutorial scholars. His career began in 1997, and with a degree in Oenology from the University of Adelaide he has worked in wineries in France, Italy, Hungary, Canada and Germany, his domestic experience spanning the Adelaide Hills, the Hunter Valley, Clare Valley and Coonawarra.

Bellarmine Wines

Est 2000
1 Balyan Retreat, Pemberton, WA 6258
Open By appt
Getting there 3.5 hours' drive from Perth CBD
Contact (08) 9776 0667; info@bellarmine.com.au; www.bellarmine.com.au
Region Pemberton
Lat 34°27'S
Elev 170m
E° Days 1468
Harvest 8 March–25 April

Estate vineyards 20ha
Varieties planted Merlot (5), chardonnay (3), pinot noir (3), riesling (2.5), sauvignon blanc (2.5), shiraz (2.5), petit verdot (1.5)
Dozens produced 6000 May increase to 9000.
Exports To China and Hong Kong through Riversdale Fine Wines (ph) +61 3 9043 2036; ryan@ac-smartlink.com.
Winemaker Dr Diane Miller

Key wines

Riesling Dry
How it is made: Is made in the classic fashion, cold-fermented in stainless steel with selected cultured yeasts, then bottled once stabilised after the end of fermentation.

How it tastes: Has fragrant citrus blossom aromas, and a crisp, clean, minerally palate, which progressively builds complexity over 5–10 years. Minimum 10 years' cellaring potential.

Best vintages: 2013, 2012, 2011, 2009, 2004

Shiraz
How it is made: This is an exciting cool-climate style, unknown in Australia before 1980. The grapes are harvested in the night, meaning an unnaturally slow start to fermentation, which ultimately peaks at 30°C. The wine is pumped over twice daily, and the total time on skins is between 7 and 10 days before being pressed. The mlf takes place in tank, the wine thereafter spending 12–14 months in French oak (15% new, 30% 1 year old, and 55% older).

How it tastes: Strong, black berry fruit, spice and black pepper aromas and flavours, yet is only medium-bodied and typically only 14.5% alc/vol. Cellar to 10–20 years from vintage.

Best vintages: 2012, 2011, 2010, 2009, 2008

Bellarmine Wines

Bellarmine Wines was founded by German-born but now Australian resident Dr Willi Schumacher and wife Gudrun. His background as a long-time wine collector and connoisseur led to the desire to plant a vineyard and produce estate-grown wine somewhere in the world. His search for suitable land began in the early 1990s, but it was not until 2000 that the Schumachers found what they were looking for: a magnificent 220ha property in the remote Pemberton region, with the Lefroy River running through it. Willi Schumacher had studied geology, and when the results of the soil tests came back, the decision to buy the property was immediate.

The source of the name Bellarmine is unusual. It was the name given to German wine jugs in the 16th century, the widespread use of jugs reflecting the fact that wine (which has no bacteria with the potential to harm health) was safer to drink than water (which was easily contaminated). The jugs had an etching of a bearded man thought to be Cardinal Bellarmine, who had helped English King Henry VIII separate church and state. As well as being a wine collector of note, Willi Schumacher began collecting antiques when only 12 years old, and has many Bellarmine jugs (among other antiques). Thus the Bellarmine wine labels have a sketch of the bearded Cardinal's face.

The full-time winemaker and general manager of the business is Dr Di Miller, who was a fully qualified veterinarian before moving to winemaking in 1999, and joining Bellarmine in 2004. Between the end of 2000 and 2002, 44,000 vines were planted on 20ha of the most suitable soil. The very cool Pemberton region had already proved its ability to produce high-quality chardonnay, pinot noir and sauvignon blanc, but as one might expect, the Schumachers were anxious to see how suited it was for riesling; shiraz was to follow a year or so later.

The consistency of the quality of all the wines is exceptional, but that of the riesling must be the most satisfying for the Schumachers. In the German tradition, it is produced in three styles: Dry, Half-Dry and Select. Botrytis plays no role in these wines: the difference derives from the amount of grape sugar left unfermented. Thus the Dry has 13% alc/vol, the Half-Dry 12% alc/vol, and the Select 9.5% alc/vol.

The soil is red gravel over limestone, and is not particularly rich. Thus it is not hard to limit yield to 5 tonnes/ha (or 32 hectolitres/ha); this low production, coupled with precise canopy management and the cool climate, is a key reason for the quality of the wines.

The merlot and petit verdot were mainly sold in Germany as single varietal wines, but in 2012 the varieties were blended and labelled Batavia after a sailing vessel that sank in 1629 off the West Australian coast. By pure chance, a number of Bellarmine jugs were recovered from it.

Best's Wines

Est 1866
111 Best's Road, Great Western, Vic 3377
Open Mon–Sat 10–5, Sun 11–4
Getting there 2.5 hours' drive from Melbourne CBD
Contact (03) 5356 2250; info@bestswines.com; www.bestswines.com
Region Grampians
Lat 37°17′S
Elev 240–440m
E° Days 1377
Harvest 7 March–14 May
Estate vineyards 34ha
Varieties planted Concongella Vineyard 19.7 ha, planted to shiraz, merlot, dolcetto, cabernet sauvignon, cabernet franc, petit verdot, pinot noir, pinot meunier, and riesling, and including the 1.1ha Nursery Block planted to 39 varieties (8 still unknown)
Rhymney Vineyard 16.41 ha, planted to shiraz, riesling, pinot noir and pinot meunier
Leased or contracted vineyards 30ha
Varieties planted NFP
Dozens produced 20 000 No increase planned.
Exports To China through Pran Cellar Australia (ph) 8621 5178 0108; tina@cellaraustralia.com and to Hong Kong through Macro Asia Wines & Spirits (ph) 852 2791 6332; www.macroasia.com. Also to the UK, Ireland, Belgium, Switzerland, Canada, Singapore, Malaysia, Taiwan and Japan.
Winemaker Justin Purser

Key wines

Bin No. 1 Shiraz
How it is made: The grapes are part estate-, part contract-grown, and the fermentation takes place in both open and closed fermenters. It is typically matured for 10–12 months in proportions of predominantly French old oak barrels, large-format casks, and 10% new French oak barrels. The amount produced varies widely according to vintage, from 940 dozen bottles to 3900 dozen bottles.

How it tastes: Dense crimson-purple when young, with luscious black cherry/blackberry fruit on the bouquet and medium-bodied palate, the oak totally integrated, the tannins fine. Cellar to 15 years from vintage.

Best vintages: 2011, 2010, 2008, 2006, 2005

Bin No. 0 Shiraz
How it is made: 100% estate-grown, with open fermentation preceded by pre-ferment cold soak. It is pressed to a mix of new and used predominantly French oak, in which it spends 18 months prior to bottling. 110–1790 dozen made.

How it tastes: Bright crimson; a fragrant bouquet, with notes of spice and pepper to its black fruit core, then a beautifully textured and structured palate, fruit, oak and tannins in perfect harmony. Cellar to 25 years from vintage.

Best vintages: 2010, 2008, 2006, 2005, 2004

Best's Wines

Best's Wines, in the Great Western subregion of the Grampians, oozes history from every pore. In the 1850s brothers Joseph and Henry Best set up a business as butchers at Ararat, and miners being by nature hungry, the business flourished. Joseph began planting a vineyard in 1865; Henry took up a 30ha property on nearby Concongella Creek and started planting in 1866.

In 1920 Henry Best died, and his son Charles sold the business (including the right to use the Best's name) to local vignerons William Thomson and his son Frederick. They were already the owners of the St Andrews Vineyard and winery, established by them in 1892.

In 1924 William Thomson died, leaving Frederick as the sole owner; the depressed economy of the time led to the sale of the St Andrews winery in 1927, but in 1930 he was able to take advantage of the Great Depression to buy a small vineyard called Misery Farm next to Lake Boga at Swan Hill on the Murray River. He composed a couplet, '1929 – not so fine; 1930 – very dirty', reflecting the fact that the Concongella Vineyard and winery had been placed in the hands of receivers. But there was no buyer, and somehow Frederick scraped together enough money to retake possession, and to rename Misery Farm as St Andrews.

In 1938 Eric Vivian (Viv) Thomson was born, the third generation of the family to grow and make wine. Frederick Thomson died in 1949, and Viv enrolled in the viticulture and Oenology faculty of the Roseworthy Agricultural College, joining the family business as its first qualified winemaker. In 1964 son Benjamin (Ben) was born, later to become the fourth generation of winemakers in the family, and the following year Viv appointed Trevor Mast as the first external winemaker.

A series of talented winemakers have built the reputation of Best's over the ensuing 50 years, the size of the business also growing with additional vineyards and a much-enlarged winery. Today it is a particularly successful producer of exemplary shiraz at three quality/price levels, headed by the Thomson Family label, followed by Bin 0, and, thirdly, Bin 1. Its riesling and chardonnay are also consistently good, the occasional releases of pinot meunier are the best of this variety made in Australia.

Many would say its unique asset is a 1.02ha block of 2400 vines comprising 32 varieties – this was planted as a nursery by Henry Best in 1866. Some of the varieties no longer exist in France, and several others have defied all attempts at identification by French experts. Others are well-known varieties which have produced cuttings of mainstream varieties (pinot meunier and pinot noir, for example), which have in turn provided plantings of exceptional quality. From time to time there are sufficient plantings of 1866 pinot noir and pinot meunier to produce a commercial quantity of wine, sometimes a blend of the two varieties. Regardless, these are the oldest pinot noir and pinot meunier vines in the world, pre-dating phylloxera in France. Phylloxera has not affected the Grampians, and these and most other vines there are planted on their own roots.

Bindi Wine Growers

Est 1988
343 Melton Road, Gisborne, Vic 3437 (postal)
Open Not
Getting there NA
Contact (03) 5428 2564; bindiwine@gmail.com; www.bindiwines.com.au
Region Macedon Ranges
Lat 37°25′S
Elev 300–700m
E° Days 1149
Harvest 12 March–7 May
Estate vineyards 6ha
Varieties planted Pinot noir (4), chardonnay (2)

Leased or contracted vineyards 2ha
Varieties planted Shiraz (Heathcote)
Dozens produced 2000 No increase planned.
Exports Exports to China through Longfellows Wine Export (ph) +61 3 9428 5444; insurance@longfellows.com.au and to Hong Kong through Watson's Wine (ph) 852 2606 8828; info@watsonswine.com. Also to the UK, the US, Quebec, Japan and South Korea.
Winemaker Michael Dhillon, Stuart Anderson (Consultant)

Key wines

Original Vineyard Pinot Noir
How it is made: Hand-picked and (when required) sorted in the vineyard, it is totally destemmed and gently worked in small, open vats, usually with indigenous yeasts running the fermentation. It spends 15–17 months in French oak barriques (around 25% new). 375 dozen made.

How it tastes: The bouquet is notably perfumed, always with red and black cherry, sometimes with wafts of exotic spices which become more prominent with age. The palate provides a delicious and seductive wine. However, the depth increases as a spicy texture comes into play, providing a reward for those with patience. Cellar to 7 years from vintage.

Best vintages: 2012, 2010, 2006, 2005, 2000

Block 5 Pinot Noir
How it is made: Is made in similar fashion to the Original Vineyard, but comes from an area of only 0.5ha, and is matured in oak (35% new) for 15–17 months. Despite this higher level of new oak, it in no way intrudes on the varietal fruit expression. 175 dozen made.

How it tastes: Crystal-clear crimson in its youth, it has a pronounced spicy background to its black cherry and plum fruit on both the bouquet and palate; there is a parade of intense fruit girdled by firmer tannins than those of the Original Vineyard and, unlike for that wine, patience is required here for it to fully open its heart. Cellar to 10+ years from vintage.

Best vintages: 2012, 2010, 2006, 2005, 2000

Bindi Wine Growers

'The best things come in small packages' might well be the motto for Bindi. It started in a small farming village in Punjab in northern India, where Darshan Singh Dhillon was born on 2 October 1937. He was the youngest of six children, and the family's micro-sized farm was insufficient to support the children and their education, so his father had moved to Malaya to start a rubber tree plantation, returning home every two years to see the child he had fathered two years prior.

When partition of India and Pakistan occurred in 1947, the village, being close to the border, found itself in the middle of the violence and deaths (600 000) caused by the conflict between the Muslim and Hindu populations either side of that border. Darshan and his youngest sister were sent to a safer town, and in 1950 the family was reunited in Malaya, with ample income from the mature plantation. In 1958 he came to Australia seeking to qualify for the faculty of Civil Engineering at Melbourne University. This meant two years at Ballarat Grammar School, from where he went on to obtain his engineering degree.

During this time at Ballarat he was nicknamed Bill, but, far more importantly, was mentored by a brilliant mathematics and physics teacher, Kostas Rind. Rind had come to Australia from Lithuania to escape Russian persecution, and became a lifelong friend. He also introduced Bill Dhillon to the culture and pleasure of fine table wine.

Bill met and married wife Kaye during his time at university, and they acquired a 170ha sheep farm, and in 1972 built the Gisborne Squash Courts and the Wool and Wheel craft shop. Following Kaye's death in 1985, Bill decided the property should become self-sustaining, and in 1988 he began the planting of chardonnay and pinot noir. Fifteen hectares of eucalypts for high-grade furniture timber were also planted, with the remainder of the property maintained as remnant bushland and indigenous grassland.

At 500m above sea level, and in the cool southern location of the Macedon Ranges, chardonnay and pinot noir are by far the most commonly planted varieties; from the early 1990s Stuart Anderson, who retired to Macedon after selling his Bendigo winery, Balgownie Estate, became a consultant. He has great intelligence, vast experience, and a world view of wine, and has formed a mental partnership with Michael Dhillon, Bill's son and the Bindi winemaker and viticulturist.

Michael's unremitting attention to detail to the area's different soils and in the vineyard is exactly what you would encounter in the best Burgundy estates. The carefully used winemaking options also mirror those of Burgundy, albeit with choices appropriate for this (Australian) site.

Composition Chardonnay comes from a 1.5ha block on 480-million-year-old base rock, with shattered quartz over silt soil, sandstone and clay, the topsoil with some volcanic content (4 million years old). Quartz Chardonnay comes from a 0.5ha block, planted in 1988, at the same time as Composition, at the top end of the planting area, with more quartz; both wines are made the same way, the difference due to the soil.

Apart from the Original Vineyard Pinot Noir, the Composition Pinot Noir and the Block 5 (the latter 0.5ha on a sheltered, north-facing, very quartz-riddled site), Block K Pinot Noir, planted in 2001, is waiting in the wings as the vines mature, the grapes being included in Composition in the meantime. Michael Dhillon believes it will eventually produce the best pinot noir Bindi can create.

Boireann Winery

Est 1998
**26 Donnellys Castle Road, The Summit,
Qld 4377**
Open Fri–Sun 10–4
Getting there 2.5 hours' drive from
Brisbane CBD
Contact (07) 4683 2194;
boireannwinery@bigpond.com;
www.boireannwinery.com.au
Region Granite Belt
Lat 28°40'S
Elev 810m
E° Days 1717
Harvest 10 February–20 March

Estate vineyards 1.6ha
Varieties planted Cabernet sauvignon,
shiraz, merlot, petit verdot, mourvedre,
cabernet franc, viognier, tannat,
barbera, nebbiolo
Dozens produced 800 No increase
planned.
Exports Wines are not currently
exported.
Winemaker Peter Stark

Key wines

Shiraz Viognier

How it is made: The two varieties are co-fermented (viognier less than 10%), open-fermented, basket-pressed and matured in French oak barriques.

How it tastes: It is a fragrant, supple, smooth and medium-bodied wine, drinking well when young or mature, its bouquet and palate lifted by the impact of the viognier. Cellar to 20 years from vintage.

Best vintages: 2013, 2008, 2006, 2005, 2002

The Lurnea

How it is made: It is usually a blend of cabernet sauvignon, merlot, cabernet franc and petit verdot. Like the Shiraz Viognier, it is open-fermented and not filtered, and is also matured in French oak.

How it tastes: The wine has more structure than the Shiraz Viognier, but is still only medium-bodied. Both these wines are prime examples of Peter Stark's attention to detail. Cellar to 20 years from vintage.

Best vintages: 2013, 2008, 2006, 2005, 2002

Boireann Winery

Peter Stark had worked for a major Australian bank in Rockhampton, Queensland, for many years, but was made redundant in the early 1990s – along with others around Australia. The termination payment was enough for him and his wife Therese to sell their home and move to the far more appealing climate of the Granite Belt. Says Peter, 'Rockhampton has the same humid weather every day of the year, whereas the Granite Belt has four seasons.'

They purchased the property in 1994, and brought their collection of 500 bottles of Australian wine with them; they were keen consumers of Australian wine, but purely amateurs. Their income came from a small bed and breakfast business on the property, leaving them with time on their hands. While they had not intended to plant vines and make wine, there was sufficient land for a small vineyard, and Peter began reading books on viticulture and winemaking, and talking to other winemakers in the Granite Belt. In the Australian fashion, they have always been happy to give advice on any question or problem he might have.

In 1995 he planted 400 vines of cabernet sauvignon as a trial, intending simply to make wine for home consumption, and for guests to drink at the bed and breakfast facility. The wine was made in one small shed with the bare minimum of equipment, but was so good it led to the planting of shiraz and merlot in 1997, petit verdot and mourvedre in 1998, cabernet franc and grenache in 1999, viognier in 2000, and tannat, barbera and nebbiolo in 2002. Subsequent grafting of pinot noir to additional tannat, and of the grenache to sangiovese, has proved successful.

The winery now has a bottle storage area, an insulated, temperature-controlled barrel storage cellar, and two equipment storage buildings, housing the grape crusher, press and wine filter, and tractor plus vineyard equipment.

Right from the outset, Peter Stark has made wines of great purity and varietal expression; he clearly has an excellent palate, and fully understands the importance of having a very clean winery and the attention to detail which is needed to achieve such beautiful wines. After frost decimated the crop in 2010 he installed frost protection, and in that year purchased grapes from other growers. It proved that it is his personal skill, not some magic in the soil, that makes these wines what they are.

He has also become interested in those two difficult varieties, sangiovese and nebbiolo, and he and Therese have been to Italy twice to gain direct knowledge about the way those varieties are grown and made. He is quietly confident that he can tame nebbiolo if there are no vintage issues, and given his record, I believe him.

Finally, they sell out each year within six months, most of the wine going to their wine club members, 'The Boireann Bunch'. The Granite Belt has 44 other wineries, and offers much for both general and wine tourism, so a visit is strongly recommended. If you are interested in tasting and buying wine, an email or phone call will let you know whether any or all of the wines are then available.

Brokenwood

Est 1970
401–427 McDonalds Road, Pokolbin,
NSW 2321
Open 7 days 9.30–5
Getting there 2 hours' drive from
Sydney CBD
Contact (02) 4998 7559;
sales@brokenwood.com.au;
www.brokenwood.com.au
Region Hunter Valley
Lat 32°54′S
Elev 76m
E° Days 1823
Harvest 31 January–11 March

Estate vineyards 20ha
Varieties planted Shiraz
Leased or contracted vineyards 200ha
Varieties NFP
Dozens produced 100 000 No increase
planned.
Exports To China through
Empire M (ph) 8621 5866 0563;
sales@empirem.net and to Hong
Kong through Macro Asia Wines
& Spirits (ph) 852 3191 2001;
www.macroasia.com. Also to the UK,
the US, Canada, Cambodia, Japan
Malaysia, the Maldives, Singapore,
Sweden and Vietnam.
Winemaker Iain Riggs, Simon Steele

Key wines

Graveyard Shiraz
How it is made: Hand-picked, a 4-day cold soak, then 4–5 days' ferment at 26–28°C;
3-tonne open-fermenters enable hand-plunging twice a day; pressed off and run to
oak and mlf in barrel, 100% French, including 10% larger format (500l) puncheons;
approximately 40% new oak in total. 500 dozen made.

How it tastes: Full but clear purple-crimson; an imperious wine, its power so
relaxed you might walk by without stopping to look; blackberry, licorice and
leather are sheathed in quality oak, the tannins exceptionally fine, but perfectly
balanced. Can be enjoyed within 5 years from vintage, but will cellar for 40 years
or more (under screwcap).

Best vintages: 2011, 2009, 2007, 2006, 2005

ILR Reserve Semillon
How it is made: There is nothing of any particular importance in making the wine:
cultured yeast is used, the fermentation lasting around 7 days at 15–17°C to ensure
completion of the fermentation with no residual sugar remaining. Within 3 months
of vintage, the wine is lightly fined and filtered. What makes the wine special is the
very high quality semillon purchased to make it, and the magic of not less than
6 years' maturation in bottle. 500 dozen made.

How it tastes: Although the wine never comes into contact with oak, it develops
extraordinary richness and depth, with honey, toast and cashew flavours akin to
barrel-fermented white wines. Its naturally high levels of acidity, coupled with its
low alcohol (around 11% alc/vol) gives it great longevity; it will cellar well for at
least 20 years from vintage.

Best vintages: 2007, 2006, 2005, 2004, 2003

Brokenwood

Three Sydney lawyers who had graduated from Sydney University in 1961, and known each other for six years, became committed consumers of the best wines then available in Australia. In the latter part of the 1960s their wine horizon extended to France and beyond under the guidance of the late Len Evans AO, OBE.

I was one of those three, and I persuaded my friends that we should buy land, plant a vineyard and build a winery in the Hunter Valley, the nearest wine region to Sydney. My motive and rationale for this audacious idea was that it would prevent legal practice taking over my life, seven days a week, a situation confronting any junior partner (as I then was) in a Sydney law firm. So in 1970 we purchased a 4ha block of land covered by trees and enlisted help from friends as we cleared the trees, ploughed the heavy clay soil, planted the vines (1971), built a very small tractor shed, and in 1973 made the first vintage of 175 dozen bottles.

Because we had extremely good cellars of old French wines (ex Christie's of London) and I could cook, we were able to enlist a growing number of friends to give their weekends and holidays (during bottling and vintage) free of cost to us. An enduring part of this business has been the continuing involvement of the owners, who drink well, eat well, share a communal dormitory without complaint, and work whenever they are asked to do so. The history of Brokenwood since those early years has seen an unbroken increase in the production and quality of its wines, although I played no part in that success after 1983, for I left Sydney to live and work in Melbourne.

A parting gift, as it were, was the hiring of Brokenwood's first employee (and first winemaker with an Oenology degree) in mid-1982, a 27-year-old winemaker from McLaren Vale who had established his reputation as an outstanding winemaker of the all-but-unknown blend of semillon and sauvignon blanc, and of chardonnay. Iain Riggs has been CEO of the business since that time, and, through a rare mix of winemaking, wine marketing, financial and people management skills, has given Brokenwood its reputation as one of the best medium-sized wineries in Australia.

In 1978 we had made a Hunter Valley/Coonawarra blend of shiraz and cabernet sauvignon, inspired by a similar blend made 20 years earlier. It set the precedent for Brokenwood's wine portfolio of today: the only vineyards owned by Brokenwood are 20ha of Hunter Valley shiraz, the best of which goes to make the truly iconic Graveyard Shiraz. All the superb Hunter Valley semillon comes from contract-grown grapes from a number of subregions in the Hunter Valley. The ILR Reserve Semillon, released when it is six years old, is the white partner to the Graveyard Shiraz.

These two wines are made in strictly limited quantities; Brokenwood also produced other top-class single-vineyard semillons and shirazs from the Hunter Valley and elsewhere across Australia. However, the major part of production comes from the varietal range of pinot gris, semillon, unwooded chardonnay, chardonnay, nebbiolo, pinot noir, sangiovese, cabernet sauvignon merlot and shiraz, grown variously in McLaren Vale, Beechworth, King Valley, Cowra, Orange and the Canberra District. These wines may be single-region or blends; the largest volume is for two regional varietal blends called Cricket Pitch White and Cricket Pitch Red.

Brookland Valley

Est 1984
Caves Road, Wilyabrup, WA 6280
Open 7 days 10–5
Getting there 3 hours' drive from Perth CBD
Contact (08) 9755 6042; wineshop@brooklandvalley.com.au; www.brooklandvalley.com.au
Region Margaret River
Lat 33°57′S
Elev 40–90m
E° Days 1552
Harvest 26 February–8 April

Estate vineyards NFP
Varieties planted As with other wineries that are part of a much larger wine business under single ownership, vineyard resources are shared across all brands in the group.
Dozens produced NFP
Exports To China through Shanghai CWC Wine Company (ph) 8621 3252 8715; Enquiries@ accolade-wines.cn and to Hong Kong through Accolade Wines Hong Kong HKEnquiries@accolade-wines.com; www.accolade-wines.com. Also to Samoa, Christmas Island, Fiji and Papua New Guinea.
Winemaker Courtney Treacher

Key wines

Reserve Chardonnay
How it is made: Estate-grown, hand-picked, chilled and then whole-bunch-pressed. The juice is wild yeast barrel-fermented in French oak (60% new), and left on yeast lees for 8 months, undergoing mlf in this time, with some lees stirring.

How it tastes: Light straw-green; a wine of extreme finesse and elegance, seemingly taking its cue from Tasmania and/or the Yarra Valley; it has great length and line, early-picked grapes providing natural acidity and low pH to soak up the oak from barrel fermentation, yet in no danger of crossing into sauvignon blanc territory, stone fruits the key driver. Cellar to 10 years from vintage.

Best vintages: 2012, 2010, 2009, 2005, 2002

Estate Cabernet Sauvignon Merlot
How it is made: Hand-picked grapes are sorted prior to being destemmed and crushed; fermentation is in open-top fermenters with specific cultured yeast, with 10 days on skins before being basket-pressed. The wine is then taken to a mix of new, 1-year-old and 2-year-old French oak for 15 months' maturation, and is lightly fined with egg whites before being bottled.

How it tastes: Bright, relatively light, crimson-purple; a very attractive example of the blend, something which comes easily in Margaret River; cassis, redcurrant and a dab of oak flow through the medium-bodied palate, tannins simply pointing the way to the finish. Both terroir and variety are allowed to speak. Cellar to 20+ years from vintage.

Best vintages: 2011, 2010, 2009, 2008, 2004

Brookland Valley

In 1984 Dr Tony Jordan and Brian Croser, then partners in the leading wine consultancy business Oenotec, were retained to identify the location for, and then oversee the establishment of, Brookland Valley. This led to the initial estate plantings of cabernet sauvignon, chardonnay, semillon and sauvignon blanc. It soon gained a high reputation for its wines, and also for its cellar door, Gallery of Wine Arts, and restaurant situated on Caves Road, in the heart of Margaret River.

In 1997, the founders, Malcolm and Dee Jones, accepted an offer by Houghton (part of the then BRL Hardy Group) to acquire 50% of the business, which saw a significant increase in its estate vineyards. Hardys moved to full ownership in 2004, giving Brookland Valley access to group-owned vineyards spread across five of the six subregions of Margaret River identified by the godfather of the region, Dr John Gladstones.

Now part of Accolade, its operations are totally integrated with those of Houghton, albeit with dedicated vineyards for the Reserve Chardonnay and Cabernet Sauvignon.

The sheer consistency of the quality of its wines, from the bottom tier to the top as at 2013, and with wines strategically priced at intermediate levels, all offering excellent value for money, led me to make Brookland Valley 'Winery of the Year' in my *2009 Australian Wine Companion*.

A major reason for its success is that it has continued to focus solely on the core varieties that do so well in Margaret River, and are recognised as classic in all parts of the wine world. The two wines at the top of the pyramid are the Reserve Chardonnay and Reserve Cabernet Sauvignon; next are the Estate Chardonnay and Estate Cabernet Merlot. The Unison label, a relatively recent introduction, sits in the mid-range of price, and offers chardonnay, sauvignon blanc semillon and cabernet sauvignon. Verse 1, the entry-point label, offers chardonnay, semillon sauvignon blanc, shiraz and cabernet merlot.

A succession of highly gifted winemakers have been responsible for the quality of the Brookland Valley wines, all of which have been made at Houghton since 1997. The first was Paul Lapsley, who left to become chief winemaker at Coldstream Hills in 1998. He was followed by Larry Cherubino. Both men went on to even higher positions, Lapsley as chief winemaker for Hardys/Accolade, Cherubino as a very successful consultant, setting up his eponymous brand with wife Edwina, and (since 2009) chief winemaker for Robert Oatley Vineyards.

Current winemaker, Courtney Treacher, is also responsible for the Moondah Brook wines.

Brown Brothers

Est 1885
Milawa-Bobinawarrah Road, Milawa, Vic 3678
Open 7 days 9–5
Getting there 2.5 hours' drive from Melbourne CBD
Contact (03) 5720 5500; info@brownbrothers.com.au; www.brownbrothers.com.au
Region King Valley
Lat 36°20'S
Elev 200–800m
E° Days 1618
Harvest 20 February–4 May
Estate vineyards 596.22ha
Varieties planted Cienna (81.23), shiraz (60.94), chardonnay (50.46), dolcetto (46.21), pinot gris (38.04), crouchen (35.1), prosecco (32.6), gordo blanco (31.04), orange muscat (27), riesling (26.74), tarrango (22.5), merlot (22.13), cabernet sauvignon (21.82), chenin blanc (15.48), sauvignon blanc (15), pinot noir (14.7), tempranillo (11.15), plus smaller plantings of vermentino, durif, pinot meunier, malbec, flora, petit verdot, graciano, gewurztraminer, mondeuse, carmenere, gamay, viognier, montepulciano, nero d'Avola, savagnin, aglianico, sagrantino, schioppettino, gruner veltliner
Dozens produced 1 million May increase to 1.05 million.
Exports To China and Hong Kong through ASC Fine Wines (ph) 862 160 561 999 (China); (ph) 852 3923 6720 (Hong Kong); www.asc-wines.com. Also to all major markets.
Winemaker Wendy Cameron, Joel Tilbrook, Cate Looney

Key wines

Patricia Cabernet Sauvignon
How it is made: The Patricia range is Brown Brothers' best, honouring the late Patricia Brown, who outlived husband John Charles. It is estate-grown, and fermented in small, open vats with cultured yeast, with twice daily pumpovers. It spends 18 months in French oak barriques, around 75% new. It is racked to tank for 3–6 months, before light filtration and bottling, and is then matured in bottle for another 2 years. Nil to 750 dozen made.

How it tastes: Clear, deep colour; the bouquet and palate have a complex range of blackcurrant fruit, black olive, cedary oak aromas and flavours. The wine is full-bodied, but the tannins are ripe and well balanced, drawing out the length of the finish. Cellar to 15 years from vintage.

Best vintages: 2008, 2005, 2003, 2002, 2000

Cienna
How it is made: Cienna, a unique red grape, is a cross between cabernet sauvignon and the Spanish variety sumoll, bred in Australia in 1972 for planting in hot, dry conditions. Brown Brothers is the only producer, with 81ha planted in two Riverland estate vineyards, plus contract-grown grapes. It is made as a low-alcohol, lightly sparkling style. 90 000 dozen made.

How it tastes: Brightly coloured, the luscious red fruits are sweet but vibrant, thanks to the CO_2, and to the balanced acidity. Not designed to be cellared.

Best vintages: 2012, 2009, 2008, 2004, 2000

Brown Brothers

Brown Brothers stands alongside Tyrrell's and Yalumba, sharing with those wineries a history dating back to the mid-19th century, an unbroken line of family ownership, and commercial success on a significant scale. The rich Brown Brothers story commences in 1852 when 18-year-old law clerk George Harry Brown arrived in Melbourne. Like so many others, he found the lure of gold irresistible and went to Bendigo to join the search. He was unsuccessful, and joined with four others to travel further north and buy a property at Hurdle Creek near Milawa. In 1857 a Scot named John Graham arrived at Milawa and purchased 50ha. George Brown met and married Graham's schoolteacher daughter, and on her father's death the couple moved to the Milawa property.

John Graham had planted table grapes, and George Harry Brown extended the plantings with wine varieties. His son John Francis Brown (born in 1867) made the first wine on the property, using an old Canadian-style barn which John Graham had built. It still stands, and is used for maturing the fortified wines of Browns. In 1900 an additional winery was built, part of which remains. It was incorporated into the winemaking complex which has grown over the ensuing 100+ years.

In 1915 phylloxera finally made its way from Rutherglen to the Milawa area of the King Valley. Of the numerous vineyards around Milawa destroyed by phylloxera, only the Brown vineyard of 16ha was replanted. John Charles Brown, eldest son of John Francis, left school in 1933 and made his first vintage in 1934. It was due to the extraordinary foresight of this gentle, kind and compassionate man that Brown Brothers was transformed from a quiet and sleepy family winery at the end of the 1950s to one of Australia's leading mid-sized wineries, with a production of over 1 million cases. He died in May 2004, his 70th vintage at Milawa.

His second-youngest son, Ross Brown, joined the company in 1970, and was responsible for development of Australia's leading cellar door (with 100 000 visitors a year) and its associated Epicurean Centre. His marketing responsibilities led to frequent trips overseas and within Australia, and to his leading role in Australian and Victorian tourism bodies.

In 2001 he was appointed CEO, and in 2010 took the far-sighted decision to buy Tasmania's largest winery and vineyard owner, Tamar Ridge. It was the most recent (and at A$32 million, by far the most important) acquisition of vineyards, and complements Brown Brothers' mainland vineyards (at various altitudes in the King Valley, and in Heathcote).

The company grows 36 varieties on 12 vineyards in Victoria and Tasmania, with total plantings of 899ha on 1000ha of land producing 47 different wines available at the cellar door, ranging from sparkling to table to fortified styles. The construction of what was termed the kindergarten winery (in fact a small-scale fermentation cellar for top-quality, limited-production wines) several decades ago underpinned the more recent production of the Patricia range, resulting in a spread of prices.

After several years of familiarisation with the Tasmanian vineyard portfolio, Brown Brothers sold the White Hills plantings of 82.9ha to Treasury Wine Estates, doubtless reducing the company's debt from the borrowing used to purchase Tamar Ridge in the first place. For further information on Tamar Ridge see page 182.

A founding member of Australia's First Families of Wine.

Burch Family Wines

Est 1986
Miamup Road, Cowaramup, WA 6284
Open 7 days 10–5
Getting there 2.75 hours' drive from Perth CBD
Contact (08) 9756 5200; hpw@hpw.com.au; www.burchfamilywines.com.au
Region Margaret River/Denmark
Lat 33°57′S
Elev 40–90m
E° Days 1552
Harvest 26 February–8 April
Estate vineyards 141ha
Varieties planted Chardonnay (42), cabernet sauvignon (30), riesling (15), pinot noir (13), sauvignon blanc (12), shiraz (11), semillon (5), merlot (5), other varieties (8); in all, 74ha in Margaret River, and 67ha in the Great Southern

Leased or contracted vineyards 329ha
Varieties planted Chardonnay (72), cabernet sauvignon (72), sauvignon blanc (55), shiraz (46), semillon (32), merlot (21), riesling (16), pinot noir (12), other (3)
Dozens produced NFP
Exports To China through Aussino (ph) 8620 3887 9081; kenneth@aussino.net and Mega Wines (ph) 8620 3888 6322; vip@megawines.com.cn and to Hong Kong through Nathan Wines Ltd (ph) 852 2321 1169; hazehm.wong@nathanfinewines.com.hk and Winerack (ph) 852 2433 9929; james@winerack.com.hk. Also to the UK, the US and other major markets.
Winemaker Janice McDonald, Mark Bailey

Key wines

Howard Park Abercrombie Cabernet Sauvignon
How it is made: The very best blocks from the Scotsdale Vineyard in Great Southern/Mount Barker are hand-picked, destemmed and passed over a sorting table. Fermentation uses cultured yeast, and the time on skins is between 10 and 15 days. Some of the wine is pressed at 3 baume and taken direct to barrique, while part is left on skins for post-fermentation maceration for several weeks. It spends 22 months in 50% new and 50% used French oak barriques. 700 dozen made.

How it tastes: A deeply coloured and very distinguished wine, showing classically powerful black fruits, with texture and structure provided by firm tannins and quality oak. Needs at least 5 years' maturation, and will cellar for 30 from vintage.

Best vintages: 2010, 2009, 2008, 2004, 2001

Howard Park Leston Margaret River Shiraz
How it is made: The grapes are either hand-picked or machine-harvested, and pass across a sorting table on their way to fermentation with cultured yeast. As with Abercrombie Cabernet, part of the must is pressed well before dryness and taken to barrel to complete fermentation, part remaining on skins for post-fermentation maceration for several weeks. This wine spends 15–18 months in predominantly French oak (30% new). 2000 dozen made.

How it tastes: A harmonious and balanced wine, offering red and black cherry and plum fruit, sustained by fine-grained tannins and a touch of cedary oak. Enjoyable now or up to 20 years from vintage.

Best vintages: 2010, 2009, 2007, 2005, 2004

Burch Family Wines

The establishment date of 1986 is correct, but needs to be put into context if the breathtaking speed of development since 1993 is to be understood. Visionary winemaker (now turned chocolatier) John Wade opened Howard Park Wines in 1986 and crushed a total of 3 tonnes of riesling and cabernet sauvignon in a converted butter factory in the town (and subregion) of Denmark, the quality validating his belief that the Great Southern region was uniquely suited to these two varieties.

He was not to know that Amy and Jeff Burch had purchased a pastoral property in Margaret River, with the Wilyabrup River meandering through it, in 1988. Being full-time drivers of a very successful flexible packaging business meant their idea of creating a vineyard and winery would have to wait.

Five years later they formed a partnership with John Wade, and his small wine-making business was transformed overnight with a move to the Denmark Agricultural College. New French oak, modern presses and new tanks were purchased. Another three years on, in 1996, the Parkhead property was bought, and construction of a large modern winery began, completed in time for the 1997 vintage. 1996 also saw the plantings of the first vines at their Margaret River Leston Vineyard.

With John Wade's exit from the partnership in 1998 the pace and scale of development increased yet again. In 1999 the Howard Park Single Vineyard series wines, Leston Shiraz and Scotsdale Cabernet Sauvignon, were released; in 2000 the large *feng shui*-designed winery and cellar door were opened on the Leston Vineyard; in 2004 the family purchased a property in Porongurup, and planted riesling, chardonnay and pinot noir in 2005, calling the vineyard Mount Barrow Vineyard, and making the first wines in 2008.

Threaded through this was the arrival of members of the family: Jeff's brother David Burch (after 16 years as a star in the Australian Ballet Company) as vineyard manager of Leston; Jeff's sister Lesley Scogna as brand ambassador for Australia, working with distributor Negociants Australia; daughter Nat Burch, with several tertiary degrees and time as a teacher, taking responsibility for exports, bottling, administration, and stock and product control; son David W. Burch, with multiple tertiary degrees, extensively involved in sales and marketing; and son Richard Burch the brand manager for the Australian east coast.

The involvement of so many blood relatives led to the renaming of the business as Burch Family Wines in 2012 (but retaining Howard Park as the brand name). But there are also three key people outside the family. The first is David Botting, chief viticulturist, with an academic and practical background that puts him at the top level of his profession in Australia. He has been at the forefront of the move towards biodynamic management of the vineyards, and part of the overall management of the business and its move to reduce its carbon footprint, thus increasing its sustainability.

Next is Burgundian winemaker Pascal Marchand, who is the French partner of the Marchand & Burch joint venture. He has direct responsibility for Marchand & Burch pinot noir and chardonnay, made from Porongurup grapes, and a range of Burgundies from Village to Grand Cru – all sealed with screwcaps.

Finally, there is the feisty and vastly experienced senior winemaker Janice McDonald, who took up the position in January 2011, and may well make the great Burch Family Wines even greater.

A founding member of Australia's First Families of Wine.

By Farr/Farr Rising

Est 1994
27 Maddens Road, Bannockburn,
Vic 3331
Open Not
Getting there NA
Contact (03) 5281 1733;
wine@byfarr.com.au; www.byfarr.com.au
Region Geelong
Lat 38°09'S
Elev 25–150m
E° Days 1377
Harvest 8 March–21 May
Estate vineyards 14ha
Varieties planted Pinot noir (8.7),
chardonnay (3.1), shiraz (1.2),
viognier (1)

Dozens produced 5000 May increase to
5500.
Exports To China through Ruby Red
Fine Wine (ph) 8621 6234 2249;
info@rubyred.com.cn and Aussino
(ph) 020 3887 9081; gzo@aussino.net; to
Hong Kong through Links Concept (by
Farr) (ph) 852 2802 2818; marketing@
linksconcept.com and Watson's Wine
(Farr Rising) (ph) 852 2606 8828;
info@watsonswine.com. Also to the UK,
Japan, Singapore, Taiwan, Canada and
Denmark.
Winemaker Nick Farr

Key wines

Farrside Pinot Noir
How it is made: Hand-picked; a substantial but various number of whole bunches
are incorporated in the open-top fermenters, and the must is plunged by foot or
hand, the temperature encouraged to reach 33°C or more; basket-pressed to a high
percentage of new French oak barriques.

How it tastes: Always a powerful, masculine pinot noir, even in wet vintages such
as 2011, with abundant black cherry/berry fruit, but with fine, savoury tannins
running through the beautifully detailed and long palate. Cellar 10–15 years
from vintage.

Best vintages: 2011, 2010, 2008

Chardonnay
How it is made: Unusually, the grape bunches are sometimes partially crushed by
foot in the picking bins to build phenolics, and the pressed cloudy juice is chilled
to 12°C before going to French oak for wild yeast fermentation and natural mlf;
lightly fined and filtered prior to bottling.

How it tastes: Always a superbly complex wine with the majesty of grand cru white
burgundies. Cellar for 10 years or more from vintage.

Best vintages: 2011, 2010, 2008, 2006, 2004

By Farr/Farr Rising

The somewhat complicated name reflects the father Gary Farr and son Nick Farr partnership, Gary having founded By Farr, and Nick having founded Farr Rising. Having run the businesses separately for some years, they joined forces, but have kept the labels unchanged.

While Geelong is home base for the vineyard and winery, both have been strongly influenced by decades of experience in Burgundy at Domaine Dujac, in Gary's case dating back to 1983. That experience is reflected in the way the grapes are grown and the way the wines are made. Thus 3.2ha of the pinot noir is a multi-clone, high-density (8000 vines/ha), low-trellis planting. The pinot noir winemaking involves open fermentation, with varying percentages of whole bunches, pigeage by hand and foot, and a leisurely approach to the initiation of the mlf.

The Geelong region as a whole is uncompromisingly cool, with a significant maritime influence. The estate vineyards are in the Moorabool Valley. Its meso-climate is shaped by prevailing winds from the western plains, keeping the vines on edge, and the maritime influence regulates the temperatures of the long days of sunshine and cool night breezes. This results in low-yielding vines that are naturally in balance.

The soils also play an important role. There are two main types: first, a rich, friable red and black volcanic loam over clays and limestone (the latter appearing in the loam in some patches); and second, a quartz gravel mixed with red ironstone in grey sandy loam with a heavy clay base. They are well drained and are of low fertility. The Farrs say these soils compare with the best sites for chardonnay and pinot noir in the world.

The By Farr wines are all made from single estate blocks; the chardonnay, shiraz and viognier were planted on the red loam House Block in 1994. The Sangreal (pinot noir) also comes from this block, with clones 114 and 115. Farrside was planted in 2001, with clones 114, 115, 113, 667, 777 and MV6 on black volcanic soils over limestone. This produces a more masculine wine; Sangreal, on the red soils, is more elegant and feminine.

Tout Pres is one of the blocks planted with 8000 vines/ha, and even though this is only a 1ha block, it has an amphitheatre-like structure, with each of the three slopes having different soils. The clones are the same as those for Farrside, but the close planting and the impact of the soil produces lush but masculine wines, with the structure found only in the most age-worthy pinots.

The Farr Rising wines are produced from both estate-grown fruit and purchased fruit, the estate-grown chardonnay and pinot noir vines having been planted in 2002 on a mixture of black volcanic soils over limestone at the bottom of the north-facing slope, and ironstone soil towards the top. The vine rows run north–south to achieve maximum light and flavour. The purchased grapes come from two sources, one with clones 114 and 115, another with clone MV6 planted in 1980.

Finally, for 10 years Nick Farr has also made Farr Rising Mornington Pinot Noir, the wines always a lot softer and sweeter than those from the Moorabool Valley.

Campbells

Est 1870
Murray Valley Highway, Rutherglen, Vic 3685
Open Mon–Sat 9–5, Sun 10–5
Getting there 3 hours' drive from Melbourne CBD
Contact (02) 6033 6000; wine@campbellswines.com.au; www.campbellswines.com.au
Region Rutherglen
Lat 36°03'S
Elev 170m
E° Days 1591
Harvest 17 February–27 March
Estate vineyards 57.4ha
Varieties planted Shiraz (19.4), cabernet sauvignon (3.3), chardonnay (2.5), trebbiano (2.5), durif (2.5), muscadelle (2.4), riesling (2.3), plus lesser plantings of viognier, semillon, merlot, malbec, gewurztraminer, ruby cabernet, roussanne, and other white and red grapes, including port varieties
Leased or contracted vineyards 16ha
Varieties planted Shiraz (10), tempranillo (2), durif (2), muscat (2)
Dozens produced 33 000 May increase to 40 000.
Exports To China through Shandong Wine World Liquor Co. (ph) 86 532 8491 2310; mark@marikma.com. Also to all major markets.
Winemaker Colin Campbell, Tim Gniel

Key wines

The Brothers Shiraz
How it is made: The grapes are crushed and the must chilled to allow a 2-day pre-fermentation cold soak, fermentation initiated by cultured yeast, and peaking at 26°C, with 10–14 days on skins. It is pressed to new puncheons (60% French oak, 40% American), where it spends 12–18 months, depending on vintage. It is not fined, and only lightly filtered; 250 dozen made, but only in the best vintages.

How it tastes: The depth of blackberry, plum and black cherry fruit reflects the quality of the grapes; this power keeps the substantial oak contribution in balance. Cellar to 20 years from vintage.

Best vintages: 2009, 2006, 2005, 2004, 2002

Merchant Prince Rare Rutherglen Muscat
How it is made: The grapes are picked at the highest baum level; cultured yeast is added immediately after crushing, and the must is pumped over twice daily for 2–3 days to extract colour and flavour before the wine is fortified, stopping fermentation. The must will then be pressed and the wine taken to a 5-level solera, level 5 the youngest, level 1 the oldest. Levels 4 and 5 are kept in old casks of 1600l, levels 3, 2 and 1 in old 500l puncheons. As wine is bottled, level 2 is used to top up level 1, levels 3 to top up level 2, and so on. Some of the wine is 80 years old, and only 5% of the level 1 solera is bottled per year, providing 100 dozen 375ml bottles.

How it tastes: Deep amber colour, grading to olive on the rim, it is exceptionally luscious, intense and rich, its density greater than most from Rutherglen; it has an exceptionally complex array of aromas and flavours, including raisin, burnt toffee and spice; great balance and length.

Best vintages: NA

Campbells

Campbells has a long and rich history, with five generations of the family making wine in the same place for 140 years. There were difficult times: phylloxera's arrival in the Bobbie Burns Vineyard in 1898; the Depression of the 1930s; and premature deaths along the way. But the Scottish blood of founder John Campbell has ensured that the business has not only survived, but quietly flourished. Indeed, there have been spectacular successes in unexpected quarters (white table wines, especially riesling) and expected success with the Rutherglen region's unique fortified wines, muscat and topaque. But even here, 99-point scores from Robert Parker and a 100-point score from Harvey Steiman (*Wine Spectator*) put Campbells in a special position, dramatically underlined with its Merchant Prince Rare Muscat receiving trophies from the Rutherglen Wine Show as Best Australian Fortified Wine and Best Australian Muscat.

The nigh on half-century, fourth-generation stewardship of Malcolm and Colin Campbell has been the most important in the history of the winery, but the five members of the fifth generation all working in various capacities in the business are well equipped to move up the ladder when Colin and/or Malcolm decide to retire. This is not a decision under consideration now, but as in any successful family business, succession planning is in place.

Colin Campbell led the formation of the 'Muscat of Rutherglen Network', its members those who make this wine. In 1998, the Network devised a four-tier classification system, with a simple varietal name for the entry level, then in turn Classic, Grand and Rare, in ascending order of age and complexity. The same structure applies to what used to be named tokay, but in deference to the EU is now called topaque; it is in fact made from muscadelle, a grape used in small amounts by the French makers of white Bordeaux, either sweet (sauternes) or dry.

He also formed the 'Durif of Rutherglen Network' to promote the dry red wine made from this variety, bred in France as a cross between syrah and peloursin by botanist Dr François Durif in the 1860s. In California it is called petite sirah, and is known for its deep colour, robust structure, and resistance to downy mildew.

Brother Malcolm took responsibility for the family's substantial general farming business and for the vineyards in 1974. Since that time, he has replanted most of the vines, and increased the vineyard area to its present level. This has seen Campbells produce very good table wines, especially shiraz and durif, at the head of a portfolio of 13 varieties resulting in 21 different wines. However, the four topaques and four muscats are the jewels in Campbells' crown.

A founding member of Australia's First Families of Wine.

Capel Vale

Est 1974
118 Mallokup Road, Capel, WA 6271
Open 7 days 10–4
Getting there 2 hours' drive from
Perth CBD
Contact (08) 9727 1986;
winery@capelvale.com;
www.capelvale.com
Region Geographe
Lat 33°33′S
Elev 10–70m
E° Days 1718
Harvest 16 February–27 March
Estate vineyards 85.25ha
Varieties planted Geographe 10.25ha
with small plantings each of verdelho,
viognier, chardonnay, petit verdot,
merlot, cabernet sauvignon, shiraz,
malbec; **Margaret River** cabernet
sauvignon (24), merlot (3), malbec (1),
sauvignon blanc (1); **Pemberton**
sauvignon blanc (15), semillon (10),
pinot noir (6); **Mount Barker** shiraz
(10), riesling (5)
Dozens produced 50 000 No increase
planned.
Exports To China through Urban Glass
Wines Co. Ltd (ph) 86 769 2282 8079;
shuyi.zhen@gmail.com and to Hong
Kong through Telford International
Company Ltd (ph) 852 2722 5066;
james_li@telford.com.hk. Also to all
major markets.
Winemaker Justin Hearn

Key wines

Regional Series Margaret River Chardonnay
How it is made: All estate-grown grapes are barrel-fermented with a mix of
cultured and wild yeasts in 100% medium-toast French oak (30% new) for
10 months. The wine is lees-stirred during its 10-month sojourn in oak. Fined
and filtered. 1350 dozen made.

How it tastes: A complex and rich chardonnay, with white peach, nectarine
and rockmelon fruit enhanced by the well-handled French oak. Does not
need cellaring.

Best vintages: 2012, 2011, 2010, 2008, 2005

Regional Series Margaret River Cabernet Sauvignon
How it is made: Produced from 100% estate-grown grapes, inoculated with
cultured yeast; cold maceration and 20% post-maceration skin contact increases
the length and complexity of the tannins. It spends 12 months in French oak
(30% new) and is lightly fined with egg whites and filtered. 4000 dozen made.

How it tastes: The medium purple-crimson colour introduces a densely packed
wine with black fruits on the full-bodied palate, oak and tannins also having their
say. Cellar to at least 20 years from vintage.

Best vintages: 2012, 2011, 2010, 2008, 2005

Capel Vale

This estate-driven Geographe region winery was established by Perth-based medical practitioner Dr Peter Pratten and wife Elizabeth. The first vines were established on the banks of the beautiful, slow-flowing Capel River, with its resident population of native mountain ducks (portrayed on the labels of the wines). The first winery was built onsite in 1979, the first vintage following in 1980. Not long thereafter, I visited the vineyard, and vividly remember the luxuriant growth of the vines. They were planted on 5-metre-deep rich, red alluvial soil over a limestone base.

The vigour of the growth of the vines paralleled the vigour of Dr Pratten in driving the growth of the business, which was successful right from the outset. Doctors are well acquainted with second opinions being sought on complex medical conditions, and Dr Pratten followed suit by obtaining expert consultancy advice on ways to control the vigour.

Likewise, having initially purchased grapes from Margaret River, he moved to extend estate vineyards to that region, in Pemberton, and in Mount Barker, the first family-owned and -run winery to spread its ownership over these four key regions. The two vineyards in Geographe share the same red soil, and have the warmest climate, which means the grapes ripen earlier than in the other regions. The Margaret River vineyard is in the centre of the region, on red lateritic soil interspersed with patches of granitic loamy soil. The vineyard faces south-west, exposing it to strong cool ocean winds, producing low yields of high-quality cabernet sauvignon. Vintage here is later than Geographe, but earlier than Pemberton.

This latter region has deep, fertile loams, and while it is cooled by the low water temperature of the Southern Ocean, summer days are warm, and there is abundant water. It is here that some of the best sauvignon blanc and semillon is grown. Mount Barker is the coolest of the four regions, with some of the oldest rocks and soils in the world. It is ideal for riesling and cool-climate shiraz, elegant but perfumed.

With this constant theme of matching variety with terroir (and climate), Capel Vale grows and makes chardonnay, riesling, sauvignon blanc, semillon (often blending those two varieties), verdelho, shiraz, cabernet sauvignon and merlot (the latter for blending with the cabernet sauvignon). There is a three-tiered volume/price structure, all varietal-based, with Debut the entry point, Regional Series in the middle, and Single Vineyard at the top. There are also limited production wines named Cellar Exclusive, only sold at cellar door or to mailing list customers.

In 2007 son Simon Pratten took over as CEO, but parents Peter and Elizabeth still keep in close touch with the business, which now has one of the most highly certified bottling plants in Australia, and export markets spread throughout Asia.

Cape Mentelle

Est 1970
Wallcliffe Road, Margaret River, WA 6285
Open 7 days 10–4.30
Getting there 3 hours' drive from Perth CBD
Contact (08) 9757 0888; info@capementelle.com.au; www.capementelle.com.au
Region Margaret River
Lat 33°57′S
Elev 40–90m
E° Days 1552
Harvest 26 February–8 April
Estate vineyards 165ha
Varieties planted Sauvignon blanc (52), cabernet sauvignon (33), semillon (30), shiraz (21), chardonnay (17), merlot (8), other (4)
Leased or contracted vineyards 50ha
Varieties planted Varieties change each year subject to vintage
Dozens produced 100 000 May increase to 130 000.
Exports To China and Hong Kong through Moet Hennessy Diageo (ph) 852 2976 1888; info@mhdhk.com. Also to the UK, the US, Singapore, Malaysia, Thailand, Vietnam, Taiwan, South Korea, Japan, Eastern Europe, Russia, India and New Zealand.
Winemaker Robert Mann, Paul Callaghan, Evan Thompson

Key wines

Trinders Cabernet Merlot
How it is made: This is in fact a Bordeaux blend of cabernet sauvignon (65%), merlot (25%), petit verdot and cabernet franc (5% each) given 30 days on skins in the fermenters, then 14 months in French barriques (20% new).

How it tastes: A wine of considerable class, the attention to detail rewarded by its bright redcurrant and cassis fruit, supported by fine-grained tannins on the medium-bodied palate. Cellar up to 15 years.

Best vintages: 2011, 2009, 2007, 2004, 2001

Cabernet Sauvignon
How it is made: Often includes a small percentage of merlot, with all the grapes rigorously sorted prior to a 30-day fermentation and maceration before basket-pressing to French barriques (40% new) for 21 months' maturation prior to blending and bottling.

How it tastes: Bright purple-crimson in its youth, it has a fragrant red and black berry bouquet, then a complex, medium- to full-bodied palate. Here cassis and notes of black olive and earth are interwoven with French oak, typical cabernet sauvignon tannins standing guard to protect a long life. Cellar for up to 20 years from vintage.

Best vintages: 2011, 2009, 2007, 2004, 2001

Cape Mentelle

One of the founding wineries of the Margaret River region, and one of its largest producers, since 2003 it is 100% owned by Louis Vuitton Moët Hennessy (LVMH) but established by David Hohnen, who also established Cloudy Bay, New Zealand's greatest maker of Marlborough sauvignon blanc. Indeed, there is no doubt that LVMH's acquisition of Cape Mentelle was in part founded on the value of its subsidiary, Cloudy Bay.

Situated just to the west of the town of Margaret River, it has always been regarded as a foremost producer of cabernet sauvignon, a reputation forged in steel when it won the most famous wine show award, Melbourne's Jimmy Watson Trophy, in 1983 and again in 1984. It was a relatively small winery at the time, and the region was still to become well known, so winning the trophy in consecutive years (with the '82 and '83 vintage wines) was of huge importance for the winery and the region alike.

At the other extreme was the zinfandel, then the only planting in Australia, prompted by Hohnen's experience in California, where he spent two years (1969–70) studying winemaking and Oenology at the UC Davis wine school. That experience also prompted – albeit much later – the annual Cape Mentelle International Cabernet Sauvignon Wine Tasting, attended by a cross-section of winemakers, retailers, journalists and wine consumers.

Cape Mentelle's growth under the benign control of LVMH has left the very attractive rammed earth winery, situated in a dell with a rivulet of fresh water, visually intact, its vastly increased fermentation and barrel storage tucked in behind the face of the winery.

Robert Mann has been senior winemaker at Cape Mentelle since December 2005. He is the grandson of the legendary Jack Mann, who stood like a colossus over the Western Australian wine industry during his long career as winemaker at Houghton's Swan Valley winery: from 1922 to 1931 (under father George Mann), then from 1932 to 1972 as chief winemaker.

Robert works in tandem with viticulturist Ashley Wood, whose interest in grapegrowing was piqued by time spent in Alsace and Bordeaux, which then led to his enrolment in the Bachelor of Viticulture degree at Charles Sturt University. On graduation, he moved to Margaret River, and spent 12 years working in vineyards across the region before moving to Cape Mentelle prior to the 2007 harvest.

As well as the responsibility for over 200ha of estate vineyards spread across three districts, he manages the annual purchase of around 50 tonnes of grapes to fill any shortage from the estate production. These (plus estate-grown grapes) go towards the bottom tier of Georgiana Sauvignon Blanc and Marmaduke Shiraz, which frequently offer outstanding value; next come a series of varietal and varietal blends (including Trinders), and at the top, Cabernet Sauvignon.

A feature is a one-hour guided tour exploring the way the wines are made both in the vineyard and the winery, and an even more interesting behind-the-scenes guided tour followed by a private wine tasting matched to a selection of local produce hosted in our historic barrel cellar. Fees are charged for these tours.

Castle Rock Estate

Est 1983
2660 Porongurup Road, Porongurup, WA 6324
Open 7 days 10–5
Getting there 4.25 hours' drive from Perth CBD
Contact (08) 9853 1035; diletti@castlerockestate.com.au; www.castlerockestate.com.au
Region Porongurup
Lat 34°40′S
Elev 250–300m
E° Days 1506
Harvest 4 March–24 April

Estate vineyards 10.5ha
Varieties planted Riesling (4), pinot noir (2.3), chardonnay (2), sauvignon blanc (1.2), cabernet sauvignon (1)
Leased or contracted vineyards 1ha
Varieties planted Shiraz
Dozens produced 3500 May increase to 5000.
Exports Wines are not currently exported.
Winemaker Robert Diletti

Key wines

Riesling

How it is made: The estate-grown grapes are crushed, and the juice is allowed to naturally settle before fermentation is initiated with cultured yeast, continuing for 2 weeks at 13°C. It is bottled as quickly as possible after vintage. Extremely fine and linear in its youth, it develops over the next 5–7 years with exceptional grace, adding both flavour and structural complexity. 1200 dozen made.

How it tastes: When young, the scented bouquet has nuances of wild flowers, herbs and lime blossom, the pristine palate with hallmark intensity and magical acidity underwriting its extreme longevity. Cellar 15–20 years from vintage.

Best vintages: 2012, 2011, 2008, 2006, 2002

Pinot Noir

How it is made: The estate-grown grapes are hand-picked, 90% destemmed, and 10% separately fermented as whole bunches, and kept separate until blending just prior to bottling. The main component is initially cold-soaked before the onset of fermentation, using part wild yeast, part cultured. Held for 7–10 days in the fermenter for post-ferment maceration. Part is pressed earlier at 2 baume, with 40% taken to new French oak, the remainder matured in used oak, kept on lees for 11 months prior to filtration and bottling. 600 dozen made.

How it tastes: Proclaims its variety immediately the bouquet is assessed; intense red berry fruits on the palate are harmoniously backed up by silky, fine tannins, the oak totally integrated and balanced. Cellar to 8 years from vintage.

Best vintages: 2012, 2009, 2008, 2006, 2002

Castle Rock Estate

Angelo and Wendy Diletti began planting the estate's vines in 1983 on a long, northeast-facing slope of the Porongurup mountain range. It is an exceptionally beautiful site, and establishing the vineyard was a labour of love, for Angelo had a full-time job at the helm of the Albany Hospital, 40km to the south-west of the vineyard. Son Robert (Rob) Diletti, now Castle Rock winemaker, clearly remembers helping plant the vines when he was six years old, and continuing to work in the vineyard during school holidays and weekends. A lesser man may have been turned off vines and wines for life, but the self-effacing, quietly spoken Rob proceeded to enrol in the Charles Sturt University winemaking course in 1995, graduating in 1998.

During the last year of that course he won the prize for the most consistent taster: all his class tasted six wines blind, and gave each points as if the wines were entries in a wine show. Later that same day the wines were retasted but in a different order; a statistical analysis proved he was the most consistent. He was to show the same ability at the 5-day hyper-masterclass of the Len Evans Tutorial, then as an associate wine show judge, and later as a senior judge.

In the meantime, the planting of the vineyard continued, riesling producing its first crop in 1986. Between then and 2000 the wines were made at the Alkoomi winery, in the latter years with Rob Diletti as assistant winemaker. The family then decided to build an onsite winery in time for the 2001 vintage. It was designed to take advantage of the slope: the grapes are received and destemmed on the upper level, then gravity-fed into the press, avoiding unwanted skin and pip extract (especially for the riesling). The winery – with state-of-the-art equipment – was completed four days before the first grapes arrived.

With typical modesty, Rob says, 'The wine quality is really determined in the vineyard. I just try to make the wine that portrays the fruit quality. There are several techniques which are important in doing this, and you need to know and under-stand these techniques. But we're human, neither magicians nor gods.' The unfailing finesse and elegance of the Castle Rock portfolio might be seen to prove his point, but the contract winemaking services he provides to a number of other producers in the Great Southern region proves beyond doubt that his skills are every bit as important as the grapes he is given to work with. I have lost track of the number of times I have been surprised at the quality of wines from small wineries in the region, so much so that I instinctively know they have been made by Rob Diletti.

On the Castle Rock home front, the riesling and pinot noir take front of stage, the riesling because of its exceptional longevity, the pinot noir because Diletti has been able to conjure up more with it with greater consistency than any other Great Southern winemaker. But Castle Rock's chardonnay and sauvignon blanc are also wines of the highest quality, and all the wines offer exceptional value for money.

Chambers Rosewood

Est 1858
Barkly Street, Rutherglen, Vic 3685
Open Mon–Sat 9–5, Sun 10–5
Getting there 3 hours' drive from
Melbourne CBD
Contact (02) 6032 8641;
chambers@chambersrosewood.com.au;
www.chambersrosewood.com.au
Region Rutherglen
Lat 36°03'S
Elev 170m
E° Days 1591
Harvest 17 February–27 March

Estate vineyards 50ha
Varieties planted Muscat (15), shiraz
(10), muscadelle (6), palomino (4),
cabernet sauvignon (2), riesling (1),
durif (1), other varieties (11)
Dozens produced 10 000 No increase
planned.
Exports To China and Hong Kong through
Zibo Barossa Commercial and Trading
Co Limited; liuhong6668@126.com. Also
to the US, New Zealand and Belgium.
Winemaker Stephen Chambers

Key wines

Muscat

How it is made: Muscat is also known as brown frontignac. The grapes are picked
as ripe as possible (from 15 baume to over 20 baume, depending on the vintage)
and partially fermented before the addition of spirit terminates the fermentation,
with alcohol of 18–20%. The wine is then aged in old oak for an indefinite number
of years, and ultimately blended with other muscat, most likely over 5 years or
up to 20 years or (in small quantities) much older (50 years or more). The art of
making rare muscat is to have a wine of exceptional concentration and richness,
that yet has some freshness (achieved with a small amount of young muscat from
a very good vintage). Bottled, the ageing process ceases, and the wine does not
deteriorate once it is opened.

How it tastes: see opposite page

Best vintages: NA

Shiraz

How it is made: The grapes are crushed and destemmed, then fermented with a
cultured yeast in a closed stainless steel tank, with pumpovers, and fermentation
temperatures 25–30°C. The wine is pressed to another tank for mlf, and then racked
to American oak puncheons for 12 months. It is fined and filtered prior to bottling.

How it tastes: A relatively light-bodied, fresh wine, with red fruit aromas and
flavours; neither oak nor tannins mask the fruit. Cellar to 5 years from vintage.

Best vintages: 2012, 2010, 2008, 2006, 2002

Chambers Rosewood

While this winery can only boast six generations of the Chambers family as owner/ winemakers, history oozes out of every corner of the humble corrugated iron winery which is home of two of Australia's greatest fortified wines – Chambers Rare Rutherglen Muscat and Rare Rutherglen Topaque. (The winemakers of Rutherglen have a self-created and administered four quality level appellation system for these wines: at the bottom, simply named Rutherglen Muscat; next Classic; then Grand; and at the top, Rare. In each case the terminology is the same for muscat and topaque.)

The lack of pretension is accompanied by fierce independence of spirit and mind. Thus when 49-year-old William Chambers, together with sons Jabez and Philip, emigrated from England in the late 1850s with little money or other assets, it was not to search for gold. Instead, they leased a 40-acre (16ha) block of land in Rutherglen intending to utilise what they had learnt in France of grape and fruit cultivation.

When gold was discovered in Rutherglen two years later, one of the gold-bearing seams was located on the property. They charged miners a fee for access, and made sufficient money to acquire the block, and more land, on which the winery and cellar door stand today. Further luck would have it that their neighbour was Anton Ruche, an exceptionally gifted winemaker, who gave advice and whose business was ultimately acquired by third-generation William Henry (Will) Chambers, an acquisition still acknowledged on invoices issued by W.H. Chambers & Son over 100 years later.

Will did not die until 1956, but in the meantime he had increased the size of Chambers Rosewood to 586 acres (283ha) and established a sheep stud. His son Arthur was more interested in the stud than the vineyard, but paid for his eldest son William (Bill) Chambers to enrol in the Oenology degree at Roseworthy Agricultural College.

He graduated with first-class honours, and had already demonstrated an exceptionally skilled palate, which he retained throughout his 21-year tenure as Chairman of Judges at the Melbourne Royal Wine Show (and Rutherglen Wine Show over the same period).

Since then his youngest son, Stephen, has become the sixth generation Chambers to assume the winemaking mantle, while also taking an active role in the farming side of the business. There is an eclectic range of table wines (including gouais, which is said by Jancis Robinson et al. in *Wine Grapes*, Ecco, 2012, pp. 419–20, to be the almost extinct parent of at least 81 distinct grape varieties in Western Europe) at extremely low prices and fortified wines ranging from cheap to (justifiably) high prices.

I once wrote of muscat: 'Like Narcissus drowning in his reflection, one can lose oneself in the aroma of a great old muscat. All this, and one has not yet felt the necessity of actually tasting the wine. That moment destroys the calm which preceded it: an old muscat has an explosive intensity of luscious flavour, combined with high acid and a twist of wood-derived volatility, which strips the saliva from the sides of the taster's mouth, leaving the flavour in undiminished magnificence for two minutes after the last millilitre has been swallowed.'

Chambers and Morris make the greatest Rare Muscats and Topaques, each mounting a convincing case to be regarded as the foremost producer of these wines, but Chambers has that touch of magic which leads many (myself included) to place it first.

Charles Melton

Est 1984
Krondorf Road, Tanunda, SA 5352
Open 7 days 11–5
Getting there 1 hour's drive from Adelaide CBD
Contact (08) 8563 3606; cellardoor@charlesmeltonwines.com.au; www.charlesmeltonwines.com.au
Region Barossa Valley
Lat 34°29′S
Elev 274m
E° Days 1571
Harvest 27 February–17 April

Estate vineyards 31ha
Varieties planted Shiraz (20), cabernet sauvignon (6.5), grenache (4.5)
Leased or contracted vineyards 30ha
Dozens produced 15 000 No increase planned.
Exports To China through MAB Australia Pty Ltd (ph) 613 9939 0787; mabaustralia@gmail.com and to Hong Kong through Northeast Wines & Spirits Ltd (ph) 852 2873 5733; www.northeast.com.hk. Also to the UK, the US, Canada, Belgium, France, Germany, Ireland, the Philippines, Russia, Thailand, Singapore and New Zealand.
Winemaker Charlie Melton

Key wines

Nine Popes

How it is made: Typically an equal blend of shiraz and grenache, and up to 5% mourvedre, the grenache component (from vines 70–130 years old) receiving more whole-bunch and whole-berry fermentation than the other varieties, but overall only 50% of the grapes are crushed, with the remainder left as whole berry or bunch. A mix of cultured (mainly) and wild yeasts are used, with a mix of hand-plunged open tanks and closed tanks with pumpover. The wine is matured in French oak barriques (usually around 20% new). The wine is not fined, and is only lightly filtered. 2500 dozen made.

How it tastes: Totally avoids confection/nougat nuances; its textured layers of black and red fruits are supported by ripe, soft tannins and integrated oak, all the components carefully calibrated to provide maximum synergy. Cellar to 10+ years from vintage.

Best vintages: 2012, 2010, 2006, 2004, 2002

Grains of Paradise Shiraz

How it is made: There are many similarities to the Nine Popes technique, one being control of alcohol to 14.5%, the second the fermentation procedures. Here, however, the new oak may rise to 30%, and is an equal blend of French and American, and the wine spends 2 years on yeast lees. 2500 dozen made.

How it tastes: It has layer upon layer of black fruits, spice and licorice, framed by ripe tannins and oak, the latter perfectly balanced and integrated. Reflecting the controlled alcohol and mid-range fermentation temperatures, the wine is very elegant and little more than medium-bodied. Cellar to 20 years from vintage.

Best vintages: 2010, 2008, 2006, 2003, 2001

Charles Melton

Actually, Charles (or often Charlie) Melton was christened Graeme Melton, and was so known when he started a planned round-Australia road trip with a mate. They were travelling in an old EH Holden ute, and when they reached the Barossa Valley, the Holden had a serious mechanical failure. Lacking the money to pay for the repairs and continue their planned journey, they looked for and found two opportunities: one pruning a vineyard, the other as a cellarhand at Krondorf. They tossed a coin, and Graeme won the winery job.

The head winemaker was the late Peter Lehmann, who for unknown reasons refused to accept Graeme as a name, instead using Charlie from the word go, and continuing to do so over the 10 years of employment that followed. During this time Charlie met his wife-to-be, Virginia, and had northern hemisphere vintage experience in the southern Rhône Valley, where his deep and abiding love of grenache, shiraz and mourvedre took shape.

In 1984 that love affair was consummated when he purchased the first grapes from old, dry-grown vines. Within a short time he had purchased a 5ha vineyard of grenache (planted in 1947) and shiraz, and built a small wooden winery and cellar door. It was a time of acute surplus of red grapes in the Barossa Valley, culminating in the state government–funded Vine Pull Scheme: paying growers for each hectare of vines they removed. This gave Charlie opportunities he could not have otherwise afforded, particularly for his emblematic Nine Popes.

This grenache shiraz mourvedre blend was so named in Charlie's belief that Châteauneuf-du-Pape meant the château/home of nine popes, and he didn't want to end up in trouble if he came too close phonetically or literally. It was all too late to do anything about it when he discovered that the true (literal) meaning is Castle of the New Pope – and he would not dream of changing it now.

With one exception, both the estate-grown grapes and those coming from the three growers come from vines between 70 and 130 years old, dry-grown, and managed with minimal use of chemicals. Indeed, one of the growers has moved to full biodynamic status. The exception is the new vineyard Charlie and Virginia have planted on the 30ha of beautifully sloping land in the high Eden Valley.

Apart from the Rose of Virginia, for long one of the best three roses in Australia, and tiny quantities of a vin santo–style barrel-aged dessert wine, Melton is solely a producer of red wines, with Nine Popes, three shirazs (Grains of Paradise, The Kirche and The Father-in-Law), Richelieu (a grenache mourvedre blend), and a cabernet sauvignon.

Assured use of predominantly French oak, sophisticated fermentation techniques, extended barrel-ageing before bottling, very high quality grapes, a determination to avoid alcohol levels over 14.5%, and extraction of soft, not hard, tannins, all come together to make wines that are as enjoyable when young as they are when fully mature, 15–20 years later.

Clonakilla

Est 1971
Crisps Lane, Murrumbateman, NSW 2582
Open 7 days 10–5
Getting there 30 minutes' drive from Canberra CBD
Contact (02) 6227 5877; wine@clonakilla.com.au; www.clonakilla.com.au
Region Canberra District
Lat 35°18′S
Elev 500–850m
E° Days 1383
Harvest 18 February–1 April
Estate vineyards 12.45ha
Varieties planted Shiraz (6.5), riesling (2.5), viognier (1.5), sauvignon blanc (0.5), pinot noir (0.5), semillon (0.2), brown muscat (0.15), chardonnay (0.1), plus grenache, mourvedre, cinsaut and roussanne (0.5 in total)
Leased or contracted vineyards 16.5ha
Varieties planted Canberra District shiraz (3.1), riesling (1), semillon (0.3);
Hilltops shiraz (13)
Dozens produced 17 000 May increase to 20 000.
Exports To China and Hong Kong through Inland Trading Co (Aust) Pty Ltd (ph) 612 6238 3882; greg@inlandtrading.com.au. Also to all major markets.
Winemaker Tim Kirk, Bryan Martin

Key wines

Shiraz Viognier
How it is made: 100% estate-grown, fermented in single-vineyard section batches (up to 18) largely in 2-tonne and 4-tonne ferments. The viognier is co-fermented (and contributes 5–6%) with 20–30% whole bunches of shiraz, the remaining shiraz destemmed on top. Wild yeast fermentation starts after 3–4 days of chilled maceration, the temperature reaching 32–34°C. An 18–22-day period on skins follows before the wine is pressed to French oak (one-third new). The mlf takes place naturally, and the wine comes out of barrel after 12 months and blended in tank, and is finally bottled in May. Approximately 2000 dozen made.

How it tastes: The bouquet is supremely fragrant, with a flowery scent, the palate instantaneously imprinting its harmony and balance; fruit, oak and tannins are all seamlessly interwoven, the length prodigious. Cellar to 20 years from vintage.

Best vintages: 2013, 2009, 2008, 2005, 2001

Hilltops Shiraz
How it is made: The grapes come from 4 mature vineyards in the Hilltops region and are largely machine-picked, but with a component hand-picked for the whole bunch inclusion. Here cultured yeast is used, and the fermentation is encouraged to peak at 33–34°C; the wine stays on skins for 2.5 weeks. The wine is aged in French oak (15–20% new) and is bottled late February/early March, having been filtered immediately pre-bottling. Approximately 4000 dozen made.

How it tastes: Good colour, though not as deep as the shiraz viognier; an exercise in restraint and elegance, with finely detailed and strung beads of red and black berry fruit, silky tannins and a gentle touch of the French oak. Cellar to 20 years from vintage.

Best vintages: 2013, 2012, 2009, 2008, 2005

Clonakilla

This is one of the very greatest small, family-owned, Australian wineries, its origins a story in itself. It started in County Clare, Ireland, when a 14-year-old schoolboy, John Kirk, was given a summer vacation job of running the bar and stocking the cellars of his parents' Hydro Hotel. His formidable intelligence and curiosity led to the purchase of *Wine and Spirits: The Connoisseurs Text Book*, by Andre L. Simon.

His years of study at Cambridge University, and postdoctoral work in biochemistry at Oxford University gave him ample opportunity to expand his knowledge of the great wines of France, which he brought with him when he was invited to come to Canberra to take up a research position with the CSIRO Division of Plant Industry in 1968. This – and his linked studies in climate – caused him to compare the climate of the Southern Tablelands surrounding Canberra with great European winegrowing regions, and he found a number of matches.

When he asked why no one had planted wine grapes he was told the climate was too cold. Apart from finding it positively balmy compared with that of Ireland, England and Wales, he knew it was ideal for cool-climate grapes. So in 1971 he purchased an 18ha farm 40km north of Canberra, knowing that the soil – sandy clay loams over a base of decomposed granite – was ideal for grapes, and proceeded to plant riesling, sauvignon blanc, shiraz and cabernet sauvignon. He called the property Clonakilla, the name of his grandfather's farm in County Clare (meaning 'meadow of the church'), and in 1976 he produced Canberra's first commercial wines.

The following year he and his sons built a small winery (now the cellar door), and in 1978 found a permanent water supply by sinking a bore. Finding the right varieties took time, but the first 100% shiraz gained immediate fame, winning two trophies and two gold medals. In 1991, son Tim Kirk visited the Rhône Valley, and tasted the top Guigal wines from barrel. He wrote, 'There are rare moments in a wine lover's life when you find yourself transfixed by the extraordinary beauty of what's in the glass before you.'

In 1992 he made Clonakilla's first shiraz viognier, and since then Clonakilla has been the recipient of awards variously for Best Wine of the Year, Best Winery of the Year, Winemaker of the Year, Best First Class Red (Cellars in the Sky). The list goes on and on, every acclaim totally justified.

Demand for the wines far outstrips supply, even with: the 1998 acquisition of an adjoining 20ha property by Tim and wife Lara Kirk, and planted to shiraz and viognier; the first Hilltops Shiraz being made in 2000, from grapes from top vignerons in that region; the 2007 purchase by the Kirk family of another adjoining property, and the planting of another 1.8ha of shiraz, plus 0.4ha of grenache, mourvedre and cinsaut; and in the same year, the first vintage of O'Riada Shiraz, now composed of contract-grown grapes from Canberra, plus any estate shiraz that misses the cut for Clonakilla Shiraz Viognier.

The missing piece in this jigsaw story is Tim Kirk: he has a superb palate and is a truly exceptional winemaker. But it is his unfailing, open-hearted generosity (founded on deep religious conviction), and the soft smile that illuminates his face whenever he greets one of his legions of friends that make this man a living national treasure.

Coldstream Hills

Est 1985
**31 Maddens Lane, Coldstream,
Vic 3770**
Open 7 days 10–5
Getting there 1 hour's drive from
Melbourne CBD
Contact (03) 5960 7000;
cellardoor@coldstreamhills.com.au;
www.coldstreamhills.com.au
Region Yarra Valley
Lat 37°42′S
Elev 50–350m
E° Days 1253
Harvest 1 March–25 April
Estate vineyards 102.2ha
**Varieties planted Lower Yarra
Valley** with 48.7 ha (across 3 separate vineyards): chardonnay (22), pinot noir (12), merlot (5.8), cabernet sauvignon (5.4), shiraz (2.5), cabernet franc (1); **Upper Yarra Valley** with 53.5 ha (across 2 separate vineyards): chardonnay (26.4), pinot noir (15.2), sauvignon blanc (5), pinot gris (4.1), merlot (2.8)
Leased or contracted vineyards
Variable; up to 30ha
Dozens produced 25 000 May increase to 40 000.
Exports To China and Hong Kong through Jebsens (ph) 852 2923 8777; www.jebsen.com. Also to the UK, the US and Singapore.
Winemaker Andrew Fleming, Greg Jarratt, James Halliday (Consultant)

Key wines

Reserve Chardonnay

How it is made: From the House Block (planted 1985), the adjoining G Block and Dijon clones on the estate Briarston Vineyard. Whole-bunch-pressed when hand-picked (always House Block) and fermented in French oak barriques and puncheons (40% new). The mlf is prevented, thus eliminating the need for added acidity in the majority of vintages. The wine spends 10 months on lees with minimal additions of SO_2. Up to 1500 dozen made, sometimes none.

How it tastes: Like all top-end Yarra Valley chardonnays, this is a wine of extreme elegance and balance, the most striking feature the length of the palate, oak not obvious. The advent of screwcap provides a 5- to 20-year cellaring opportunity.

Best vintages: 2012, 2010, 2006, 2005, 2002

Reserve Pinot Noir

How it is made: Virtually all the pinot noir is hand-picked, and up to 25% of whole bunches are incorporated in the open fermenters, which are plunged after 3–5 days' cold soak, when wild yeast fermentation starts. The must is pressed before dryness and the actively fermenting wine is taken direct to barrel, remaining on gross lees for months before it is racked for the first time. It is not fined, but is crossflow-filtered. Up to 700 dozen made, sometimes none.

How it tastes: The wine is only medium-bodied, the tannins superfine, but it can thrive for 20 years or more. While the plum and red and black cherry fruit is there from the outset, the bouquet builds dramatically over the first 5 years in bottle, becoming more fragrant and more complex. As with the chardonnay, the length of the palate, and lingering aftertaste, is striking. Cellar to 10–15+ years from vintage.

Best vintages: 2012, 2010, 2006, 2004, 2002

Coldstream Hills

My wife Suzanne and I established Coldstream Hills after I moved from Sydney to Melbourne in mid-1983, ostensibly for my law firm, but also to lay the foundation for realising my dream of making high-quality pinot noir from the Yarra Valley. At that time there were far more producers of pinot noir there than in any other region, but this was not the only attraction of the Yarra Valley.

Quite apart from the suitability of its climate, the Valley has beautiful and diverse scenery, some of the vineyards, such as Coldstream Hills, on steep hillsides. The younger red volcanic soils of the Upper Yarra Valley offer opportunities for high-quality sparkling wine, as well as table wine; its somewhat cooler and wetter climate ripens the chardonnay and pinot noir grapes (the dominant varieties) later than the Lower Yarra Valley.

The proximity to Melbourne, either by expressway for cars, or by train to Lilydale, the main town in the Valley, was another attraction. Between 1985 and 1988 I commuted to Melbourne by train every day, using the hour-long trip for legal work or wine writing.

In 1985 I made the first vintage of Coldstream Hills, renting space in a Mornington Peninsula winery, and buying grapes from Yarra Valley growers. Having made red wine at Brokenwood in the Hunter Valley for 11 vintages, and at the highly regarded Domaine Dujac in Burgundy, in 1983, I knew how to make red wine, and pinot noir in particular. But I didn't know enough about making chardonnay, and enlisted the aid of Dr Tony Jordan, who was the CEO and chief winemaker at Domaine Chandon before becoming Moët et Chandon's international technical wine director for its ventures around the world.

The early vintages of Coldstream Hills were phenomenally successful in wine shows and in press reviews, success which in 1996 led to a takeover offer by Southcorp – by this time Coldstream Hills was listed on the Stock Exchange. Coldstream Hills is now part of Treasury Wine Estates, having greatly benefited from the financial resources of first Southcorp, and ultimately Treasury, which built what was not far short of a new winery in 2010, a plaque on the wall reading 'The James Halliday Cellar'.

In the early 1990s, with support from a leading stockbroker and close friend (who died some years ago), Coldstream Hills was able to set up two investor-funded vineyards in the Upper Yarra Valley, with the purpose of supplying Coldstream Hills with grapes (principally chardonnay and pinot noir, but also sauvignon blanc and merlot). In 2013 Treasury negotiated an agreement to buy the two vineyards outright, giving Coldstream Hills total security for grape supplies to underpin its future growth.

Coldstream Hills has enjoyed a stable and long-serving winemaking team headed by winemakers Andrew Fleming (chief) and Greg Jarratt (senior). Conspicuous show success for pinot noir, chardonnay and sparkling has continued unabated, and it is a happy place to be.

Its strategic spread of vineyards across both the Lower and Upper Yarra Valley allow it to make highly regarded sauvignon blanc, shiraz, merlot and cabernet sauvignon. But the Reserve, Single Vineyard and varietal releases of chardonnay and pinot noir are the lifeblood of the business.

Craiglee

Est 1976
Sunbury Road, Sunbury, Vic 3429
Open Sun & public hols 10–5, or by appt
Getting there 35 minutes' drive from
Melbourne CBD
Contact (03) 9744 4489;
patatcraiglee@hotmail.com;
www.craiglee.com.au
Region Sunbury
Lat 37°45′S
Elev 275m
E° Days 1410
Harvest 7 March–28 April

Estate vineyards 9ha
Varieties planted Shiraz, viognier,
cabernet sauvignon
Dozens produced 2500 No increase
planned.
Exports Wines are not currently
exported to China and Hong Kong.
Exported to Ireland.
Winemaker Patrick Carmody

Key wines

Chardonnay
How it is made: The hand-picked bunches are crushed and pressed, the wine barrel-fermented with cultured yeast in French oak barriques (20–25% new) and matured for 11 months. The wine is sterile-filtered prior to bottling. 500 dozen made.

How it tastes: Bright, pale straw-green in colour, it has great intensity to its white stone-fruit/grapefruit flavours on both the bouquet and palate; in each instance the barrel fermentation adds complexity but without threatening the integrity of the fruit; excellent length and balance is a feature of an elegant wine. Cellar to 7 years from vintage.

Best vintages: 2010, 2009, 2008, 2005, 2002

Shiraz
How it is made: The hand-picked grapes are predominantly crushed, but some whole bunches are kept separate and included in the ferment. The maximum temperature is kept to 30°C, and part (vintage-dependent) may be pressed to barrel for the final stages of fermentation, the remainder kept on skins until the fermentation is complete. The wine spends 12–15 months in barrique, and while it is not fined, it is sterile-filtered. 1250 dozen made.

How it tastes: The wine always has a brilliantly clear purple-crimson hue in its youth, the bouquet highly fragrant with an array of spicy/peppery red and black cherry fruits precisely reflected in the light- to medium-bodied palate. It has immaculate balance and length, and history shows it has great longevity, even if delicious to drink when young. Cellar to 20+ years from vintage.

Best vintages: 2010, 2009, 2008, 2005, 2002

Craiglee

Craiglee, 15 minutes' drive from Melbourne's Tullamarine Airport, was established by James S. Johnston, a member of the Victorian Parliament and one of the founders of the *Argus* newspaper. In 1863 he planted 7ha, initially to a large number of varieties, but he ultimately rationalised these to concentrate on shiraz and riesling.

In common with most of the cool-climate regions of Australia, it went out of production in the late 1920s, but the four-storey bluestone winery (using gravity wherever possible) is still in immaculate condition, although the ever-vigilant Department of Health decreed that the Carmody family (who purchased the property from the Johnstons in 1961) could not use it for winemaking as (strange though it may seem) it does not conform to present-day health regulations.

Nearby Goona Warra Vineyard was established in the same year (1863) by James Goodall Francis, who became Premier of Victoria in 1870. The winery, like Craiglee, was built with bluestone. Totally restored, it now houses the wine cellar and great hall (used for events and functions). The name, incidentally, means black swan in local Indigenous dialect (depicted on the original Goona Warra label, and used today), not to be confused with South Australia's Coonawarra (meaning honeysuckle).

An 1872 Craiglee Hermitage (10.5% alc/vol) won an award in Vienna, and a cache of the wine was discovered (under soil) in the winery in the 1950s. It was sold by the leading wine merchant of the day, Tom Seabrook. I was fortunate to be able to taste a number of bottles over the decades: some were remarkably fresh and wonderful to taste, others (unsurprisingly) tired and oxidised.

With the support of then Victorian State Government viticulturist Murray Clayton, son Pat Carmody persuaded the family to re-establish a vineyard. He had embarked on his tertiary education in 1971, duly completing a four-year Agricultural Science degree, followed by a year obtaining his Diploma of Education. He then became a teacher, embarked on a third degree in wine science at Charles Sturt University, and began planting the vineyard on the deep black volcanic soils of the area – all in 1976.

While shiraz has always been the heart of Craiglee's wine production, there was a flirtation with sauvignon blanc (since grafted to shiraz and a little viognier), pinot noir (strangely unsuccessful and since removed), and all but a small amount of cabernet sauvignon likewise. Thus the two main wines are shiraz and chardonnay, with lesser amounts of shiraz viognier and cabernet sauvignon, the last (possibly) a hedge against global warming.

Quietly spoken Pat Carmody is a self-effacing gentleman of the old school, but rightly proud of the great inheritance he, his wife Dianne and sons David and Tom share. A visit to the vineyard is always a privilege, if only to breathe in the atmosphere of the bluestone cellar.

Crawford River Wines

Est 1975
741 Hotspur Upper Road, Condah, Vic 3303
Open By appt
Getting there 3.75 hours' drive from Melbourne CBD
Contact (03) 5578 2267; info@crawfordriverwines.com; www.crawfordriverwines.com
Region Henty
Lat 38°08'S
Elev 15–100m
E° Days 1213
Harvest 26 March–11 May

Estate vineyards 10ha
Varieties planted Riesling (4.5), then smaller plantings of cabernet sauvignon, cabernet franc, merlot, semillon and sauvignon blanc
Dozens produced 3500 No increase planned.
Exports Wines are not currently exported to China and Hong Kong. Exported to the UK.
Winemaker John and Belinda Thomson

Key wines

Riesling

How it is made: Depending on the vintage, a combination of crushed grapes and whole-bunch-pressed fruit is used; a neutral, cultured yeast takes the fermentation through at 12°C in temperature-controlled stainless steel tanks. The wine spends up to 3 months on lees before being sterile-filtered and bottled, but not fined. 1300 dozen made.

How it tastes: Bright straw-green in its youth, with a fragrant, lime-infused bouquet, then a palate welding ripe lime/citrus fruit to a framework of minerally acidity and low pH. Has tremendous length and lingering aftertaste. Cellar to 20+ years from vintage.

Best vintages: 2012, 2010, 2009, 2006, 2004

Cabernet Sauvignon

How it is made: A blend of up to 95% cabernet sauvignon, up to 5% cabernet franc, and perhaps a touch of merlot. It is picked in small batches, and there will be a combination of whole berry and crushed fruit in the very small (2-tonne) open fermenters, each lot kept separate until blending. A pre-fermentation cold soak of up to 7 days is followed by wild yeast initiation, then followed up by cultured yeast additions. The time on skins varies considerably, with a small percentage of barrel ferment, and mlf either in tank or barrel. 500 dozen made.

How it tastes: Blackcurrant, cedar and cigar box aromas, then a firm palate, with overtones of Bordeaux, the tannins savoury but fine. Cellar to 15 years from vintage.

Best vintages: 2012, 2010, 2008, 2006, 2004

Crawford River Wines

John Thomson is the fourth generation of his family to graze sheep and cattle on this large property, his ancestors having arrived in the Henty region in 1852, and acquired the property in 1872. A hundred or so years later, between 1966 and 1968, he enrolled in Commerce at Melbourne University; it was here that his interest in wine grew. Nonetheless, when he returned to the family property to farm, he had no thought of becoming a vigneron. But another seven years later, the uncertainty of the wool market led him to look at some diversification of farming activities, so in 1975 he planted 0.8ha each of riesling and cabernet sauvignon, their roots in an unusually complex, mineral-rich soil base. Gravelly, basalt-derived loam overlays permeable clay which in turn lies above a limestone base created by an ancient risen seabed.

The following year he enrolled in the extension (non-residential) winemaking course of what is now Charles Sturt University. He completed the degree without stress, making the first small vintage in the tractor shed in 1979. By 1980 the winery walls and roof were in place, and (when released) the 1981 riesling and cabernet were both listed at Stephanie's, then Melbourne's leading restaurant. It was clear from the outset that John Thomson had an intuitive feel for winemaking.

This immediate success might suggest that this is an easy place in which to grow vines and make wine, but it's not. While the maritime climate depends on the sea only 50km to the south, that sea is the very cold Southern Ocean, and there is nothing to break the winds coming from it. The winery and striking cellar door are on top of a small hill, and the vines benefit from the gentle slope running down from the crest of the hill, which in turn provides a panoramic vista, and increases the impact of the southerly winds. Indeed, this is the coldest region on the Australian mainland.

All of the key viticultural tasks are done by hand: picking, pruning, leaf-plucking, shoot-thinning and bunch-thinning. Moreover, no insecticides or herbicides are used, so all the disciplines necessary to obtain organic or biodynamic status are already observed.

John Thomson has been assisted by wife Catherine from the outset, and by elder daughter Belinda since 2004, when she returned home after gaining degrees in Viticulture and Oenology, and working in several European regions. Since 2008 she has divided her time between Spain and Crawford River, doing two vintages each year. In 2010, younger daughter Fiona took responsibility for national sales and marketing.

Riesling not only occupies the greatest surface area, but provides more individual wines than the other estate plantings. The most important is simply called Crawford River Riesling; then there is Young Vines Riesling (from the block planted in 2000), next the curiously named Serendipitous Riesling, late-picked, but not with botrytis, and made in the Rheingau (rather than Mosel) style, with fruit, low-level sweetness and acidity tightly bound together. All it needs is several decades. Finally, there is the intermittent release of Nektar, intensely luscious and sweet, yet with great varietal purity.

All of the wines are made and bottled on the estate, with minimal interference and movement, and the same attention to detail as in the vineyard. Crawford River is a remote place, and cellar door visitors need to ring first to make an appointment, but when they arrive they will find a top-class, architect-designed facility, which was built in 2000. It's worth the trip.

Cullen Wines

Est 1971
4323 Caves Road, Wilyabrup, WA 6280
Open 7 days 10–4.30
Getting there 3 hours' drive from Perth CBD
Contact (08) 9755 5277; enquiries@cullenwines.com.au; www.cullenwines.com.au
Region Margaret River
Lat 33°57'S
Elev 40–90m
E° Days 1552
Harvest 26 February–8 April
Estate vineyards 33.54ha
Varieties planted Chardonnay (11.47), cabernet sauvignon (11), sauvignon blanc (7.73), merlot (1.28), semillon (1.2), cabernet franc (0.4), malbec (0.36), petit verdot (0.1)
Leased or contracted vineyards 21.32ha
Varieties planted Petit verdot (5.43), sauvignon blanc (4.6), semillon (3.97), merlot (3.08), malbec (3.04), verdelho (1.2)
Dozens produced 20 000 No increase planned.
Exports To China and Hong Kong through Links Concept Company Limited (ph) 852 2802 2818; marketing@linksconcept.com. Also to the UK, the US, Canada and numerous others.
Winemaker Vanya Cullen, Trevor Kent

Key wines

Kevin John Chardonnay
How it is made: The grapes are hand-picked over a number of days, hand-sorted, and whole-bunch-pressed, and fermented with indigenous (wild) yeasts in French barriques, two-thirds new, the remainder one year old. It spends a further 5–9 months (according to the vintage) in those barrels before it is bottled after a light filtration.

How it tastes: It fills the mouth with its complex, yet supple and round, white fruit flavours, mineral-like acidity drawing out the exceptionally long finish. Cellar to 15 years from vintage.

Best vintages: 2010, 2009, 2005, 2004, 2001

Diana Madeline
How it is made: This is a cabernet-dominant blend (usually two-thirds of the total), the remainder merlot, petit verdot, malbec and cabernet franc. It is fermented with indigenous yeasts, then matured in French oak barriques (50% new). 2500 dozen made.

How it tastes: It has deep, bright colour; it is medium- to full-bodied, with small black berry fruit and fine-grained tannins. It has effortless grace, and is sure to develop beautifully for 30 years (or more).

Best vintages: 2010, 2009, 2005, 2004, 2001

Cullen Wines

Owned by the Cullen family since its inception, this winery, and its estate-owned vineyards, is the foremost biodynamic producer in Australia thanks to the total commitment of managing director and chief winemaker Vanya Cullen, the daughter of the late founders Dr Kevin Cullen (with a very busy medical practice) and wife Diana, known as Di.

The family lived on a sheep and cattle farm, and when it was decided to plant 7.3ha in 1971, it was Di who was responsible for the vineyard, and in due course the winemaking. In 1977 Cullen Wines made history when it was the first Margaret River winery to win a trophy, and not just any trophy – it was for Best Wine in the Canberra National Wine Show.

Kevin and Di Cullen were the recipients of many awards, and in 1995 were jointly declared Western Australian Citizen of the Year, their names engraved on a plaque on St Georges Terrace, Perth's major road (sections barred to cars). Kevin passed away in 1994, Di surviving until 2003, and the age of 80.

Vanya Cullen has followed in the footsteps of her parents: She made the *Qantas Wine Magazine* Winemaker of the Year in 2000, is a member of the Qantas wine selection panel, and in 2008 was the UK magazine *Drinks Business*'s Woman of the Year.

Since the estate plantings began, concern for the environment led to the minimal use of chemical sprays, but in 1998 the move to organic certification began. Drains were put in (the vineyards are not irrigated, but the winters provide high rainfall), cover crops were planted, and extensive composting was used. In 2003 the vineyard was given A Grade Organic certification by the Biological Farmers Association of Australia. The move to biodynamic certification followed soon thereafter.

Vanya Cullen's university degree was in music, and I believe that background – as well as her family upbringing – has guided her path. She also made the winery the first in Australia to achieve carbon neutral status. Whether biodynamic management (increasingly common in France, especially Burgundy) provides benefits over and above those achieved by organic management will always be controversial, but the supreme quality of the Cullen wines is beyond argument.

While her parents (and her numerous brothers and sisters) frequently tasted great wines from France's great wine regions, Vanya has moved to another level. She regularly visits France, and worked the 1987 vintage at Domaine Drouhin.

The two icon wines are the Kevin John Chardonnay and the Diana Madeline (a cabernet sauvignon blend), with a Cullen Vineyard Sauvignon Blanc Semillon the third 100% estate-grown wine. The Mangan Vineyard, owned by Vanya's brother Rick and partner Bettina Mangan, is also certified biodynamic and not irrigated; it provides a vineyard-designated Sauvignon Blanc Semillon and Malbec Petit Verdot Merlot. The bottom tier of the Cullen winery encompasses a Margaret River Red and Margaret River White, sourced from the two vineyards, and of exceptional quality and likewise value for money.

Curly Flat

Est 1991
263 Collivers Road, Lancefield,
Vic 3435
Open W'ends 12–5 or by appt
Getting there 1 hour's drive from
Melbourne CBD
Contact (03) 5429 1956;
mail@curlyflat.com; www.curlyflat.com
Region Macedon Ranges
Lat 37°25′S
Elev 300–700m
E° Days 1149
Harvest 12 March–7 May

Estate vineyards 12.3ha
Varieties planted Pinot noir (8.5),
chardonnay (3.1), pinot gris (0.7)
Dozens produced 6000 No increase
planned.
Exports To China through Longfellows
Wine Export (ph) 61 3 9428 5444;
insurance@longfellows.com.au and to
Hong Kong through Watson's Wine (ph)
852 2606 8828; info@watsonswine.com.
Also to the UK and Japan.
Winemaker Phillip Moraghan,
Matt Regan

Key wines

Pinot Noir
How it is made: The estate-grown, hand-picked grapes are 80% destemmed and 20% left as whole bunches, with wild yeast fermentation; the open fermenters are either foot-plunged (whole bunches) or plunged daily. After pressing, the wine spends 20 months in French oak (33% new) and is crossflow-filtered but not fined. 1300 dozen made.

How it tastes: Clear red-purple colour; the bouquet has spicy/savoury nuances and some oak running through the plum and red cherry fruit; the palate is perfectly balanced and of great length. Cellar to 10 years from vintage.

Best vintages: 2012, 2010, 2006, 2005, 2003

Chardonnay
How it is made: The estate-grown, hand-picked grapes are whole-bunch-pressed, the juice inoculated with cultured yeast, then taken to French oak (up to 50% new), lees-stirred in the first 3 months of a total of 17 months. Crossflow-filtered and, like the pinot noir, held for 12 months in bottle prior to release. 2700 dozen made.

How it tastes: Gold-green hue; the bouquet offers nectarine, grapefruit and lemon blossom, the palate with generous fruit, a spine of acidity and the right amount of toasty oak. A harmonious wine with excellent length and complexity. Cellar to 10 years from vintage.

Best vintages: 2011, 2010, 2008, 2004, 2002

Curly Flat

Phillip Moraghan and Jenifer Kolkka began the development of Curly Flat in 1991. It stemmed from Phillip's experiences while studying in Switzerland, a fertile incubation for tackling the very cool, high-altitude, Macedon Ranges. Also, Switzerland is no more than two hours' autoroute-drive from Burgundy, the wines of which totally enthrall Phillip.

When he returned to Australia, he and Jeni set their hearts on Macedon. To gain experience, they worked on a voluntary basis with other wineries, and thus met their lifelong friend and mentor, the late Laurie Williams. A Macedon Ranges pioneer, he instilled in them the need for ultimate attention to detail in all aspects of viticulture if they were to succeed.

Phillip began studying viticulture, reading every book he could lay his hands on, and worked vintages at the celebrated Ponzi Vineyards in Oregon, and Russell Hearn's group on Long Island, New York. After an 18-month search across the cool regions of Australia, and with Laurie Williams' help, Phillip and Jeni found a perfect property. It has long slopes that catch the very last rays of sunshine in autumn, a key factor in the quality of the grapes the vineyard was to produce.

The first vines were planted in 1991, and by 2000 had reached their present amount, 12.3ha. The decision was made to use a lyre trellis, roughly in the shape of a V, which opens up the canopy to sunlight and air movement more than any other system, by splitting the canes into two separate planes.

The downside of the lyre is that every activity has to be done by hand: every shoot, every leaf, and every bunch of grapes has to be inspected and manipulated through the six-month growing season. In winter, all pruning is likewise done by hand. This means that five full-time vineyard workers, with a combined experience of 34 years, tend the vines, twice the number used for most similarly small vineyards, and 10 times that of large vineyards with mechanisation.

The first wine was made in 1998 in a neighbouring winery, an arrangement that continued until the 2002 vintage. Prior to that year's harvest, a lavish two-storey winery was built, and Phillip Moraghan took responsibility for the winemaking. That said, he has retained consultants to advise on both the viticulture and the winemaking practices.

In addition to the vineyard workers, there are two winemakers responsible to Phillip, and four marketing, sales and administration personnel under Jeni's control. I know of no other winery in Australia with 13–14 full-time employees engaged in making and selling 6000 dozen bottles a year. Even more surprising are the modest prices of the wines given their extreme quality and the cost of production. The explanation is that there are no wholesale prices: every bottle is sold by email or to visitors to the cellar door or by export.

This quest for knowledge, and the desire to make better wines in the future, is not unique to Curly Flat. But the investment in time and in money is without parallel. So has it all been worthwhile? The answer is a resounding yes: these are beautifully made wines of exceptional consistency.

Dalwhinnie

Est 1976
**448 Taltarni Road, Moonambel,
Vic 3478**
Open 7 days 10–5
Getting there 2.25 hours' drive from
Melbourne CBD
Contact (03) 5467 2388;
enquiries@dalwhinnie.com.au;
www.dalwhinnie.com.au
Region Pyrenees
Lat 37°05′S
Elev 220–375m
E° Days 1440
Harvest 24 February–14 April
Estate vineyards 25.7ha
Varieties planted Shiraz (14.7),
cabernet sauvignon (4),
chardonnay (2.6), pinot noir (2.4), plus
smaller plantings of cabernet franc,
merlot, sangiovese and viognier
Dozens produced 4500 No increase
planned.
Exports Exports to China through
Pran Cellar Australia (ph) 86 21 5178
0108; tina@cellaraustralia.com and to
Hong Kong through Inland Trading
Co. (Aust.) Pty Ltd (ph) 612 6238 3882;
greg@inlandtrading.com.au. Also to the
UK, Canada, Malaysia, Singapore and
Russia.
Winemaker David Jones, Gary Baldwin
(Consultant)

Key wines

Moonambel Shiraz and Moonambel Cabernet

How they are made: The estate-grown, hand-picked grapes are either crushed and destemmed (80%) or kept as whole bunches (20%), equally spread across the four 2-tonne open fermenters. After a 7–8-day fermentation, the wine is left in contact with the skins for 1 week prior to pressing and then taken to French (Burgundy) oak barriques (30% new) for 17 months' maturation. 1400 dozen made of the shiraz, 650 dozen of the cabernet.

How they taste: The shiraz is a typical deep crimson-purple; intense dark berry fruit aromas join with quality French oak on the bouquet, the supple, medium-bodied palate adding perfectly balanced and integrated tannins; top-class finish and aftertaste; purity and power. The cabernet is deeply coloured when young; medium- to full-bodied, the wine has red and black fruit aromas which are then reflected on the fore-palate; tightens up on the finish with tannin grip that relaxes as the years go by. Both will cellar to 25 years from vintage.

Best vintages: 2010, 2008, 2006, 2004, 2000

Dalwhinnie

History does not relate whether Ballarat architect Ewan Jones knew how precious the 130ha property he purchased in 1972 would prove to be when he began planting the vineyard in 1976. It is situated in a unique amphitheatre rising to just under 600m at the foot of a higher range of hills, sloping down to its opening, thus allowing free air drainage at night-time and making the vineyard frost free.

The first vines planted were the contour block of cabernet sauvignon, and the Grand Piano block of shiraz, the two varieties which have been the lifeblood of the business through to the present day. Chardonnay, the third string to the bow, followed in 1990; the small amounts of merlot and cabernet franc were also early plantings.

Ewan Jones decided from the outset that the financial cost, and the time commitment, of building a winery were not justified, and when the first vintage arrived in 1980, Gary Farr, then winemaker at Yellowglen, was entrusted with the winemaking.

The wines made that year were not released until September 1983, but their quality was exceptionally good given the youth of the vines, and the lack of experience in knowing when to pick, and how the grapes should be vinified. That said, Gary Farr went on to prove to be an extremely good winemaker, first at Bannockburn (from 1978) and since 1994 with his own vineyard and winery (*see page 54*).

In 1983 eldest son David Jones took on management of the vineyard. With wife Jenny, he has owned it since 1994. The onsite winery was built in 2001, giving total control of all aspects of viticulture and winemaking.

A 30-year retrospective tasting of every wine made between 1980 and 2009 underlined the consistency of the very high quality of the shirazs and cabernet sauvignons (and also of the chardonnay, by far the best made in the Pyrenees region).

There is no question this is a distinguished site, what the French would call great terroir. This is reflected in the meso-climate, which is cooler than other parts of the Pyrenees, yet traps enough sunlight and warmth to ensure full ripening of the grapes.

The soil also brings to mind the French saying, 'If the soil was not the best in the world, it would be the worst.' In other words, the lean and hungry soil is ideally suited to vine growing, but to nothing else.

This quality is reinforced by the 100% dry-grown, organic practices used in managing the vineyard. Moreover, there are now four clones of shiraz, and each is picked and vinified separately. The VSP (vertical shoot position) trellis system is a further contributor to grape quality.

The shiraz is released in four price levels when vintage conditions are sufficiently good. At the bottom, The Hut; then Moonambel; third is the duo of Southwest Rocks and The Pinnacle; and finally tiny quantities of The Eagle. There is only one cabernet released each year.

d'Arenberg

Est 1912
Osborn Road, McLaren Vale, SA 5171
Open 7 days 10–5
Getting there 40 minutes' drive from Adelaide CBD
Contact (08) 8329 4888; winery@darenberg.com.au; www.darenberg.com.au
Region McLaren Vale
Lat 34°14′S
Elev 50–200m
E° Days 1680
Harvest 14 February–14 April
Estate vineyards 198.8ha
Varieties planted Shiraz (89.9), grenache (31.7), cabernet sauvignon (23), viognier (6.6), mourvedre (5.3), merlot (5), sauvignon blanc (5), plus smaller plantings of petit verdot, roussanne, tempranillo, chambourcin, marsanne, riesling, cinsaut, sagrantino, chenin blanc, carignan, sangiovese, graciano, petit manseng, aglianico, souzao, tinta cao, touriga nacional, durif and chardonnay
Leased or contracted vineyards Varies from year to year.
Dozens produced 270 000 No increase planned.
Exports To China through Kerry Wines (ph) 8621 6032 2999; info.PRC@kerrywines.com and to Hong Kong through Watson's Wine (ph) 852 2606 8828; info@watsonswine.com. Also to all major markets.
Winemaker Chester Osborn, Jack Walton

Key wines

The Dead Arm Shiraz
How it is made: The somewhat forbidding name comes from a fungal disease called *Eutypa lata*, which causes arms of old vines to die and no longer produce foliage or grapes. Cultured yeasts are used with open fermenters fitted with boards to keep the cap submerged; towards the end of fermentation, the boards are removed, and the must is foot-trodden, with temperature peaking at 30°C. The wine finishes its fermentation in, and then spends 20 months in, a mix of new and old French oak barriques, and is neither fined nor filtered.

How it tastes: Typically a deep, inky purple-crimson in its youth, the fruit powerful and rich, but lifted by the regional input of a touch of bitter chocolate, and some savoury/spicy notes. Cellar to 20+ years from vintage.

Best vintages: 2012, 2010, 2008, 2004, 2002

The Ironstone Pressings Grenache Shiraz Mourvedre
How it is made: A blend of grenache, shiraz and mourvedre from various vineyards, the components separately fermented, using the same approach as for Dead Arm. Matured in old French and American oak barriques for 10 months. Neither fined nor filtered.

How it tastes: Demonstrates the complexity that can be derived from this Southern Rhône–style blend, some briary/spicy/earthy nuances before vibrant red and black cherry fruits come through on the finish and aftertaste. Cellar to 8 years from vintage.

Best vintages: 2012, 2010, 2009, 2004, 2002

d'Arenberg

D'Arenberg has reinvented itself on several occasions, with major changes in direction, but has always been in the ownership of the Osborn family. In 1912 Francis Osborn purchased the first vineyard; some of the vines had been planted in the 1890s. He was originally a grapegrower, before moving in 1928 to make a vintage port and a massive dry red, with all the pressings returned, and sold to the Emu Wine Company for export to the UK. Francis's son d'Arenberg (universally known as d'Arry) was born in 1926 and joined his father in 1943, and had progressively taken over responsibility for the business before Francis's death in 1957.

He decided the time had come for the winery to establish its own brand; he was determined to have a label which would make a statement, and with the Houghton White Burgundy label and its diagonal blue stripe as an influence, the striking d'Arenberg label, with its diagonal red stripe, was developed. In 1965 the first release appeared under the d'Arenberg label, which soon became famous, thanks to the 1967 d'Arenberg Burgundy (mainly grenache) winning seven trophies and 25 gold medals in Australian wine shows. When the 1968 cabernet sauvignon won the Jimmy Watson Trophy at Melbourne in 1969, d'Arenberg had well and truly arrived. In 1978 d'Arry was awarded the Queen's Jubilee Medal; in 1995 he was invested as a Patron of the Australian Wine Industry; and in 2004 he was awarded a Medal in the Order of Australia for his services to the wine industry.

By 1983 production had risen to the then-significant level of around 38,000 cases, and d'Arry's son Chester, a Roseworthy (now Adelaide University) graduate in Oenology, had arrived. He progressively took over winemaking and management responsibilities.

The changes, and accompanying growth, in the d'Arenberg business, the result of the near-frenetic drive of Chester, are by far the largest reinvention of the business. He has increased production from 38 000 dozen bottles to 270 000 dozen, and introduced a kaleidoscopic range of wines from the 26 different varieties grown on the 199ha of estate vineyards. He has immersed himself in the extremely complex terroirs of McLaren Vale, leading to a detailed map of all the different soils, and underlying geological bedrock, of the region. He has moved decisively to minimal input viticulture, using the principles of organic viticulture: no insecticide or herbicide sprays, no fertilisers and no soil cultivation. All this comes together to provide a dynamic ecosystem in the soils.

A consummate marketer and communicator as well as a gifted winemaker, he regularly visits many of the over 60 countries to which the d'Arenberg wines are exported. His love of vividly coloured shirts, and his wild mane of hair, mark his progress wherever he goes. This should not lead anyone to ignore his winemaking philosophies and practices. He likens his winemaking approach to the art of sculpture, with a hands-on process demanding an intimate knowledge of and feel for the raw materials before starting to mould the sculpture.

He seeks to make red wines that have great fragrance, fruit-flavoured palates, and balanced texture, free from too much oak, and with ripe tannins. Shiraz, grenache and cabernet sauvignon are the keys to the core of the business, unusual white wines (especially very sweet, botrytised Sauternes style) are also made. And the name of every wine has a story attached to it, explained at great length on the back label.

A founding member of Australia's First Families of Wine.

De Bortoli Wines (Yarra Valley)

Est 1987
Pinnacle Lane, Dixons Creek, Vic 3775
Open 7 days 10–5
Getting there 1 hour's drive from Melbourne CBD
Contact (03) 5965 2271; yarra@debortoli.com.au; www.debortoliyarra.com.au
Region Yarra Valley
Lat 37°42′S
Elev 50–350m
E° Days 1253
Harvest 1 March–25 April
Estate vineyards 237ha
Varieties planted Pinot noir (68), cabernet sauvignon (45), chardonnay (39), shiraz (33), sauvignon blanc (20), merlot (9), semillon (5), riesling (4), sangiovese (3), nebbiolo (3), pinot gris (2), vermentino (2), viognier (2), gewurztraminer (1), pinot blanc (1)
Dozens produced 350 000 No increase planned.
Exports To China and Hong Kong through De Bortoli Wines Asia (ph) 613 9761 4100; dbw_asia@ debortoli.com.au. Also to the UK, the US and other major markets.
Winemaker Stephen Webber, Sarah Fagan, Andrew Bretherton

Key wines

Melba Reserve
How it is made: The grapes come from the Old Hill and Old Back blocks planted in 1971, limited to 15 bunches per vine. The grapes are crushed into 6-tonne fermenters, and the natural fermentation is kept to a minimum of 25°C, spending 25 or so days on skins. The wine is pressed into new French oak barrels and used casks for 14 months' maturation. 300 dozen made.

How it tastes: The aim is to make a wine with elegance, balance and length, with fruit the driving force, oak and tannins playing a support role. The bouquet has a fragrant array of red fruits which meet savoury tannins on the palate. Needs 5 years minimum and will cellar for up to 25 years from vintage.

Best vintages: 2012, 2006, 2005, 2002, 2001

Noble One Botrytis Semillon
How it is made: This wine has won more trophies and gold medals than any other table wine in Australian history, and is more a reflection of the vintage than any other, not made at all in the years when the botrytis infection fails to take hold or is contaminated by black mould. The grapes come from a number of Riverina vineyards with a history of producing the most suitable grapes, and the fermentation (in new French oak) of each vineyard is kept separate, allowing blending choices prior to bottling. Unusually, sold in 3 bottles sizes: 3000 dozen 375ml; 1300 dozen 500ml; 700 dozen 750ml.

How it tastes: Glowing yellow-gold colour; exceptionally rich, sweet and opulent, with flavours of mandarin, cumquat, honey and vanilla balanced by acidity; a true Sauternes style of the highest quality. Cellar to 10 years from vintage.

Best vintages: 2010, 2008, 2004, 2001, 2000

De Bortoli Wines (Yarra Valley)

This is run as a separate part of the De Bortoli family's far-flung wine business, headquartered in the Riverina, but with a vineyard and winery in the Hunter Valley, large vineyard holdings (170ha) in the King Valley, and by far the largest estate plantings in the Yarra Valley, with a winery to match.

Leanne De Bortoli is a director of the parent company, and manager of the Yarra Valley operations; her husband, Stephen Webber, is chief winemaker. From the moment De Bortoli arrived in the Valley by purchasing Chateau Yarrinya in 1987, it has worked tirelessly to promote the Valley as a whole as well as its own business.

Its growth over the intervening years has been quite remarkable, its vintage intake rising from a mere 35 tonnes to over 4200 tonnes. One might assume that wine quality must have taken a back seat during that massive increase in volume, but the contrary has happened. Part of this achievement has been due to the introduction of the second label, Windy Peak, in 1990, offering less costly wines, but still with a touch of class. It is the only label from this business that uses grapes both from the Yarra Valley and King Valley, but it always discloses the origin of the grapes.

The second step was the introduction of the Gulf Station label in 1994, using 100% Yarra Valley grapes, largely estate-grown. It is priced between Windy Peak and the De Bortoli Estate wines, once again offering excellent value for money. Next up the quality (and price) ladder is the full range of Estate Grown varieties led by chardonnay, sauvignon blanc, pinot noir, syrah and cabernet sauvignon. At the top, limited quantities of Reserve Release varietals are made in the vintages with exceptionally good parcels of grapes, and even smaller amounts of ultra-premium Melba Reserve (a cabernet-dominant blend).

The wines have won numerous awards – the Estate Grown Chardonnay 19 trophies and 45 gold medals from the 2000 to 2009 vintage wines, the Estate Grown Pinot Noir twice winning the Trophy for Best Pinot Noir at the Royal Sydney Wine Show, the 1996 Gulf Station Reserve Syrah the most coveted trophy in Australia, the Jimmy Watson Memorial Trophy. The winemakers, too, have received conspicuous honours, Steve Webber made *Gourmet Traveller Wine Magazine*'s Winemaker of the Year in 2007, second-in-command Sarah Fagan winning the magazine's Young Winemaker of the Year award in 2009.

Equally important in the eyes of Leanne De Bortoli and Steve Webber has been a major change in the underlying philosophy of the business. Their belief is that sustainable vineyard practices will deliver exceptional fruit quality to the winery as well as real environmental benefits. De Bortoli makes its own compost, makes compost teas, uses cover crops, and has reduced the use of herbicides and insecticides.

In the winery a 'less is more' approach has been adopted. Movements of wine are carried out by gravity wherever possible, wild (indigenous) yeasts have taken the place of cultured yeasts, and the amount of new oak has been reduced. Says Webber, 'Every bottle contains the preservation of site, season and variety. Character and personality in wine comes from the imperfections of nature.'

A founding member of Australia's First Families of Wine.

Delatite

Est 1982
26 High Street, Mansfield, Vic 3722
Open 7 days 11–5
Getting there 2.5 hours' drive from Melbourne CBD
Contact (03) 5775 2922; info@delatitewinery.com.au; www.delatitewinery.com.au
Region Upper Goulburn
Lat 37°03'S
Elev 250–800m
E° Days 1350
Harvest 12 March–30 April

Estate vineyards 25ha
Varieties planted Riesling (7.7), pinot noir (3.5), gewurztraminer (3.3), pinot gris (3.3), chardonnay (2), tempranillo (1.5), malbec (1.1), cabernet sauvignon (1), merlot (0.6), shiraz (0.5), graciano (0.5)
Dozens produced 10 000 May increase to 16 000.
Exports To China and Hong Kong through Longfellows (Shanghai) Trading Co., Ltd (ph) 8621 5058 8537; info@longfellows.com.cn. Also to Denmark, Japan and Malaysia.
Winemaker Andy Browning

Key wines

RJ Shiraz

How it is made: Is only made in the best vintages. The grapes are crushed into open fermenters, and chilled to prevent the onset of fermentation for 8 days, whereafter the must is warmed (since 2009 no cultured yeast has been used); the must is hand-plunged but pumpover and rack-and-return can also be used. The wine is basket-pressed and spends 24 months in a mix of new French and American oak barrels.

How it tastes: A fragrant bouquet and light- to medium-bodied palate with notes of warm spice and black pepper to the principal flavours of red and black cherry, and fine tannins and oak balance to the finish of a high-quality, cool-climate shiraz. Cellar for 15–20 years from vintage.

Best vintages: 2010, 2008, 2006, 2000, 1994

Pinot Noir

How it is made: Open fermenters are used for 85% destemmed grapes and 15% whole bunches, chilled to 10°C and cold-soaked for a week, whereafter fermentation with wild yeasts commences, with the must hand-plunged and pumped over, followed by a further 10 days on skins before basket-pressing and maturation in new French oak.

How it tastes: Good colour; a spicy bouquet of dark cherry and a touch of bracken/ fern; the palate is tense and lively, with fresh acidity and fine tannins persisting on the finish and aftertaste. Cellar to 7 years from vintage.

Best vintages: 2010, 2006, 2002, 2000, 1998

Delatite

When graziers Robert and Vivienne Ritchie were encouraged by Brown Brothers (in 1968) to plant riesling, gewurztraminer, sylvaner, chardonnay, pinot noir, shiraz, merlot, malbec and cabernet sauvignon, the very fact of so many varieties being trialled tells what a step into the unknown this was. It is even more remarkable that the only variety to be abandoned was sylvaner, and that pinot gris, graciano and tempranillo have since been planted.

When the vines came into bearing, and the grapes (by prior agreement) purchased by Brown Brothers, the wines were sold with the Delatite Vineyard name featured on the label. By the latter part of the 1970s, the Ritchies started planning to make their own wines. Daughter Rosalind (Ros) studied Oenology at what is now Charles Sturt University, and wine consultant Oenotec (Dr Tony Jordan) designed the winery that was completed in 1982, and continued giving consultancy advice thereafter.

The Ritchies also had the foresight to repurchase five vintages (1977 to 1981) of Delatite Cabernet Shiraz, so when they obtained their producer's licence in 1982, they had four vintages to offer. That ceased to be so important when the 1982 Cabernet Sauvignon, 1982 Gewurztraminer and 1982 Riesling won seven gold medals between them; if that were not enough, the 1983 Riesling won four gold medals and the Trophy for Best Victorian Wine at the 1983 Royal Melbourne Wine Show.

Delatite continued to make exceptional riesling and gewurztraminer, always noted for their finesse and purity, and very good chardonnay; the red wines were more variable, struggling for full flavour ripeness in the cooler vintages. In 2001 the Ritchies began using biodynamic practices in the vineyard, progressively increasing the scope of those practices through the remainder of the decade. Coincidentally, with those changes, since 2004 there has been a shift to earlier vintages, which has assisted the ripening of the red wines, especially the shiraz.

There have also been a series of changes in ownership and management since Ros Ritchie retired in 2005 to start Ros Ritchie Wines. In late 2007 David Ritchie purchased the winery from his parents; in 2009, winemaker Andy Browning was appointed; and in 2011 the Vestey family of the UK (owners of Coombe Farm) acquired a majority shareholding in a new company which owns the winery, wine stocks, vineyards, and some additional land for future vineyard expansion over and above the 7ha currently being brought into production.

David Ritchie's family is a minority shareholder in the new company, and he continues to manage the business. In the meantime, the Vestey group has purchased The Lane winery in the Adelaide Hills, and as at 2013 was looking for further appropriate investments in small to medium-sized wineries in Australia.

Devil's Lair

Est 1981
Rocky Road, Forest Grove via Margaret River, WA 6285
Open Not
Getting there 3 hours' drive from Perth CBD
Contact 1300 651 650; www.devils-lair.com
Region Margaret River
Lat 33°57'S
Elev 40–90m
E° Days 1552
Harvest 26 February–8 April

Estate vineyards 130ha
Varieties planted Chardonnay (50), cabernet sauvignon (30), sauvignon blanc (20), merlot (10), shiraz, semillon and other varieties (20)
Dozens produced 250 000 No increase planned.
Exports Exports to China and Hong Kong through Jebsens (ph) 852 2923 8777; www.jebsen.com. Also to the UK and Canada.
Winemaker Oliver Crawford

Key wines

Devil's Lair Chardonnay
How it is made: The estate-grown grapes are hand-picked, and chilled in a cool room before being whole-bunch-pressed, and taken direct to barrel for fermentation, with sometimes wild, sometimes cultured yeast to initiate fermentation and mlf. A barrel-by-barrel selection is made at the end of 9 months' maturation.

How it tastes: The wine is more elegant than many Margaret River chardonnays. Nectarine, white peach, apple and grapefruit are framed by perfectly balanced barrel fermentation characters providing some creamy cashew nuances. One piece of unusual advice from Devil's Lair is to decant the wine if it is being drunk while young. Cellar to 10 years from vintage.

Best vintages: 2013, 2009, 2006, 2002, 1995

Devil's Lair Cabernet Sauvignon
How it is made: Mainly machine-harvested, but with some hand-picked material to introduce a level of whole-berry fermentation. Typically has a merlot (occasionally tempranillo) component of up to 14%. It is warm-fermented, and once pressed is taken to French oak (40% new), where it undergoes the mlf and matures for 15 months.

How it tastes: Like the chardonnay, is a very refined and elegant wine, but also displays the power of top-class cabernet sauvignon. The palate is built around the core of blackcurrant fruit and the firm cabernet tannins that cool-grown cabernets always have, and demands patience. The inclusion of merlot, tempranillo or other compatible soft tannin varieties gives balance. Cellar to 20 years or more from vintage.

Best vintages: 2011, 2010, 2005, 2000, 1999

Devil's Lair

Devil's Lair was founded by a renowned beermaker, Phil Sexton; not any beer, for Matilda Bay/Redback was one of the early craft beers, exciting the attention of Carlton United Breweries, which took on the distribution, and then made an offer too good to refuse for the entire operation. This gave him the capital to set up Devil's Lair, and lure his beermaker, Janice McDonald, to become his chief winemaker.

Sexton is a master marketer, creating one of the most talismanic label designs, untouched 30 years down the track, and was the first to put the winery website address on the side of each cork. In late 1996 he once again received an offer too good to refuse, this time from Southcorp, and here intersections began to develop quickly. In mid-1996, Southcorp had made a successful stock exchange takeover offer for Coldstream Hills, founded by me, and I was appointed by Southcorp as group winemaker responsible for Devil's Lair (among other Southcorp wineries).

Almost overnight, Sexton arrived in the Yarra Valley and planted his Giant Steps Vineyard on the same hill as Coldstream Hills, only a few kilometres away. That is now well in the past for me and Sexton, and even more so for Devil's Lair. One parting contribution which I had a role in before stepping down as Southcorp group winemaker was the identification of a large adjacent property as an ideal vineyard site, which increased the estate vineyards to 130ha.

The story of the continuous success of Devil's Lair on a grand scale has been due to some very talented winemakers, since July 2008 led by quietly spoken but hugely talented Oliver Crawford, with well over 20 years' experience, and by viticulturist Simon Robertson, who has been at Devil's Lair since 1993, and guided the expansion of its vineyards. The increase in production from 40 000 dozen to 250 000 dozen is all the more remarkable given that Devil's Lair is tucked away out of sight, and despite the very large and beautiful blue water lake immediately in front of the winery, has no cellar door facilities, and is thus not open to the public.

There is a very neat and easy-to-follow hierarchy of Devil's Lair labels: at the bottom, the large production Fifth Leg White, Rose and Red varietal wines; next the Hidden Cave core regional varieties; then an offshoot, Dance with the Devil alternative varieties, priced only a little higher; then the two wines on which Devil's Lair's reputation was made (and continues to this day), Chardonnay and Cabernet Sauvignon, at a price twice that of Dance with the Devil; and finally Ninth Chamber Chardonnay, only made in small quantities in the best vintages at a price twice that of the two preceding wines.

All of these names are spun around the fossilised remains of a Tasmanian Devil found in a local cave; the brilliant cave art–like Devil portrayed on the label, together with a separate unconnected fifth leg; and the absolute insistence that the printing of the label is of the highest quality. It's the attention to detail that can make all the difference.

Domaine A

Est 1973
Tea Tree Road, Campania, Tas 7026
Open Mon–Fri 10–4
Getting there 30 minutes' drive from Hobart CBD
Contact (03) 6260 4174; althaus@domaine-a.com.au; www.domaine-a.com.au
Region Southern Tasmania
Lat 42°53'S
Elev 55m
E° Days 1195
Harvest 3 April–26 May

Estate vineyards 11ha
Varieties planted Cabernet sauvignon (6.4), pinot noir (1.5), merlot (1.5), sauvignon blanc (1.3), cabernet franc (0.4), petit verdot (0.1)
Dozens produced 5000 No increase planned.
Exports Exports to China and Hong Kong through Watson's Wine (ph) 852 2606 8828; info@watsonswine.com. Also to the UK, Switzerland, Japan, Taiwan and Singapore.
Winemaker Peter Althaus

Key wines

Pinot Noir

How it is made: The grapes are destemmed, and 50% crushed, then open-fermented, peaking at 32°C, with 10 days' skin contact before being pressed to French oak, where it remains for 18 months before being bottled, whereafter it spends up to 2 years in the winery prior to release. Like all the Domaine A wines, it is not fined, filtered, or cold-stabilised, and no acid additions are used. 400 dozen made. Cellar to 10 years from vintage.

How it tastes: This is a full-bodied, long-lived pinot with a core of plummy black fruits and persistent, fine-grained tannins.

Best vintages: 2010, 2009, 2008, 2005, 2002

Cabernet Sauvignon

How it is made: This wine normally has 90% cabernet sauvignon, 4% each of merlot and cabernet franc, and 2% petit verdot. It spends 3 years in new French oak, and is matured in the cellar for a further 2 years prior to release. Its alcohol ranges between 13.5% and 14% alc/vol. 500 dozen made on average each vintage.

How it tastes: It is full-bodied, the spicy blackcurrant fruit always with powerful, albeit fine-grained tannins and integrated French oak. Cellar to 20 years from vintage.

Best vintages: 2010, 2008, 2006, 2005, 2000

Domaine A

George Park, a senior officer with Tasmania's Hydro Electric Commission, and wife Priscilla, were the third vignerons in the state's 20th-century history when they established half a hectare of 11 close-planted varieties in 1973 (after Jean Miguet of Provence Vineyard in 1956 and Claudio Alcorso of Moorilla Estate in 1958). Despite his lack of formal training, the tiny size of the vineyard, and the then unheard of variety zinfandel (and other obscure varieties), George dominated the admittedly very small Tasmanian wine classes at the Royal Hobart Wine Show. Another hurdle was the absurd requirements first proposed by the State Department of Health for his intended micro winery.

He had begun a rationalisation and expansion of the vineyard when the Swiss-born, raised and educated Peter and Ruth Althaus purchased Stoney Vineyard in 1989 and renamed it Domaine A. They immediately began the design and building of a multi-level gravity-flow winery, largely built into the side of the hill on which the 11ha vineyard is planted. All of the structural components are made of massively thick off-form concrete, eliminating the need for air conditioning.

The winery has space for much greater production by normal Australian standards, the barrels all at floor level only, not stacked three or more levels high, as is usual in most Australian wineries. It is as clinically clean and precisely ordered as all things Swiss.

If it were possible, the attention to detail evident in the winery is even more obvious in the meticulously managed vineyard. It has an ideal northeasterly slope, with 200-million-year-old Jurassic dolerite over limestone on the higher parts, and sandy gravel on the lower slopes. The low to moderate fertility is ideal, making the management of the canopy of the close-planted vines (6000 per hectare) easier than it might otherwise be, and reducing the need for extensive crop thinning.

That said, capturing every bit of sunlight during the long daylight hours of summer is important for all Tasmanian vineyards. In the case of cabernet sauvignon, Domaine A's major variety, it is doubly so. It is the most challenging grape for the cool Tasmanian climate, and no other producer in the state is as successful as Domaine A. Even here, however, it has a far more European feel to it than any other Australian cabernet, and is often misunderstood.

The wine that deserves more attention (and praise) than it in fact receives is the Lady A sauvignon blanc, which is totally different from any other Australian or New Zealand wine of this variety. Even though the planting is only 1.3ha, it is progressively picked and barrel-fermented in small batches in new French oak. It is kept in those barrels on lees for 12 months before being bottled, and then held in the ultra-cool winery for a further two years before being released.

The winery, and its practices, call to mind the monasteries of bygone centuries in Burgundy, where the passage of time was of no consequence, but the attention to detail, and observation of each passing day in the summer and autumn were of overwhelming importance.

Domaine Chandon

Est 1986
727 Maroondah Highway, Coldstream, Vic 3770
Open 7 days 10.30–4.30
Getting there 1 hour's drive from Melbourne CBD
Contact (03) 9738 9200; info@domainechandon.com.au; www.chandon.com.au
Region Yarra Valley
Lat 37°42'S
Elev 5–350m
E° Days 1253
Harvest 1 March–25 April

Estate vineyards 107.6ha
Varieties planted Chardonnay (55), pinot noir (52.6)
Leased or contracted vineyards 70ha
Varieties planted NFP
Dozens produced NFP
Exports To China and Hong Kong through Moët Hennessey (ph) 8621 2211 9999 (China); (ph) 852 2976 1888 (Hong Kong); rebecca.bian@mhdchina.cn (China); yeenleng.moh@mhdk.com (Hong Kong). Also to the UK and other major markets.
Winemaker Dan Buckle, Glenn Thompson, Adam Keath

Key wines

Vintage Brut

How it is made: Typically a blend of 50% pinot noir, 47% chardonnay and 3% pinot meunier drawn from numerous cool-climate vineyard sites. Each parcel is pressed and fermented separately, and when the slow process of blending the base wine begins, over 40 individual cuvees will be tasted and their percentage contribution to the final base wine will be determined. Under Australian law, up to 15% of the final assemblage can be of prior vintages (but vintage champagne has to be 100% of the stated vintage). After 3 years on lees the bottle is disgorged.

How it tastes: The Vintage Brut has 7 g/l of sugar, less than most vintage champagnes, simply because its acidity is lower. The chardonnay component is the slowest to fully express itself, but is crucial to the freshness of the wine on entry to the palate, the pinot noir (and meunier) giving the weight and creamy complexity/ brioche flavour and texture on the finish. Cellar to 5 years from release.

Best vintages: 2012, 2010, 2008, 2006, 2002

Prestige Cuvee

How it is made: While the same process is used to make both the Vintage Brut and this wine, there are 4 crucial differences. First, no meunier is used, the base wine being typically 58% chardonnay and 42% pinot noir. Second, only very cool regions provide the grapes: the Yarra Valley, Strathbogie Ranges, King Valley, Macedon Ranges and Tasmania. Third, part of the base wine is taken through mlf. Fourth, the wine spends up to 9 years on lees.

How it tastes: This is one of the richest and most complex traditional method wines made in Australia, contrasting toasty/brioche/spice flavours with a bright and cleansing shaft of citrus-like acidity on the finish. Cellar to 3 years from release.

Best vintages: 2004, 2002, 1996, 1995

Domaine Chandon

I was involved in various ways in the establishment of Domaine Chandon in 1986. Initially in discussions with senior management of Moët et Chandon in Epernay in 1983 about the suitability of the Yarra Valley for growing chardonnay and pinot noir for sparkling wine; thereafter (as a lawyer) responsible for incorporating the company in Victoria, and becoming its first nominee director; then securing the services of my friend and wine consultant, Dr Tony Jordan, as its first winemaker and Australian CEO; and even providing its Yarra Valley office until its own offices (and thereafter winery) were built on its Green Point property. Moreover, I live only 8km away from that property.

So I have watched as its striking winery and tasting/reception area were built; become friends with Richard Geoffroy (now Dom Pérignon *chef de cave*) on his many trips to Australia in the early years of Chandon's production of sparkling wines; seen the establishment of its Green Point vineyards, and vineyards in the Strathbogie Ranges; and watched its move into table wines, and its ever-spreading access to contract-grown grapes, including Tasmania.

While there were some difficult periods in the early parts of its life, and restrictions on the countries to which it could export its wines (so it didn't compete with Moët's champagnes) the ownership has not been intrusive into areas properly the province of local management. Thus the Z*D Blanc de Blancs and the Chandon Blanc de Noirs have stainless steel crown seals.

The reward has been stability in the winemaking and viticultural teams, and consistently very good sparkling and table wines. The sparkling range starts with non-vintage Brut and non-vintage Brut Rose, and cover the full gamut from Zero Dosage (Z*D) to Vintage Blanc de Blancs, Tasmanian Cuvee, Yarra Valley Cuvee, Vintage Rose, Vintage Brut, with occasional Prestige Cuvee and Late Disgorged wines. Finally, there is the off-dry Cuvee Riche, primarily designed for fresh fruit or cake desserts, but not rich or creamy dishes. A pinot noir shiraz sparkling is also made.

The table wines first released in 2008 are centred around chardonnay and pinot noir grown in the Yarra Valley, and shiraz from either the Yarra Valley or Heathcote. The quality and style of these wines has steadily increased, with greater emphasis on varietal expression and elegance.

As is the case in Champagne, Domaine Chandon casts its net widely for components of both its vintage and non-vintage sparkling wines. Grapes are sourced from regions as diverse as the Yarra Valley, King Valley, Goulburn Valley and Macedon Ranges in Victoria, along with Adelaide Hills (South Australia), Great Southern (Western Australia) and the Coal River Valley (Tasmania). The wines are made using the traditional method of the secondary ferment taking place in the same bottle as that sold after disgorgement.

The beautiful Green Room used for tastings and light food has a spectacular vista over the adjoining vineyards, thence to the mountain range beyond, and receives 200 000 visitors a year.

Duke's Vineyard

Est 1998
**Porongurup Road, Porongurup,
WA 6324**
Open 7 days 10–4.30
Getting there 4.25 hours' drive from
Perth CBD
Contact (08) 9853 1107;
dukes@bordernet.com.au;
www.dukesvineyard.com
Region Porongurup
Lat 34°40'S
Elev 250–300m
E° Days 1506
Harvest 4 March–24 April

Estate vineyards 10ha
Varieties planted Riesling, shiraz,
cabernet sauvignon
Dozens produced 3500 May increase
to 8000.
Exports Wines are not currently
exported.
Winemaker Robert Diletti

Key wines

Riesling
How it is made: The grapes are hand-picked and whole-bunch-pressed, fermentation taking place in stainless steel at about 13°C. The wine is stabilised and filtered before bottling within months of vintage. The Magpie Hill Reserve is a vineyard selection of the best block, the vinification the same as that of the Single Vineyard.

How it tastes: The clarity and finesse of the wine is accentuated by its bone-dry lingering finish; perfectly balanced lime, apple and mineral aromas and flavours guarantee cellaring up to 20 years, and needing a minimum of 5 years to start showing its best.

Best vintages: 2013, 2012, 2004, 2002, 2001

Cabernet Sauvignon
How it is made: The grapes are hand-picked, sorted and crushed, then warm-fermented with cultured yeast incorporating as much oxygen in the ferment as possible; 7 days post-ferment maceration, then into French oak (at least 50% new) for 18 months' maturation, with a coarse filter pre-bottling. The Magpie Hill Reserve is a 'local' clone selected from original Porongurup plantings.

How it tastes: Strong purple-crimson; a complex wine with layers of interleaved cassis fruit and French oak, lengthened by fine-grained tannins. Cellar to 20 years from vintage.

Best vintages: 2013, 2012, 2008, 2007, 2004

Duke's Vineyard

When Hilde and Ian (Duke) Ranson sold their clothing manufacturing business in 1998, they were able to plan their long-held dream of establishing a vineyard as a retirement activity. After a protracted search, they found a 65ha farm nestling at the foot of the monolithic mountain that sits atop the region. The first vine was planted on 5 August 1999, Duke's 60th birthday.

Right from the outset, they decided that they would do all the vineyard work involved in establishing their 10ha of vines, and in running a Suffolk sheep stud on the remaining land, with only one extra worker. Their major concession to reality was to have the wine made by Robert Diletti, of the nearby Castle Rock winery. Diletti is one of Australia's most gifted winemakers, and the first vintage in 2001 won a gold medal, the start of a cascade of awards, including Best Wine of Show at the Royal Sydney Wine Show in 2006.

They also chose to plant the three varieties most suited to the region: riesling, shiraz and cabernet sauvignon. The vines are planted on a long northerly slope, the rows running north–south on the well-drained lateritic loam at an altitude of 220m.

An early project was the design and construction of a tasting room, insulated bottled wine storage, and an art gallery that would make the best use of the spectacular views of the Stirling and Porongurup ranges. Hilde is a successful artist, and she conceived the idea of a scalloped roof line, rising and falling in curves, the external surface covered in blue cladding, at once repeating the curves of the hills yet merging into the surrounding countryside.

The only problem was that no builder they asked was prepared to tackle what was involved. Finally, in 2002 the Ransons decided to take on the construction themselves, and the concrete foundations and floor were laid 'with a little help from our friends'; they sub-contracted the rest of the project.

Porongurup is a wild and beautiful region, well off the beaten track. It is a vinous Garden of Eden, except for one thing: birds, and in particular, silvereyes. These tiny birds peck holes in the grapes to extract some of the juice, making an entry point for wasps and bees to follow. Anyone who has smelt or tasted bird-pecked grapes will know how acetic the grapes are, and how even a small amount in a fermenter can spoil the wine.

To make matters worse, they pay no attention to shotguns, making up for this lack of intelligence by finding the smallest gap or hole in the netting that has to cover the entire vineyard. The one real defence is provided by nature in some years: abundant flowering of the red gums provides all the nectar the birds need. Such an event occurred in 2012, and the Ransons breathed a sigh of relief – until a flock of 100 crows landed.

Is Duke thinking about his second retirement? From time to time he has intimated he might be, but on the other hand, he has ambitions to increase production to 8000 cases by 2017. And given the quality and the enticingly low prices of the wines, I can see no reason why he should have any difficulty in selling that higher production.

Forest Hill Vineyard

Est 1965
Cnr South Coast Highway/Myers Road, Denmark, WA 6333
Open 7 days 10–4
Getting there 4.5 hours' drive from Perth CBD
Contact (08) 9848 0000; info@foresthillwines.com.au; www.foresthillwines.com.au
Region Great Southern
Lat 34°56′S
Elev 20–150m
E° Days 1512
Harvest 4 March–22 April

Estate vineyards 63.3ha
Varieties planted Cabernet sauvignon (18.4), chardonnay (16.4), sauvignon blanc (9.4), riesling (8), shiraz (7.3), malbec (2.6), gewurztraminer (0.8), tempranillo (0.4)
Leased or contracted vineyards 260ha
Dozens produced 25 000 May increase to 40 000.
Exports To China through Sunfield Wines (ph) 8620 8903 3829; sunfield@live.com.au. Also to Taiwan and Singapore.
Winemaker Clémence Haselgrove

Key wines

Estate Chardonnay

How it is made: The hand-picked grape bunches are refrigerated overnight then whole-bunch-pressed, the juice already cool, and transferred direct to Burgundy-made barrels (30% new), the cloudy juice cool-fermented in a temperature-controlled barrel room. The mlf is prevented to retain the natural acidity, the wine spending 10 months in barrel. 1200 dozen bottles made.

How it tastes: The bouquet offers citrus blossom and white peach aromas, the generous yet finely structured palate with a mix of white peach, grapefruit and a framework of minerally acidity. Cellar to 10 years from vintage.

Best vintages: 2011, 2010, 2008, 2007, 2006

Estate Cabernet Sauvignon

How it is made: Machine-picked grapes are crushed into 8-tonne fermenters, the must chilled to allow pre-fermentation cold soak before being warmed up for fermentation to commence, pumped over with aeration twice daily, the temperature controlled to 25°C, and the wine pressed just prior to the end of fermentation. This approach is intended to prevent extraction of excessive tannins from the skins. The mlf takes place in barrel, with a total maturation time of 20 months in French oak. 1600 dozen bottles made.

How it tastes: Skilled winemaking results in a deep crimson-coloured wine, the bouquet with both redcurrant and blackcurrant fruit, the medium- to full-bodied palate framing the fruit with cedar and cigar box oak, and firm but balanced tannins. Cellar with confidence to 20 years from vintage.

Best vintages: 2012, 2011, 2010, 2007, 2005

Forest Hill Vineyard

While Forest Hill rightly claims to have the oldest cool-climate vines (planted in 1966) in Western Australia, it is widely acknowledged that it was the vision of the West Australian government a decade earlier that indirectly led to the planting. In 1955 it invited the world-renowned Professor Harold Olmo of the University of California, Davis Campus, to visit the state and report on those regions he considered most suited to the production of fine table wines. He was particularly impressed with the Great Southern region.

What is less well known is that in the early years of the 20th century the government had endeavoured to interest Penfolds in establishing vineyards in the Mount Barker subregion. When it declined, a Correction Centre was established instead. In the 1930s it is said that the legendary winemaker Maurice O'Shea (of Mount Pleasant, in the Hunter Valley) suggested it could be suitable; he had never been to Western Australia, let alone the Great Southern, but he had studied the available climate and soil data. The Swan Valley legend, Jack Mann, visited several times between World Wars I and II, not to look for vineyard sites, but to play cricket; nonetheless, he also recognised the potential.

In 1962 the Department of Agriculture put a process in train that led to its employees Dorham Mann (son of Jack) and Bill Jamieson selecting the Springvale property owned by the Pearse family for a trial planting of 1ha each of riesling and cabernet sauvignon. A 10-year lease to the department in place, the first vines were planted in 1965, but failed; the next year was successful, and the first bunch of riesling was ceremoniously picked in 1972.

In 1975, the final year of the lease, Dorham Mann, now the winemaker at Sandalford, made the riesling, which won nine trophies and 12 gold medals, more than any single West Australian wine, and unlikely to be challenged in the future.

Over the 1980s, shiraz, malbec, sauvignon blanc, chardonnay and gewurztraminer were planted, and the riesling and cabernet sauvignon plantings were expanded. In 1989, Betty Pearse accepted an offer of $1 million from the late Robert Holmes à Court, and in 1996 Perth businessman Tim Lyons and family in turn purchased the vineyard, embarking on a major upgrade and rejuvenation of the plantings. In 2005 a new cellar door, spacious restaurant and winery were built 4km outside Denmark. The following year French-born and trained winemaker Clémence Haselgrove and viticulturist husband Lee Haselgrove took responsibility for production.

With large estate plantings, and the luxury of being able to pick and choose from the much larger contract-grown fruit supply, Forest Hill has a three-tiered structure in place, with the limited amounts of Block 1 Riesling, Block 5 Cabernet Sauvignon, Block 8 Chardonnay, Block 9 Shiraz at the top; then the Estate varietal range; and last, the large volume Highbury Fields varietals. What is more, Forest Hill already has the grape resources to expand its production to 40 000 cases. It's a good position to be in.

Frankland Estate

Est 1988
Frankland Road, Frankland, WA 6396
Open Mon–Fri 10–4, public hols &
w'ends by appt
Getting there 4 hours' drive from Perth
CBD
Contact (08) 9855 1544;
info@franklandestate.com.au;
www.franklandestate.com.au
Region Frankland River
Lat 34°22'S
Elev 200–300m
E° Days 1574
Harvest 28 February–14 April

Estate vineyards 35.3ha
Varieties planted Riesling (8), shiraz (8),
chardonnay (4), cabernet franc (4),
merlot (4), cabernet sauvignon (3),
mourvedre (1), malbec (1), sauvignon
blanc (0.8), marsanne (0.5), viognier
(0.5), petit verdot (0.5)
Dozens produced 20 000 No increase
planned.
Exports To Hong Kong through
Valdivia Wines Ltd. (ph) 852 2555 7431;
claudia@valdiviawines.com.hk. Also to
all major markets.
Winemaker Hunter Smith, Brian Kent

Key wines

Isolation Ridge Shiraz and Olmo's Reward (red blend)
How they are made: The estate-grown grapes are typically cold-soaked for 24–36
hours prior to the commencement of fermentation, which builds to 28°C before
they are cooled and controlled to preserve maximum aromatic and varietal fruit
expression. The wines then spend 18–20 months in French oak on lees, with
minimal filtration prior to bottling. 1200–1400 dozen made.

How they taste: The Isolation Ridge Shiraz is strong purple-crimson when young;
a complex, medium- to full-bodied wine, with a symbiotic and synergistic union
between its abundant black fruits and plentiful ripe, velvety tannins. Cellar to
20+ years from vintage. Olmo's Reward is an estate-grown blend of cabernet franc,
merlot, cabernet sauvignon and malbec, with cabernet franc and merlot the major
components, making it a rare assemblage. It pays homage to the right bank of
Bordeaux, its small black and red berry fruits with fine-grained savoury tannins
and integrated oak. Cellar to 20 years from vintage.

Best vintages: 2011, 2010, 2008, 2007, 2004

Frankland Estate

Barrie Smith and wife Judi Cullam purchased their 400ha wool-growing farm in 1974 in a part of the country that even Australians regard as remote. And when they decided to embark on a diversification venture in 1988 there were no neighbours just around the corner to provide advice if anything went wrong.

They had several things going for them. They had undertaken a tour of French vineyards in 1985, and had worked two vintages at Château Sénéjac in Bordeaux. Equally importantly, the vineyard's isolation means it is largely free of vine pests and diseases (and gives rise to the name of its top-tier shiraz). Its location adjacent to the region's eponymous river, and the Southern Ocean 40km to the south, promotes air movement during the night as well as the day, in summer drawing up ocean-cooled breezes.

As well as moderating the climate and reducing the risk of frost, the air movement makes fungal disease relatively easy to control with sulphur and copper sprays. Flocks of guinea fowl scour the vineyard by day eating bugs and insects that might otherwise damage the foliage or crops. In winter, sheep keep the grass down and provide a source of manure. Add in a range of composting and mulching techniques, and recycling of winery waste, and it's easy to see how the vineyard has achieved certified organic status.

While both Barrie and Judi have been centrally involved in hands-on building of the business, Judi has been the driving force behind the biennial Frankland Estate International Riesling Tasting, bringing keynote speakers and producers from many parts of the world. It is an important part of the International Riesling Coalition (also pioneered by Frankland Estate) which sees major similar events held annually around the world.

It hardly need be said that the quality of Frankland Estate's rieslings (with individual vineyard releases and an off-dry riesling of the highest calibre) are consistently excellent. Thus they have taken some of the attention away from the Estate's red wines, a decade ago arguably of lesser quality than the rieslings, but now needing no excuses at all.

Barrie and Judi's two children are now actively involved in the business. Daughter Elizabeth Smith graduated with a Bachelor of Science (Honours) in Agricultural Science from the University of Western Australia, and subsequently completed further studies in viticulture at Charles Sturt University. She also worked vintages in California, Spain and New Zealand, and divides her time between nurturing young wines and young children.

Son Hunter Smith has a Bachelor of Business (Agricultural Management) and is involved in every aspect of the wine business, including finance and marketing, and is also responsible for managing the wool-growing farm.

Freycinet

Est 1980
15919 Tasman Highway via Bicheno, Tas 7215
Open 7 days 10–5 (Nov–Apr), 10–4 (May–Oct)
Getting there 2 hours' drive from Launceston CBD, or 2.25 hours' drive from Hobart CBD
Contact (03) 6257 8574; freycinetwines@bigpond.com; www.freycinetvineyard.com.au
Region East Coast Tasmania
Lat 41°20'S
Elev 5m

E° Days 1233
Harvest 16 March–19 May
Estate vineyards 14.83ha
Varieties planted Chardonnay (4), pinot noir (2.94), sauvignon blanc (2.78), riesling (2.42), cabernet sauvignon (1.81), merlot (0.35), cabernet franc (0.27), shiraz (0.2), schonburger (0.06)
Dozens produced 8500 No increase planned.
Exports Wines are not currently exported to China and Hong Kong. Exported to the UK and Singapore.
Winemaker Claudio Radenti, Lindy Bull

Key wines

Pinot Noir
How it is made: There is little pest and disease impact in the vineyard, and autumn is usually mild and dry, so sprays are kept to a minimum. However, shoot-thinning, leaf-plucking, fruit-thinning and hand-picking add to the cost but deliver top-quality fruit. The focus of winemaking is to showcase the fruit purity. The grapes are destemmed into a rotary fermenter, and approximately 4% whole bunches are incorporated, together with a pure yeast culture. Fermentation peaks at 32°C, and is concluded in 8 days, and the wine is matured for 15 months in French oak barriques (30% new). The wine is filtered and bottled with the protection of screwcaps. The 2012 vintage is the 26th. 600 dozen made.

How it tastes: The fragrance of the bouquet intensifies as the wine ages, as do the multiple layers of fruit in the mouth, with a silky sweetness to the flavours; the tannins are evident, as is the oak, but it is the integrity of the fruit that is so imposing. Cellar to 30 years from vintage.

Best vintages: 2012, 2010, 2009, 2007, 2000

Chardonnay
How it is made: The grapes are hand-picked, and 70% is crushed followed by immediate pressing, then cold-settled before inoculation with a pure yeast culture (ex Champagne) and, once the fermentation is underway, transferred to French oak barriques (20% new). 30% of the fruit is whole-bunch-pressed, and the cloudy juice inoculated with yeast, then straight to barrel for fermentation, providing Burgundian-like complexity, then matured for 10 months and lightly fined prior to bottling. 1350 dozen made.

How it tastes: The barrel fermentation, lees stirring and occasional mlf tame the often fierce Tasmanian acidity, resulting in a nectarine, white peach and melon-flavoured wine, the oak influence subtle, the finish long and distinguished. Cellar to 15 years from vintage.

Best vintages: 2012, 2009, 2007, 2006, 2005

Freycinet

The connection between owning a Tasmanian abalone fishing licence and a pioneering East Coast vineyard and winery may not be immediately obvious. But when Geoff Bull purchased and cleared what was to become the Freycinet Vineyard in 1978, he was also the owner of a commercial abalone fishing licence which provided the funds necessary for his wine enterprise.

He had no background in grapegrowing and, even if he had, it would have been extremely difficult to visualise the unique macro-climate that would become apparent once the first vines (planted by him the following year) came into production. The first 4ha were planted in two blocks called The Hill and The Paddock; the magic that emerged came from the gentle slopes they were perched on, in what is a small, sheltered valley, closed at the top end, open at the bottom.

It has been described as an amphitheatre, and as a heat trap. The slopes provide enhanced sunlight interception and warmth during the day, and cold air drainage in spring nights that might otherwise cause great damage. These two influences mean the otherwise marginal climate (that is, too cool) is ideal for pinot noir, chardonnay and riesling.

In 1995 two more vineyard sites were planted. The first is 300m down the valley, on a more gentle north-to-east-facing slope. Its 4ha are planted to the same three varieties, but managed to provide grapes for the second-tier Louis range. This comprises a sweeter riesling, an unwooded chardonnay, and an earlier-drinking (but delicious) pinot noir.

The third vineyard site, known as Synotts, is 4km west of the amphitheatre, and is a classic continental site, providing the grapes for the outstanding traditional method vintage sparkling wine (pinot noir and chardonnay) aged on lees for 8 years.

Finally, in 2013 Freycinet acquired part of the neighbouring Coombend property. It is 42ha, and extends to the Tasman Highway (and a likely cellar door location), with a mature 5.75ha vineyard (planted to sauvignon blanc, cabernet sauvignon, riesling, cabernet franc and shiraz), and a 4.2ha olive grove.

Daughter Lindy Bull helped her parents establish the original vineyard, and enjoyed the experience. So she graduated as a Bachelor of Applied Science in Oenology from Roseworthy Agricultural College (now Adelaide University) in 1989, the first Tasmanian female to graduate as a winemaker. After gaining experience making wine in the Clare Valley, New Zealand and France, she travelled to Goundrey Wines in the Great Southern of Western Australia, and there met (for the first time) another Tasmanian-born winemaker who had obtained his degree in Oenology from the same college in 1982, and whose domestic and international winemaking experience was even greater than hers.

His name was Claudio Radenti, and in 1992 they both returned to Freycinet, partners in life and in wine, now with three children. When Claudio smiles, his face is suffused with a gentle joy, and he has plenty to smile about with Lindy – herself with a wonderful personality – and their children.

All the Freycinet Vineyard wines are of consistently high quality, none more so than the Pinot Noir, Chardonnay and Radenti sparkling.

Geoff Weaver Wines

Est 1982
2 Gilpin Lane, Mitcham, SA 5062 (postal)
Open Not
Getting there NA
Contact (08) 8272 2105;
weaver@adelaide.on.net
www.geoffweaver.com.au
Region Adelaide Hills
Lat 34°00′S
Elev 500–550m
E° Days 1359
Harvest 12 March–30 April

Estate vineyards 13ha
Varieties planted Riesling, sauvignon blanc, chardonnay, pinot noir
Dozens produced 4650 No increase planned.
Exports To Hong Kong through Watson's Wine (ph) 852 2606 8828; info@watsonswine.com.
Winemaker Geoff Weaver

Key wines

Sauvignon Blanc

How it is made: Using 100% estate-grown, hand-picked grapes, the wine is made in two very different styles. The first is conventional, cold-fermented with cultured yeast in stainless steel tanks, and bottled early. The second is only made in some vintages, with wild yeast, lees contact and oak-fermented; it is very complex, and can develop very well in bottle.

How it tastes: One of the most elegant sauvignon blancs on the market; has a fragrant bouquet and fresh palate, the finish dry and almost savoury. Cellar for up to 10 years from vintage.

Best vintages: 2012, 2010, 2009, 2005, 2000

Chardonnay

How it is made: Hand-picked, estate-grown grapes; the wine is 100% barrel-fermented in new and used French oak with cultured yeast and extended contact with yeast lees, and is taken through mlf, an approach adopted by many makers in the Adelaide Hills.

How it tastes: The wine is powerful, yet subtle, with juicy, vibrant fruit, and excellent length and balance. Cellar up to 12 years from vintage.

Best vintages: 2012, 2010, 2009, 2005, 2000

Geoff Weaver Wines

This family-owned and managed winery was established in 1982 by Geoff and wife Judy Weaver. Geoff studied for and obtained a degree in agricultural science from Adelaide University in 1970, but after a brief period working in the Orlando winery commenced his second degree, in Oenology, from Roseworthy College (now part of Adelaide University), graduating in 1973.

He has painted landscapes since 1973, one of which is on the beautiful labels adorning the Weaver wines. He says painting leads him to engage fully with the land, and in doing so to appreciate the grandeur and the subtlety, the full glory, of nature. Each painting is of a place that is important to him, and captures a particular moment.

His artistic approach, and his belief in the beauty of nature, is directly reflected in the wines he makes, each vintage a particular moment captured in his wines. It also explains his gentle personality, quiet voice, and the great elegance of the wines he makes.

But there is another side to this gifted winemaker. After starting his career at Orlando, he joined Thomas Hardy & Sons Pty Limited in 1975 as chief white wine maker, and in 1988 was appointed chief winemaker for the Thomas Hardy group, responsible for the intake (crush) of 120 000 tonnes of grapes, then 10% of the entire Australian vintage.

Woven through this distinguished career was the slow and steady growth of his family vineyard at Lenswood, high in the Adelaide Hills at an altitude of 500–550m. With help from his father, he worked on weekends, holidays and in the evenings, planting riesling, chardonnay, cabernet sauvignon and merlot in 1983, sauvignon blanc in 1987 and pinot noir in 1992.

Hardy's knew about his vineyard development, and raised no objection, even though it led to his early 'retirement' in 1992 to focus entirely on the family vineyard and winemaking. One moment he was responsible for a vintage of 120 000 tonnes of grapes, the next 70 tonnes from 11ha of vineyards.

This was a lifestyle decision, not very different from mine to leave the large Australian law firm of which I was a senior partner. In each case there was a major financial sacrifice. Weaver was (and remains) in demand as a consultant, as do other senior winemakers of large wineries when they decide to follow their dreams.

The vines are planted on sloping hillsides with ancient low-fertility soils, and are not irrigated. While attention to detail is of paramount importance, the yields are low, and the grape flavours are intense. He makes the wines at the nearby Shaw + Smith winery, an arrangement that benefits both businesses, his vast experience helping the winemaking team at Shaw + Smith.

Giaconda

Est 1985
30 McClay Road, Beechworth, Vic 3747
Open By appt
Getting there 3 hours' drive from Melbourne CBD
Contact (03) 5727 0246; sales@giaconda.com.au; www.giaconda.com.au
Region Beechworth
Lat 36°21'S
Elev 300–720m
E° Days 1435
Harvest 18 February–3 April

Estate vineyards 5ha
Varieties planted Chardonnay (3), shiraz (1), pinot noir (0.6), nebbiolo (0.4)
Dozens produced 3500 No increase planned.
Exports To China and Hong Kong through Summergate Fine Wines (ph) toll free 800 820 6929; info@summergate.com. Also to the UK and the US.
Winemaker Rick Kinzbrunner

Key wines

Chardonnay

How it is made: This wine is arguably Australia's greatest; in my annual *Australian Wine Companion*, the 2010 vintage was ranked equal second, and in the 2014 edition, the 2011 vintage was ranked first (in a field of 943), and the '96 was by far the greatest chardonnay of that vintage, a great classic. Its vinification is very similar to that used by most Burgundians: total barrel fermentation of cloudy juice initiated by wild yeast, and maturation in new, high-quality French oak.

How it tastes: It is almost inevitable that the exceptionally complex wine is strongly reminiscent of grand cru white Burgundy. The mouthfeel is staggeringly deep, yet full of energy, driving the wine through to an exceptionally long finish. Cellar to 15 years from vintage.

Best vintages: 2011, 2010, 2005, 2004, 2002

Estate Shiraz

How it is made: It is open-fermented, and given extended maceration, with wild/natural yeast for both the primary and secondary mlf. It is neither filtered nor fined.

How it tastes: It is medium-bodied, with ripe tannins and supple texture, with a strong spicy/peppery undercurrent to its black fruit flavours. Cellar to 20 years from vintage.

Best vintages: 2010, 2008, 2005, 2004, 2002

Giaconda

I have long been struck by the similarities between Rick Kinzbrunner of Giaconda and Phillip Jones of Bass Phillip. Both have been profoundly influenced by Burgundy, Kinzbrunner by white Burgundy (and its chardonnay), Jones by red Burgundy (and its pinot noir). Both have implicit belief in the overriding importance of terroir; both use biodynamic practices in their vineyards; both use a non-interventionist approach in the winery, either minimising pumping or, in the case of Giaconda, using gravity flow – after creating a large granite underground cellar in 2008. The vineyard is managed biodynamically, and solar panels have meant the winery has not used external electrical power.

Kinzbrunner's university degree in mechanical engineering had been put to one side when, in 1970, he began a 10-year odyssey across the world. The first small step was to New Zealand, before a move to California to study Oenology at the UC Davis Campus. While undertaking the degree course, he worked at leading wineries including Stag's Leap, Simi and Matanzas Creek. In France, he worked at Château Pétrus for a vintage.

He returned to Australia in 1980 to join Brown Brothers as assistant winemaker, and in 1982 purchased the present-day property 9km south-west of Beechworth, not far from the since-abandoned Everton Hills Vineyard pioneered by Brown Brothers.

Planting began the same year, initially with chardonnay, cabernet sauvignon, merlot, cabernet franc and a little pinot noir. In 1985 the first crop was harvested, and Giaconda was on the way. From that first day, the 3ha of chardonnay have been the lifeblood of the business. So much so that the Bordeaux varieties have been removed, and 1ha of shiraz has been planted, along with 0.4ha of nebbiolo. Pinot noir (0.6ha) has been an erratic performer but an additional 0.3ha has been planted with a new clone on a particularly cool spot in the vineyard, and Kinzbrunner expects it will improve the quality of the pinot. Likewise, he has made progress with that most difficult of all grapes, nebbiolo. Rather than the granitic soils of its first planting, it is now being grown on red shale soils.

When it comes to promotion and the sale of their wines, Phillip Jones of Bass Phillip and Kinzbrunner have similar attitudes. Each sells his annual production immediately on release of the wines, much by direct sale to mail/email customers, reserving small amounts for top restaurants and a few fine wine retailers.

Perhaps the most striking coincidence is that Beechworth, with a handful of wineries, is only slowly gaining recognition as a fine wine region. The vast area of Gippsland, home to Bass Phillip, is so sparsely populated by wineries that it is technically a zone, with no official regions.

The future varietal production of Giaconda is in the lap of the gods. Chardonnay must surely remain its greatest wine. The pinot noir has (quite legally) used a percentage (never exceeding 15%) of Yarra Valley pinot, but this will gradually decrease as the new planting comes into production.

The taste of mature nebbiolo is often likened to that of pinot noir, and Kinzbrunner is ageing three vintages of nebbiolo in the cellar, a pattern to be continued in the future. It has seldom performed well in Australia, but one should not take Kinzbrunner's winemaking skills lightly. This may suggest that shiraz is the odd man out, but I believe it is the most likely to sit at the feet of the chardonnay in future decades.

Grant Burge

Est 1988
279 Krondorf Road, Barossa Valley, SA 5352
Open 7 days 10–5
Getting there 1 hour's drive from Adelaide CBD
Contact (08) 8563 3700; admin@grantburgewines.com.au; www.grantburgewines.com.au
Region Barossa Valley
Lat 34°29′S
Elev 274m
E° Days 1571
Harvest 27 February–17 April
Estate vineyards 392.5ha
Varieties planted Shiraz (136.1), cabernet sauvignon (70.5), chardonnay (43.6), merlot (42.5), grenache (20.9), mourvedre (14.6), riesling (13.7), white frontignac (13.2), semillon (11.5), pinot gris (6.1), petit verdot (5.2), tempranillo (3.7), pinot noir (3.2), viognier (2.1), plus smaller plantings of palomino, pedro, bastardo, cinsaut, black muscat, graciano, red frontignac and muscat rouge
Dozens produced 400 000 May increase to 600 000.
Exports To China through Shanghai Yanlong International Trade Co. Ltd (ph) 8621 6309 3285; info@SYLITC.com and to Hong Kong through Enoteca Co. Ltd (ph) (852) 2526 2008; central@enoteca.com.hk. Also to all major markets.
Winemaker Grant Burge, Craig Stansborough, Matt Pellew

Key wines

Meshach Shiraz
How it is made: Most of the grapes come from the estate Filsell Vineyard, the vines nearing 100 years old. Smaller parcels come from even older vineyards. The grapes are crushed, and fermented until 1° baume is left, before transfer to barrel (80% American, 20% French) for the completion of fermentation. After fermentation is complete, the wine is racked off gross lees and returned to the barrels for 22 months before bottling. It is then held for 2 years before release. 1500 dozen made.

How it tastes: A wonderfully rich and plush shiraz, with black fruits, oak and dark chocolate surging through the palate, the tannins soft and integrated, the oak evident but balanced. Cellar to 20 years from vintage.

Best vintages: 2012, 2010, 2006, 2004, 2002

Shadrach Cabernet Sauvignon
How it is made: The most important component comes from the estate Corryton Park Vineyard, high in the Eden Valley, with richer fruit from the Barossa Valley floor blended seamlessly into the wine. The major part is fermented for 8 days before being pressed, the rest given extended maceration to develop structure and longevity. It spends over 21 months in new and 2-year-old French oak before bottling. It is held in bottle for 2 years prior to release. 1500 dozen made.

How it tastes: The wine has remarkable synergy to its flavour, structure and texture, resulting in a supple, ultra-smooth and beautifully balanced exercise in blackcurrant/cassis fruit, the tannins fine and balanced, the finish of great length. Cellar to 25 years from vintage.

Best vintages: 2012, 2010, 2009, 2006, 2005

Grant Burge

The history behind Grant Burge and his eponymous winery is rich enough to qualify for the iconic television series, *Australian Story*. It began when noted tailor John Burge immigrated to the Barossa Valley from Hillcot, Wiltshire, England, in 1855 with wife Eliza and their two sons, Meshach and Henry. The family created a flourishing farm, with wheat, sheep and grapevines, continued in due course by Meshach. In 1883 he married Emma, and they had eight children. First-born Percival established Wilsford Winery in 1928, and had two sons, fourth-generation Noel and Colin, the latter marrying Nancy. Their son was fifth-generation Grant Burge, born in 1951.

The pace did not slacken thereafter. In 1978 Grant and then business partner Ian Wilson acquired the Krondorf Winery from Dalgety Wine Estates, then exiting the wine industry. Burge was the winemaker, Wilson the marketer. It was a potent combination, and in 1983 Krondorf was listed on the Australian Stock Exchange. It was so successful that Mildara, led by the ultimate market genius Ray King, made a takeover offer which was accepted, making Burge and Wilson wealthy men.

Conventional thinking at the time was that brands were more important than vineyards, but Grant and Helen Burge have always thought outside the square. They promptly purchased the vineyards that Krondorf had assembled with part of the proceeds of its share issue: the price was right, and they continued buying vineyards at knock-down prices as the over-supply of grapes led to the Vine Pull Scheme of the 1980s.

When Grant Burge Wines was formed in 1988, it had the largest family-owned vineyards in the Barossa and Eden valleys. By 1999 it was crushing 8000 tonnes of grapes, four times as much as Krondorf at the time it was purchased by Mildara. It had its business headquarters and cellar door at the historic and fastidiously restored Moorooroo Cellars, its winery at the Illapara facility. But by the end of the year, the wheel had turned full circle with the acquisition of the already-upgraded Krondorf winery.

It became the white wine–making facility, Illapara the red winery. Behind all of this there have been refinements in the style of the red wines, the heart of the Grant Burge business. Grant says the first era, from 1988 to 1995, saw the generous use of air-dried, high-quality American oak to bolster a rich and robust flavour profile with alcohol levels less than 15%; the second era, from 1996 to 2001, saw more mocha-accented oak, and greater extract of fruit flavour; the third era has seen a move for some wines to new French oak, and a shortening of time in oak from 30 months to 20–22 months.

A new era on an altogether different front has seen elder son Toby become vineyard manager, daughter Amelia being groomed for marketing responsibilities, and youngest son Trent joining the winemaking team at Illapara in 2006. This is long-range succession planning: as at 2013 there was no sign of either Grant or Helen relinquishing control of the excellent business their formidable work ethic has created.

Grosset

Est 1981
King Street, Auburn, SA 5451
Open Wed–Sun 10–5 from Sept for approx 6 weeks
Getting there 1.5 hours' drive from Adelaide CBD
Contact (08) 8849 2175; info@grosset.com.au; www.grosset.com.au
Region Clare Valley
Lat 33°50′S
Elev 398m
E° Days 1493
Harvest 14 February–24 March

Estate vineyards 22ha
Varieties planted Riesling (18), cabernet sauvignon (1.5), semillon (1), cabernet franc (0.5), other (1)
Leased or contracted vineyards 5ha
Varieties planted Adelaide Hills pinot noir (2), chardonnay (2), sauvignon blanc (1)
Dozens produced 11 000 No increase planned.
Exports To China through Ruby Red Fine Wine (ph) 8621 62342249; info@ rubyred.com.cn and to Hong Kong through Watson's Wine (ph) 852 2606 8828; info@watsonswine.com. Also to the UK, the US and other major markets.
Winemaker Jeffrey Grosset, Brent Treloar

Key wines

Polish Hill Riesling
How it is made: Made using only free-run juice, and employing a neutral yeast to maintain natural fruit characters and expression of variety and place; fermented to dryness, and using no fining agents.

How it tastes: A wine of exceptional purity and elegance, with faultless balance to the lime and mineral flavours. Cellar to 20 years from vintage with total confidence.

Best vintages: 2012, 2011, 2010, 2005, 2002

Gaia Cabernet Sauvignon Cabernet Franc
How it is made: Generally a 75/25% blend (sometimes with 5% merlot) coming from the highest vineyard (570m) in the Clare Valley. Destemmed and crushed, with some whole berries; then fermentation in tank over 7–8 days with gentle cap plunging; matured in French oak barriques (45% new) for 18 months. One-year bottle maturation before release.

How it tastes: Deep crimson; a medium-bodied wine with a fragrant bouquet and supremely elegant palate with blackcurrant and cedar flavours, the fine-grained tannins giving the structure and balance for long ageing. Cellar 25–30 years from vintage.

Best vintages: 2010, 2009, 2006, 2004, 2002

Grosset

Jeffrey Grosset is a perfectionist, and has the patience – and politeness – of a saint. It far transcends the current mantra of attention to detail, although that, too, is part of his DNA. Given this, the perfection of the wines he makes should not come as a surprise.

His career had some unexpected turns after he completed a 5-year, double diploma (Viticulture and Oenology) at Roseworthy Agricultural College (now Adelaide University) in 1975. He first spent 18 months at Seppelt Great Western before accepting an assistant winemaker position at a German winery near Freiburg with a 1000-tonne crush. He arrived to find the French senior winemaker designate had changed his mind, leaving Grosset in charge of the entire winery.

The experience doubtless helped when, on his return to Australia in 1977, he joined the winemaking team at Lindemans Karadoc winery, then processing 30 000 tonnes each vintage. He had spent 3 years there when he learnt from his family that the Farmers Union milk depot at Auburn had closed, and was on the market for a nominal sum.

The stone building had been modernised internally in 1960 to the high standards required for food, leaving the front untouched; all he had to do was remove the 'Butter and Iceworks' sign on the front, and substitute 'Grosset Wines'. From 30 000 tonnes to 12 tonnes (his first crush) in 1981 is what for some might be a bridge too far, but not for Jeffrey Grosset.

Today he makes 11 000 cases from a crush of not much more than 150 tonnes from the 27ha of grapes in the Clare Valley and Adelaide Hills, and although he routinely sells out each year, he has no intention of increasing the price.

All the Clare Valley wines come from estate plantings yielding under 6 tonnes/ha. The two most famous wines are the Polish Hill Riesling and the Springvale Watervale Riesling; a recent addition to the portfolio has been the Alea Off-Dry Clare Valley Riesling, in a Mosel Valley style. The other Clare Valley wine is his resplendent Gaia.

From the Adelaide Hills grapes grown under long-term contract he makes exquisite chardonnay and pinot noir; the final wine is the Semillon (Clare Valley) Sauvignon Blanc (Adelaide Hills) blend.

Inevitably, he has been recognised around the world: inaugural Winemaker of the Year by *Gourmet Traveller Wine Magazine* in 1998; one of the world's Top 10 White Wine Makers (*Decanter Magazine*, UK); one of the '50 most influential winemakers' (*Wine & Spirits*, US); and in 1998 Riesling Maker of the Year in a Riesling summit in Hamburg, Germany.

Those who know him are not surprised by the tenacity he showed in successfully forcing the major wineries in Australia to drop the linked 'Rhine Riesling', and restrict riesling to that variety; his vision in leading the move to screwcaps by all the Clare Valley riesling makers in 2000; his commitment to the environment by achieving a zero carbon footprint for the winery through a revegetation program of 2ha per annum; converting his vineyards to organic status; and establishing the Grosset Gaia Fund to provide grants to organisations supporting youth, the arts and the environment.

Hardys

Est 1853
202 Main Road, McLaren Vale, SA 5171
Open Mon–Fri 10–4.30, Sat 10–5,
Sun 11–5
Getting there 40 minutes' drive from
Adelaide CBD
Contact (08) 8329 4124;
theteam@hardys.com.au;
www.hardys.com.au
Region McLaren Vale
Lat 34°14′S
Elev 50–200m
E° Days 1680
Harvest 14 February–14 April

Estate vineyards NFP
Varieties planted As with other
wineries that are part of a much larger
wine business under single ownership,
vineyard resources are shared across all
brands in the group.
Dozens produced NFP
Exports To China through Shenzhen
Nanyu Brother Investment Co. Ltd (ph)
86 150 1266 0700; 462977789@qq.com
and to Hong Kong through Accolade
Wines Hong Kong: HKEnquiries@
accolade-wines.com; www.accolade-
wines.com. Also to all major markets.
Winemaker Paul Lapsley (Chief)

Key wines

Eileen Hardy Chardonnay

How it is made: The grapes come from Tasmania and Yarra Valley, and the juice is fermented using a mix of wild or cultured yeasts for different lots, and is carried out in French oak barriques (50% new, 50% second use) and taken through 80% mlf. It typically spends 9–10 months in barrel and is lightly fined before bottling.

How it tastes: Has beautifully harmonious texture, structure, balance and length, fruit to the fore backed up by fine, lingering acidity. Cellar to 10 years from vintage.

Best vintages: 2010, 2008, 2005, 2004, 2002

Eileen Hardy Shiraz

How it is made: The grapes come from old vines in the Upper Tintara district of McLaren Vale. Different parcels are fermented with either wild or cultured yeast, the fermentation completed in open stainless steel fermenters before being taken to French oak barriques (25% new) for 16 months' maturation. It is lightly fined, but not filtered.

How it tastes: Power, balance, length and harmony are also the key words for this wine, blackberry and satsuma plum with nuances of spice and aniseed completing the picture. Cellar to 30 years from vintage.

Best vintages: 2010, 2008, 2005, 2004, 2002

Hardys

When a 20-year-old farmer from Devon, England, disembarked at Port Misery in South Australia on 15 August 1850, with £30 cash and a few personal possessions in a wooden box, he could not have imagined that he was to found a family dynasty that would build one of Australia's largest wine companies.

His name was Thomas Hardy, and he was to die on 10 January 1912, leaving one son and three grandsons, collectively heading an ever-expanding Hardy family clan – the sixth generation is still involved with the company. He moved at a hectic pace; in 1851 he drove cattle overland to feed the miners flocking to the recently discovered goldfields; in 1853 he returned to Adelaide with enough money to buy a property on the banks of the River Torrens; by 1857 he had made his first wine in an underground cellar he had excavated at night after working in the fields by day; and by 1859 he had exported wine to England while actively building his share of the domestic market.

In 1876 he was the only bidder for the Tintara Winery, caught in an economic downturn, and sold by its receivers. He recouped the total price from the first year's sales of the wine stocks that came with the purchase. Exactly 100 years later (in 1976) Thomas Hardy & Sons acquired the Emu Wine Company, its brand and vineyards in South Australia, but more importantly Houghton, then and now Western Australia's largest winery.

The next acquisition brought another wheel of history full circle. Back in 1850 Thomas Hardy had accepted his first offer of employment with another émigré from Devon, John Reynell, Hardy noting in his diary, 'Although it was low wages ... I have no doubt I shall be able to better myself.' He indeed did, and in 1982 the company he founded acquired Walter Reynell & Sons Limited, making Reynell's bluestone winery, barrel stores and offices, set in park-like gardens, its head office.

At a personal level, the blood of the Hardys ran thick. The chain of command ran from Thomas to Robert to Tom Mayfield, then Kenneth to Thomas Walter to Sir James, all bearing the Hardy surname. The fifth generation is represented by winemaker Bill Hardy, the sixth by Alix Hardy, who was employed in 2007.

The Hardy business had continuously grown while all this was happening, but its 1992 merger with the South Australian Riverland company Berri Renmano Limited came at a time of economic stress in Australia. It resolved short-term problems, but by early 2003 BRL Hardy Limited (as the merged companies became known) was taken over by Constellation Brands of the US to form the largest wine company in the world.

In 2008 Constellation Wines began the process of unwinding what had turned out to be a highly priced acquisition, selling wineries and vineyards, but in the majority of instances retaining the brands. In January 2011, Constellation Brands sold 80% of the capital of Constellation Wines Australia to CHAMP Private Equity, renamed Accolade Wines in June 2011. The Australian brands owned by Accolade are Amberley, Banrock Station, Bay of Fires/House of Arras, Berri Estates, Brookland Valley, Goundrey, Hardys, Houghton, Leasingham, Moondah Brook, Renmano, Reynella, Stanley, Tintara and Yarra Burn.

All of this has not harmed the standing of Hardys, which in July 2013 was named the second most powerful wine brand in the world (after E&J Gallo winery) by the 2013 Intangible Business Report. Nor has it meant that the quality of its wines has suffered.

Henschke

Est 1868
1428 Keyneton Road, Keyneton,
SA 5353
Open Mon–Fri 9–4.30, Sat 9–12, public
hols 10–3
Getting there 1.5 hours' drive from
Adelaide CBD
Contact (08) 8564 8223;
info@henschke.com.au;
www.henschke.com.au
Region Eden Valley
Lat 34°35′S
Elev 450m
E° Days 1460
Harvest 20 March–30 April
Estate vineyards 114ha
**Varieties planted Hill of Grace
Vineyard** (Eden Valley, 400m) oldest
shiraz planted 1860s; 8ha in total, 4ha
shiraz; yield 2.5 t/ha; **Mount Edelstone
Vineyard** (Eden Valley, 400m) planted
1912; 16ha shiraz; yield 6 t/ha; **Eden
Valley Vineyard** (high in the Mount
Lofty Ranges, 500m) planted 1968; 32ha
riesling, shiraz, semillon, cabernet
sauvignon, chardonnay, sauvignon
blanc, gewurztraminer, cabernet franc,
merlot, viognier; yield 5 t/ha; **Lenswood
Vineyard** (Adelaide Hills, 550m) planted
1982–87; 13ha chardonnay, riesling,
pinot noir, merlot, cabernet sauvignon,
sauvignon blanc; yield 6 t/ha
Dozens produced 50 000 No increase
planned.
Exports To China through Shanghai
Torres Wine Trading (ph) 8621 6267
7979; alberto@torres.com.cn and to
Hong Kong through Watson's Wine (ph)
852 2606 8991; CandiceCh@asw.com.hk.
Also to the UK, the US and other major
markets.
Winemaker Stephen Henschke

Key wines

Mount Edelstone Shiraz
How it is made: It is composed of separately open-fermented and matured parcels
from each of the blocks on the vineyard, and is only blended shortly prior to
bottling. The must is pressed towards the end of fermentation, which is finished
in barrel, and matured in predominantly French oak (both new and used) for
21 months; not fined, and only lightly filtered.

How it tastes: A perfectly balanced and composed wine, with black and red cherry
fruits complexed by lesser notes of plum and blackberry; the tannins are superb,
the oak of high quality, and totally integrated on the very long, silky finish of this
outstanding medium-bodied shiraz. With Vino-Lok closure, likewise cellar for
30–50 years from vintage.

Best vintages: 2010, 2009, 2006, 2005, 2002

Keyneton Euphonium
How it is made: Typically a 70/18/12% Eden Valley blend of shiraz, cabernet
sauvignon and merlot, each parcel open-fermented in the same way as the other
Henschke dry red wines, the varietal components kept separate through the
maturation phase in a mix of new and used French oak.

How it tastes: A strong crimson-purple colour; it has an array of black fruits,
plum, spice and a dash of dark chocolate, the oak and tannin contributions both
important, pivotal to the texture, structure and longevity of the wine. Cellar to 30
years from vintage.

Best vintages: 2010, 2009, 2006, 2005, 2002

Henschke

By the very fact of their inclusion in this book, all the wineries, and the wines they make, are of very high standard, the best Australia has to offer. But some stand out even in this exalted group, and one of those is the family-owned Henschke, its fame in turn generated by its Hill of Grace Shiraz.

The history of the family dates back to Johann Christian Henschke, who arrived in South Australia from Silesia in 1842. His son Paul Gotthard planted vines on the small farm his father had established at Keyneton. Following his death in 1914, his son, Paul Alfred, extended the vineyard and the cellars, but the worldwide depression of the 1930s and World War II led to a reduction in winemaking. It was not until 1949 that 25-year-old Cyril Henschke persuaded his father to renovate and extend the cellars, and winemaking became the major activity.

Cyril's second move was to bottle and label Mount Edelstone Shiraz, the first vintage in 1952. Until that time all wine had been sold in bulk, and Hill of Grace continued to be sold this way until 1958. The present generation of winemaker Stephen and viticulturist Prue is the fifth, and they did not assume control until 1979, following the sudden death of father Cyril.

There is no question that Cyril's contributions were of great importance, but the fame of Henschke, and its success across a wide range of varietal wines grown in the Eden Valley, and at the Abbott's Prayer vineyard they established at Lenswood in the Adelaide Hills, are due to this very talented duo. And, happily, waiting in the wings are their three children, Johann, Justine and Andreas. Johann has already completed university studies in Australia and Germany, and travelled extensively.

Quietly spoken Stephen's credentials as a winemaker are beyond doubt, and he is happy to leave viticulture to Prue, who has taken the vineyards to full biodynamic status. But her patient selection of vine-by-vine cuttings for propagation, then further propagation from cuttings from the first selections, is remarkable. She has also been a long-term advocate for and user of heavy straw mulch under the vines to build bacterial activity and conserve moisture. Both Prue and Stephen have won numerous and important accolades.

It is ironic that Hill of Grace should capture almost all the limelight. The Mount Edelstone vineyard is itself now 100 years old, and – unlike the Hill of Grace – is planted purely to shiraz. While the price of Mount Edelstone is much less than that of Hill of Grace, the quality is not.

There are also other red wines that most winemakers would be proud to have as their best. Leading these is the Cyril Henschke blend of cabernet sauvignon (predominantly), cabernet franc and merlot, matured in 40% new French oak. The Tappa Pass Eden Valley Shiraz is as powerful and long-lived as it is stylish; Johann's Garden is a grenache, viognier, shiraz blend; Henry's Seven, a shiraz, grenache, viognier, mourvedre blend; and Stone Jar Tempranillo Graciano.

Moreover, Henschke makes two superlative rieslings, one from the Adelaide Hills, one from the Eden Valley, and excellent pinot gris, semillon, gewurztraminer and sauvignon blanc.

A founding member of Australia's First Families of Wine.

Hentley Farm Wines

Est 1999
Cnr Jenke Road/Gerald Roberts Road, Seppeltsfield, SA 5355
Open 7 days 10–5
Getting there 1 hour's drive from Adelaide CBD
Contact (08) 8562 8427; info@hentleyfarm.com.au; www.hentleyfarm.com.au
Region Barossa Valley
Lat 34°29'S
Elev 274m
E° Days 1571
Harvest 27 February–17 April

Estate vineyards 40.1ha
Varieties planted Shiraz (27.8), grenache (6.5), cabernet sauvignon (4.4), zinfandel (0.8), viognier (0.6)
Dozens produced 10 000 May increase to 15 000.
Exports To China through Chongqing Yunze Import & Export Co. (ph) 8623 6187 5590; info@yunzewine.com and to Hong Kong through 12 Bottles Company Limited (ph) 852 2546 7628; hello@cuvees.com. Also to the US, Canada, New Zealand, Singapore, Malaysia, the Philippines, Russia and Vietnam.
Winemaker Andrew Quin

Key wines

Clos Otto Shiraz and The Beast Shiraz

How they are made: The wines are made in near-identical fashion, thus emphasising the character of the vineyard blocks from which they come. Moreover, while they are single blocks, they are generally split across 4–5 fermenters, allowing the use of a combination of cultured and wild yeast fermentations. The grapes are crushed and open-fermented until a temperature spike of 30°C is achieved. The juice is then run out of the fermenters, chilled, and returned to the fermenter with a resultant 18°C temperature, maintained by cooling plates throughout the remainder of the period on skins. The wine is then pressed and taken to high-quality French oak (65–80% new, vintage dependent). The wines spend a total of 22 months in oak. The wine is bottled without fining or filtration, and the whole process could easily be that of a pinot noir. 450 (Clos Otto) to 650 (The Beast) dozen made.

How they taste: The wines are exceptional in many ways, none more than in the decision not to add any acid, and accept the high pII and low acid balance that the vineyard naturally produces. This adds to the softness of the always mouthfilling fruit; the alcohol is never an issue, nor is the essentially full-bodied structure. The aromas and flavours range through blackberry, plum, licorice, spice, dark chocolate and a hint of earth from the savoury tannins. Cellar to 30 years from vintage, notwithstanding the limitations of the cork closures.

Best vintages: 2010, 2009, 2008, 2006, 2005

Hentley Farm Wines

No other winery in this book has achieved Top 100 Winery status in such a short period of time. Owners Keith and Alison Hentschke did not purchase the land until 1997, and did not plant any vines until 1999, nor was any wine made before 2002. It is somehow fitting that the concept of terroir did not come under the microscope prior to the 1980s in the way it is today.

Somehow fitting, because Keith Hentschke saw what others – including the most powerful wine companies in the land – did not. When Keith says, 'While our find here at Seppeltsfield [the area, not the winery] was luck, it wasn't an accident', he was neither over- nor underselling his case. For what he and Alison purchased was an old 40ha mixed farming property on the banks of Greenock Creek in Seppeltsfield, with a few ancient remnant vines not worth saving.

When you find that he had studied agricultural science and wine marketing at Roseworthy Agricultural College, and graduated with the prestigious Gramp Hardy Smith Memorial Prize (named after those who were killed in the 1938 Kyeema air crash) for the college's most outstanding student, the first piece of the jigsaw falls into place.

But even then he went off at a tangent, working for Elders, a farm supplier, valuer, sales agent and financier, then working in senior production and operations roles at Orlando, thereafter managing one of Australia's largest vineyard management companies. It was during this period that he and Alison undertook exhaustive research with Barossa winemakers on the one hand, and soil scientists on the other, seeking to identify the best terroir for shiraz.

It all pointed to the red clay loams overlaying shattered limestone of the western Barossa. An old 1950s soil map sharpened the focus, and after several years the purchase took place. Even then it took him time to assemble the team he has today. First was Greg Mader, a chef turned viticulturist with Penfolds (and over the next 12 years running a team that managed 700ha of Barossa Valley vines). Then Greg saw the young Hentley Farm vineyard, and realised that this was a very special place.

Winemaker Andrew Quin returned to Australia in 2006, after working in the northern hemisphere for some years, first in California, and thereafter with Jacques Lurton in France. Once back home, he joined the Yalumba red wine team, but when he tasted the 2006 Hentley Farm Premium Shiraz, he, too, recognised the chance of a lifetime.

It flies in the face of the near-universally held belief that only very old vines can produce truly great red wines to suggest that the 15-year-old vines of Hentley Farm are already providing grapes of the highest quality. Keith Hentschke responds by pointing out that he had a completely clean slate to choose precisely the right clones of shiraz, the right block configurations, including the orientation of the rows, the right canopy management, and the right ongoing viticultural practices.

What we are left with are wines with mesmerising richness and softness, in which the high alcohol (usually 15%) is not hot, in which the deliberate decision not to acidify the must, and thus accept the higher than usual pH levels (a decision Wolf Blass had taken 50 years earlier), and the use of French, not American, oak, are all pieces of a highly unusual jigsaw puzzle.

The one certainty is that great though the wines of Hentley Farm may be today, they will be greater still in the future.

Houghton

Est 1836
Dale Road, Middle Swan, WA 6065
Open 7 days 10–5
Getting there 30 minutes' drive from Perth CBD
Contact (08) 9274 9540; cellardoor@houghton-wines.com.au; www.houghton-wines.com.au
Region Swan Valley
Lat 31°53'S
Elev 10–40m
E° Days 1806
Harvest 3 February–14 March

Estate vineyards NFP
Varieties planted As with other wineries that are part of a much larger wine business under single ownership, vineyard resources are shared across all brands in the group.
Dozens produced NFP
Exports To China through Shanghai CWC Wine Company (ph) 8621 3252 8715; Enquiries@accolade-wines.cn and to Hong Kong through Accolade Wines Hong Kong: HKEnquiries@accolade-wines.com; www.accolade-wines.com. Also to all major markets.
Winemaker Ross Pamment

Key wines

Jack Mann Cabernet Sauvignon

How it is made: An estate-grown blend of 96% cabernet sauvignon (plus 3% malbec and 1% shiraz) from the Justin Vineyard in the Frankland River region. The grapes are crushed and taken to small, open-top stainless steel fermenters, utilising select cultured yeast. The wine spends 16 months in French oak barriques (50% new, 50% 1 year old). It is not filtered, but is egg white–fined.

How it tastes: Remarkable for its very stable, deep colour; it has faultless blackcurrant cabernet fruit, fine-grained tannins, and high-quality oak which drives the palate through to a long and satisfying conclusion. Cellar to 30 years from vintage.

Best vintages: 2012, 2011, 2008, 2007, 2004

White Classic

How it is made: The grapes are sourced from regions all across Western Australia, and the wine is typically a blend of chenin blanc, semillon, chardonnay, verdelho, muscadelle, riesling and sauvignon blanc. It is cold-fermented in stainless steel with cultured yeast, and is filtered prior to bottling.

How it tastes: Fresh and vibrant in its youth, tropical fruit characters balanced by citrus, herb and crisp acidity. While made to be enjoyed immediately it is released, has shown the ability to become richer and more complex with age. Cellar to 4 years from vintage.

Best vintages: 2013, 2009, 2006, 2005, 2002

Houghton

Houghton is Western Australia's foremost winery, its origins going back to the 1830s. On 10 January 1835 a land grant of 3240ha was made to Rivett Henry Bland; a few years later he sold the major part of the grant to a syndicate of three British officers serving in India: Houghton, Lowis and Yule. As Colonel Houghton was the senior of the three, the property was named after him, although he never came to Australia, leaving the business under the management of Yule, who subdivided it further.

In 1859 Dr John Ferguson, the colonial surgeon, purchased the home block with its small cottage and vineyard. He made 135 litres of wine in that year, some of which was offered for sale. The vineyard and cellars flourished under the control of CW Ferguson, Dr Ferguson's second son, and the property remained in the possession of the family for almost 100 years, finally being sold to the Emu Wine Company in 1950 when it became apparent that no member of the family wished to continue the business. However, prior to this the Mann family had joined forces with the Fergusons as winemakers: in 1920 George Mann left Château Tanunda and became winemaker at Houghton. He was joined in 1922 by his son Jack Mann, who became chief winemaker in 1930.

Jack Mann was a giant in physical stature, winemaking skill and utterly unforgettable sayings. Two stand out: the trilogy of CCC, Cricket, Christ and Chablis, and his oft-expressed view that any table wine worthy of consumption should be able to be blended with 50% water. He served as winemaker for Houghton for 51 consecutive vintages, a record beaten only by Dan Tyrrell (with 70) and Roly Birks (with 65).

In 1976 Thomas Hardy & Sons acquired the Emu Wine Company, which had in the interim purchased Valencia Vineyards and its substantial Gingin Vineyard, 80km north of Perth. Under Jack Mann's watch Houghton's White Burgundy, with the diagonal blue stripe across its label, became the largest-selling white wine in Australia for a period.

Houghton's viticultural holdings have been extended as far south as the Frankland River (in the Great Southern), and it purchases grapes from all the major regions south of the Swan Valley, most notably Pemberton and Margaret River, to supplement its Frankland River holdings. It has been blessed with a series of skilled winemakers since the departure of Jack Mann, its red wine flagships under the Jack Mann and John Gladstones labels of utterly impeccable quality.

Between 1985 and 1992 Houghton had three senior winemakers of remarkable talent and vision: Peter Dawson, Paul Lapsley (both to become chief winemakers of Hardys) and Larry Cherubino (now senior winemaker for Robert Oatley Vineyards as well as his own eponymous brand). The time each had at Houghton was (in the context of Jack Mann) brief, but their contribution to the breadth and quality of the Houghton wines has been the foundation for the wines of today.

Jasper Hill

Est 1979
Drummonds Lane, Heathcote, Vic 3523
Open By appt
Getting there 1.5 hours' drive from Melbourne CBD
Contact (03) 5433 2528; info@jasperhill.com.au; www.jasperhill.com
Region Heathcote
Lat 36°54′S
Elev 160–320m
E° Days 1515
Harvest 8 March–1 May

Estate vineyards 23.7ha
Varieties planted Emily's Paddock shiraz (2.85), cabernet franc (0.15); **Georgia's Paddock** shiraz (13), riesling (2.5), nebbiolo (1.3), viognier (1.1), semillon (0.6); **Cornella Vineyard** grenache (2.2)
Dozens produced 2000 No increase planned.
Exports To China through Inland Trading Co. (Aust.) Pty Ltd (ph) 612 6238 3882; greg@inlandtrading.com.au and to Hong Kong through Watson's Wine (ph) 852 2606 8828; info@watsonswine.com. Also to the UK, the US and other major markets.
Winemaker Ron Laughton, Emily McNally

Key wines

Emily's Paddock Shiraz Cabernet Franc and Georgia's Paddock Shiraz
How they are made: The grapes are hand-picked and carefully sorted, and all fermentation is initiated by indigenous (wild or native) yeasts present on the skins; no cultured yeasts are added. The wines spend 15 months in French and American oak barriques (20% new) and undergo a natural secondary mlf the following spring. There is no racking, fining or filtration until a single coarse filtration immediately prior to bottling.

How they taste: The wines are usually deeply coloured, rich and supple, with ripe tannins, and are medium- to full-bodied. Because they are not irrigated, they reflect the growing conditions each year, and both alcohol and weight can vary significantly. Cellar to 20 years from vintage.

Best vintages: 2010, 2009, 2006, 2004, 2002

Jasper Hill

In the mid-1970s food scientist Ron Laughton was operations manager for a large co-operative milk company, responsible for overseeing 13 dairy farms across Victoria. His endless driving led to many trips through Heathcote, and he became familiar with a spectacular roadside cutting of deep red soil. Investigations revealed the soil derived from 500-million-year-old Cambrian-age basaltic rock; that it was up to 4m deep, and freely drained; and that it was ideal for vines.

He and artist wife Elva decided there had to be a better life for them and their young daughters, so in 1979 they sold their Melbourne house and purchased a vineyard that had been planted with 2ha of shiraz and a small amount of cabernet franc.

The family lived in a caravan as they personally began to excavate (using dynamite) what was to become their largely underground winery cellar, burrowing into the hard, basalt rock. It was an epic undertaking, even by the standards of outback Australia, shattered rock lifted by the vineyard tractor engine, then taken from the immediate site by Elva, Ron working in the even larger and deeper hole. When that phase of work was completed, and a roof built, the family set up a temporary home (with more space than the caravan) while they built their stone house. When that was completed they returned to work on the winery buildings, partially hidden in the rock, adding fermentation facilities and ultimately a cellar door.

Early in 1982 they purchased another, larger vineyard, 1km from the first, then principally planted to shiraz and riesling, and on the same red Cambrian soil. They named the two vineyards Emily's Paddock and Georgia's Paddock in honour of their two daughters. Finally, they acquired a small property 20km north of Emily's Paddock, but with the same soil, and in 1998 planted 2.2ha of grenache.

In the early years they had to sell up to half the grapes, after the first small harvest of 1982, for precious cash flow, even though the first wine made, 1982 Georgia's Paddock Shiraz, won a silver medal at the Royal Melbourne Wine Show in 1984, and the quality of their wines was immediately recognised by critics and retailers alike.

All the vineyards have been managed using organic/biodynamic principles; the Laughtons produce their own compost, and have not used synthetic chemicals on either the vines or the soils since they purchased the three properties. Soil organic matter is high, with biodiversity in microflora, and a large earthworm population. The vines are dry-grown, reducing the yields in the all-too-frequent drought years.

The aim is to make great wine with the preservation of nature's flavours, complexities and balance by using minimal intervention in the vineyards and in the cellar. They are guided by the following observation: 'True mastery can be gained by letting things go their own way. It can't be gained by interfering,' *Tao Te Ching* (chapter 48, Mitchell translation, HarperCollins 1988).

Kilikanoon

Est 1997
Penna Lane, Penwortham, SA 5453
Open Thurs–Mon 11–5
Getting there 1.75 hours' drive from Adelaide CBD
Contact (08) 8843 4206; cellardoor@kilikanoon.com.au; www.kilikanoon.com.au
Region Clare Valley
Lat 33°50'S
Elev 398m
E° Days 1493
Harvest 14 February–24 March
Estate vineyards 150.8ha
Varieties planted Clare Valley Farehams (5.7) riesling, shiraz, cabernet sauvignon; Kilikanoon (1) cabernet sauvignon; Morrisons (21.7) riesling, shiraz; Mort's Block (5.7) riesling, shiraz, cabernet sauvignon; Trillian's Hill (24.3) riesling, pinot gris, viognier, shiraz, mourvedre; Waltons (8.1) riesling, grenache, shiraz, cabernet sauvignon; **Barossa Valley** Greens (14.5) grenache, shiraz; Crowhurst (16.4) shiraz; **Southern Flinders Ranges** Baroota (32.3) shiraz, cabernet sauvignon; Flinders (21.1) shiraz
Dozens produced 50 000 No increase planned.
Exports To China through Hua Wei (ph) 8621 3890 6651; duxia@huawei.com and to Hong Kong through Altaya Wines (ph) 852 2523 1945; info@altayawines.com. Also to most major markets.
Winemaker Kevin Mitchell

Key wines

Oracle Shiraz

How it is made: The grapes come from a small vineyard planted by a then young Mort Mitchell, Kevin Mitchell's father. It is fermented using a cultured yeast in open-top fermenters, and basket-pressed after 7–10 days; matured in French oak (50% new, 50% 1 year old) for 18–22 months. Neither fined nor filtered. 1500 dozen made.

How it tastes: Deep crimson-purple in its youth, and in a full-bodied style, the alcohol controlled, the texture opulent, balanced by fine, savoury tannins. Cellar to 30+ years from vintage.

Best vintages: 2010, 2009, 2005, 2002, 2001

Reserve Cabernet Sauvignon

How it is made: Made in virtually identical fashion to the Oracle Shiraz, except for a slightly shorter maturation (18 months in French oak). 200 dozen made.

How it tastes: Impenetrable colour, with pure cassis fruit flavours seasoned by fine French oak; the palate is juicy on entry, with densely packed tannins behind the succulent fruit; will age with grace. Cellar to 30 years from vintage.

Best vintages: 2010, 2009, 2005

Kilikanoon

Success on a grand scale for Kilikanoon has come with astonishing speed, even in a country with a dynamic and fast-changing wine industry. Moreover, this success has involved key players with very different backgrounds.

The story begins with Mort Mitchell, who has tended a group of contiguous vineyards on what has been given the name Golden Hillside since their establishment 40 years ago. The epicentre is Mort's Block, planted by him to 6ha of riesling, and now includes Meyman's, Mort's Block, Kilikanoon, Walton's Block and Morrisons vineyards on the 'Golden Slope', plus the Trillians Hill Vineyard high above Penwortham.

Enter Kevin Mitchell, Mort's son, who graduated from Adelaide University in 1990 with a Bachelor of Applied Science in viticulture, and also obtained a Graduate Diploma in Wine Technology in 1991. Over the next five years he worked with leading Australian wineries (including Orlando, BRL Hardy and d'Arenberg) and Kendall Jackson in California and Willamette Valley Vineyards in Oregon. In late 1997 he purchased the Kilikanoon property, and made the first wines that year at Torbreck Winery, an arrangement that continued until the 2005 vintage and the erection of the estate winery.

The next member to join the Kilikanoon band was Nathan Waks (in 2001), then principal cellist with the Sydney Symphony Orchestra, and who now handles export sales and is a very effective brand ambassador. He also played a vital role in putting together the syndicate that purchased Seppeltsfield from Foster's Wine Estates in 2007, and remains a shareholder and a director of both Seppeltsfield and Kilikanoon. His partner in wine was John Harding, concert master of the Hong Kong and Western Australian Symphony Orchestras. Then enter Bruce Baudinet, Chairman of and shareholder in Kilikanoon, with a background of science and property management.

While at no stage did Seppeltsfield own any shares in Kilikanoon, the latter played a vital role in bringing in yet another player when in 2009 Warren Randall became a 50% shareholder in and director of Seppeltsfield. At the same time the arrival of Warrick Duthy on the board of both companies brought the two companies even closer together. However, while the relationship was, and remains, a friendly one, Duthy and Waks agreed in February 2013 that the time had come for Kilikanoon to sell its shares in Seppeltsfield to Warren Randall, increasing the latter's shareholding to over 90%, and liberating substantial working capital for Kilikanoon.

While all this was going on, Kevin Mitchell was making outstanding wines, eliciting very high points from Robert Parker Jr, and gaining headlines with an astonishing (and unique) performance at the 2002 Clare Valley Wine Show, where Kilikanoon won six of the seven trophies awarded. Nor was this a flash in the pan; Kevin Mitchell is a fastidious winemaker, with great attention to detail, and the quality of the wines has never been higher. Thus, I made it Winery of the Year in my *2013 Australian Wine Companion*, placing it at the head (for that year) of over 2700 wineries. Most of its wines are made from the three best varieties in the Clare Valley: riesling, shiraz and cabernet sauvignon.

The decision taken in 2012 to declassify all of the 2011 Reserve, Single Vineyard wines due to the very wet vintage was very costly, but is impressive proof of Kilikanoon's determination to maintain its already high quality standards.

Lake's Folly

Est 1963
2416 Broke Road, Pokolbin, NSW 2320
Open 7 days 10–4 while wine available
Getting there 2 hours' drive from
Sydney CBD
Contact (02) 4998 7507;
wine@lakesfolly.com.au;
www.lakesfolly.com.au
Region Hunter Valley
Lat 32°54′S
Elev 76m
E° Days 1823
Harvest 31 January–11 March

Estate vineyards 12.14ha
Varieties planted Cabernet sauvignon
(5.61), chardonnay (3.46), shiraz (1.47),
petit verdot (1), merlot (0.6)
Dozens produced 4500 No increase
planned.
Exports Small exports to China and
Hong Kong; no fixed importer. Also to
Singapore.
Winemaker Rodney Kempe

Key wines

Chardonnay
How it is made: Hand-picked, partial barrel fermentation, commenced in tank
before transfer to French oak (with equal amounts of new, 2- and 3-year-old
oak) for 8 months' maturation with no mlf (to retain acidity). Neither fined nor
cold-stabilised. The annual production is 1000–1200 dozen, plus 250 dozen Hill
Chardonnay.

How it tastes: The simple approach to winemaking deliberately focuses attention
on the interaction of fruit and terroir, the flavours of stone fruit/white peach, with
some fig in warmer vintages, more grapefruit in the cooler years. The oak is never
dominant. Cellar to 12+ years from vintage.

Best vintages: 2011, 2009, 2008, 2004, 2001

Cabernets
How it is made: Petit verdot and merlot were planted following Stephen Lake's
arrival in 1990, and included in the blend from 1994 onwards. The components are
open-fermented, with gentle cap management. After pressing, the wine goes to
old oak casks before transfer to French oak barriques the following spring; as with
chardonnay, one-third is new, one-third is 1 year old, one-third is 2 years old, and
the wine spends the next 12 months in those barriques. 3000–3500 dozen made.

How it tastes: The vines are growing older, and Rodney Kempe is now master
of the winemaking, so in great Hunter Valley vintages such as 2011, the wine is
magnificent. Bright, clear crimson hue; there is a profusion of blackcurrant/cassis,
black olive, spice and red cherry fruit, French oak seen but not heard, tannins
so ultra-fine they are heard but not seen. Cellar to 30 years from vintage in the
best vintages.

Best vintages: 2011, 2009, 2007, 2005, 2003

Lake's Folly

There are many reasons why Lake's Folly should be regarded as one of Australia's most important small wineries. First is the audacity that larger-than-life (physically and mentally) Sydney hand surgeon Max Lake exhibited when he told the handful of Hunter Valley winemakers in business in 1963 that he intended to plant a vineyard and make wine with no practical or academic training. If this wasn't enough, he planted cabernet sauvignon, not shiraz, and when in 1969 he planted a white grape, it was chardonnay, not semillon.

But he was no stranger to the Hunter Valley, and his choice of cabernet sauvignon rested upon a 1930 vintage blend of 50% cabernet sauvignon and 50% petit verdot bottled by wine merchant Matthew Lang. Even more convincing was his selection of a hill of terra rossa soil, directly across the road from McWilliam's Rosehill Vineyard: this is now the Lake's Folly vineyard, ideal for red grapes, and running down into sandy flats ideal for white grapes. It is, however, an abiding mystery why the Tyrrell family should have been willing to sell such a prime piece of viticultural real estate.

The late Max Lake had an Olympian ego, and worked in many ways on the principle that if you don't ask, you don't get. This led to some astonishing marketing success with the Ritz Hotel London, Maison Troisgros, a three-star restaurant, and a deluge of praise from the crème de la crème of English wine critics, including Hugh Johnson, Michael Broadbent and (later) Jancis Robinson, the Australian critics duly lining up in support (myself included). Whether, or to what extent, Lake's approach to women was rewarded with the same degree of success is a matter of conjecture, but certainly his stylish wife Joy (who had the better palate of the two) had the patience of Job.

Some key dates along the way were son Stephen taking responsibility for wine-making in 1982; ownership passing to Peter Fogarty of the Fogarty Wine Group in 2000, and Rodney Kempe being appointed winemaker; Max Lake dying in 2009; and Fogarty adding 16ha of prime terra rossa for further plantings of cabernet sauvignon. It is a mark of his respect for the achievements of Max Lake, and thereafter Rodney Kempe as winemaker, that Peter Fogarty has been a strictly hands-off owner.

Shortly before writing these words, I was part of a small group which tasted 37 vintages of the cabernets and 29 vintages of chardonnay. Given the cork closures used for the wines, the assumption was that the chardonnays would be very uneven in quality, the reds much more resilient. In fact, it was the reverse.

There was the inevitable failure in the chardonnays, due to oxidation, but as a group they were outstanding. It was the reds (now a blend of 60% cabernet sauvignon, 20% shiraz, 10% petit verdot and 10% merlot, the percentages varying to a small degree vintage to vintage) that left me with a nagging doubt. Are they better than 100% shiraz from the same hill and of the same vintage would be? Have they fulfilled the potential they usually show when young?

The answer must be yes, given that the wines sell out for between three and five months each year, mail-list customers buying 70% of the two wines in the first few weeks each year, that 5–7% goes to the best restaurants in Australia, and that the remainder goes to cellar-door customers and a small amount to overseas customers who have heard about the legendary quality of the wines.

Leeuwin Estate

Est 1974
Stevens Road, Margaret River,
WA 6285
Open 7 days 10–5
Getting there 3 hours' drive from
Perth CBD
Contact (08) 9759 0000;
info@leeuwinestate.com.au;
www.leeuwinestate.com.au
Region Margaret River
Lat 33°57′S
Elev 40–90m
E° Days 1552
Harvest 26 February–8 April

Estate vineyards 140ha
Varieties planted Chardonnay (53),
riesling (27), cabernet sauvignon (25),
sauvignon blanc (16), shiraz (9), pinot
noir (5), semillon (3), malbec (2)
Leased or contracted vineyards 50ha
Varieties planted NFP
Dozens produced 50 000 No increase
planned.
Exports To China and Hong Kong
through ASC Fine Wines (ph) 8621 3423
9599; www.asc-wines.com. Also to the
UK, the US, Canada and other major
markets.
Winemaker Paul Atwood, Tim Lovett,
Phil Hutchinson

Key wines

Art Series Chardonnay

How it is made: Both cultured and wild yeasts are used, with fermentation in 100%
new French oak; 11 months' maturation in barrel is followed by 7 months in tank
on yeast lees; fined, filtered and stabilised before bottling.

How it tastes: Has an effortlessly powerful, intense and long palate, with grapefruit
and cashew just evident in the purity of the wine when young, complexity growing
with age. Cellar to 20 years from vintage.

Best vintages: 2012, 2011, 2010, 2005, 2002

Art Series Cabernet Sauvignon

How it is made: 7-day pre-fermentation cold soak before warming for wild or
cultured yeast, fermentation controlled to 24–28°C; mlf and maturation for 18–20
months in 50% new, 50% 1-year-old French 'Château' barrels; lightly fined and
sterile-filtered prior to bottling.

How it tastes: Refined restraint, almost to the point of austerity, marks the wine
when young; its balance and elegance ensure a brilliant maturity 15–30 years
from vintage.

Best vintages: 2012, 2011, 2010, 2008, 2005

Leeuwin Estate

For long regarded as one of the very greatest producers of chardonnay in the Margaret River, and indeed the whole of Australia; this is one of the proudest family-owned estates in the country.

Founders Denis and Tricia Horgan got off to a flying start by seeking advice by the doyen of Californian winemakers, the late Robert Mondavi, who in 1972 identified what was then a cattle farm as an ideal property. The Horgans duly purchased the land, and built their large house in a secluded forest area which has had many guests over the following decades.

A vine nursery was planted in 1974, and the initial vineyards were deep-ploughed, deep-ripped, emptied of stone, planned, pegged, measured, marked and eventually planted by hand over a 5-year period from 1975. A state-of-the-art winery was opened in 1978 with a trial vintage; in 1979 the first commercial vintage followed, and the 1980 Art Series Chardonnay won acclaim in all parts of the world.

In a brilliant and then unique marketing exercise, the London Philharmonic Orchestra was persuaded to extend a season in several capital cities and stage 'A Concert in the Trees' in 1985. It generated massive publicity in Australia and overseas, and became a 'must do' event, sold out a year in advance. I have vivid memories of the many concerts I have been lucky enough to attend, especially that with Bryn Terfel, Yvonne Kenny and the West Australian Symphony Orchestra in 1999.

In February 2001 a vertical tasting of the Art Series Chardonnays back to 1982 had a triumphant conclusion with the '85, '83 and '82 vintages all superb, and given five stars in *James Halliday Classic Wines of Australia* (published 1997); a 1994 tasting had given five stars to the '81, but this was not available in 2001.

However, the wines for the 2001 tasting had been chosen very carefully, with the more deeply coloured wines discarded. This very well known problem of random oxidation of white wines sealed with corks (a major problem in Burgundy in recent years) led to two decisions. First, to move to screwcaps for all Leeuwin Estate wines (white and red) in 2004. Second, to decant all the Museum chardonnay stock, and re-bottle the small percentage still in good condition with screwcaps.

Leeuwin Estate is not just a chardonnay producer. Its cabernet sauvignon is of very high quality, its shiraz likewise. The second label Prelude chardonnay is better than many higher-priced wines from other producers, and the riesling sells out every year, a cash-flow winner for the business. Sibling Margaret River Sauvignon Blanc Semillon is yet another string to the Leeuwin bow.

With son Justin now general manager of the business, Denis and Tricia Horgan are well and truly entitled to sit back and look with pride on their achievements.

McWilliam's

Est 1916
Jack McWilliam Road, Hanwood,
NSW 2680
Open Mon–Fri 10–4, Sat 10–5
Getting there 5 hours' drive from
Melbourne CBD
Contact (02) 6963 3400;
communications@
mcwilliamswines.com.au;
www.mcwilliamswinesgroup.com
Region Riverina
Lat 34°17'S
Elev 128m
E° Days 1719
Harvest 4 February–15 March

Estate vineyards 444ha
Varieties planted Chardonnay (162),
shiraz (115), cabernet sauvignon (34),
tyrian (19), red frontignac (17), merlot
(16), riesling (11), Canada muscat
(11), petit verdot (10), semillon (10),
pinot noir (10), white frontignac (10),
gewurztraminer (7), sauvignon blanc
(5), touriga (5), muscadelle (2)
Dozens produced NFP
Exports Exports to China and
Hong Kong through E&J Gallo
(ph) 852 2213 9110; Jonathan.Chang@
ejgallo.com. Also to all major markets.
Winemaker Corey Ryan, Jim Brayne,
Scott McWilliam

Key wines

1877 Cabernet Sauvignon Shiraz

How it is made: The precise regional and varietal composition varies from vintage to vintage, the components selected solely on the basis of extreme quality. It is a blend of cabernet sauvignon and shiraz, typically 55% cabernet sauvignon, 45% shiraz, drawn from Hilltops shiraz and Coonawarra cabernet sauvignon, occasionally with areas such as Heathcote also contributing the shiraz. The components are kept separate until the final blend is made, after extensive fermentation in predominantly French oak.

How it tastes: Always deeply coloured, with a profoundly complex bouquet full of black fruits, fine spices, well-handled oak and a suggestion of violets. The palate is densely packed and full-bodied, yet there is a lightness and grace to the palate. A prolific winner of gold medals and trophies in Australian wine shows. Cellar to 25 years from vintage.

Best vintages: 2009, 2008, 2005, 2004, 1998

Morning Light Botrytis Semillon

How it is made: The grapes are left on the vine for 2–3 months longer than the normal harvest, to allow the development of botrytis cinerea mould. They are hand-picked and pressed until the juice has settled, then inoculated with a special yeast strain capable of tolerating high sugar levels. In the early stages of fermentation, the juice is taken to new and used French oak until the desired level of residual sugar and alcohol is reached. The fermentation is then arrested, the wine remaining in barrel until the oak is fully integrated.

How it tastes: A lusciously sweet and exceptionally complex array of dried apricot, crème brûlée, mango and peach fruit is given additional complexity from the oak, with almond and biscuit characters coming through. As striking as any French sauternes. Cellar to 6 years from vintage.

Best vintages: 2009, 2008, 2006, 2004, 2001

McWilliam's

McWilliam's was founded by Samuel McWilliam when he planted vines at Corowa, on the Murray River. The family then extended its operations to Junee (south-west of Sydney) and established a substantial winery there around the turn of the 20th century. It is little known that the Junee vineyard (though not the winery) continued in production until the 1950s. The grapes were taken to McWilliam's Mount Pleasant in the Hunter Valley and the wine was made there by Maurice O'Shea, the last vintage (1952) producing a wine which 20 years later was still full of character.

It was Samuel's son, John James McWilliam, who moved decisively to the Riverina: the first water was supplied for irrigation on 13 July 1912, and within a month or so he had taken up a lease at Hanwood and planted 35 000 cuttings. By 1917 he had erected a winery at Hanwood, followed by another at Yenda in 1920. As the Murrumbidgee Irrigation Area (as it was then known) prospered, so did the McWilliams: it was the start of a long association which in the 1960s was to make the family company one of the wealthiest family companies in Australia. That was far in the future when McWilliam's acquired a fully operational winery at Beelbangera in 1944; the fourth winery, just across the Murrumbidgee River at Robinvale, was designed by Glen McWilliam in 1961. In a sign of the times, the only winery to survive is Hanwood.

The McWilliam clan is a large one, and it was not until the 1990s that any facet of the senior management of the company passed out of family hands. Four members in particular made lasting contributions to the company: John James McWilliam and wife Elizabeth, whose eight children created the family dynasty; long-term CEO Don McWilliam (since retired); and Glen McWilliam, a brilliant engineer who designed both wineries and winemaking equipment that broke new ground. Five generations, and 17 family members, have all had full-time roles in the company, all with the McWilliam surname. The family has also had the long-term services of gifted winemakers, none more gifted than Maurice O'Shea at McWilliam's Mount Pleasant (*see separate entry at page 128*).

The first CEO from outside the family to succeed was Kevin McLintock, a sales and marketing genius who structured a deal with E&J Gallo which helped the export expansion of the McWilliam's wines in Hong Kong and PRC. The company has also moved to diversify its vineyard holdings, in 1989 buying the Barwang Vineyard in the Hilltops region of New South Wales (and significantly expanding its size), in 1994 purchasing Lillydale Estate in the Yarra Valley; very importantly, between 1990 and 1994, the company progressively acquired Brand's Laira in Coonawarra, and vastly extended its vineyards; and, finally, in 2007 it acquired the Evans & Tate brand and vineyards (Margaret River) following the meltdown of that company.

The continuing feature of the exceptionally diverse regional and varietal range of the McWilliam's group wines is that, without exception, they over-deliver at their price points, which in 2013 ranged from A$7 to A$75. In that year McWilliam's appointed one of Australia's very best up-and-coming winemakers, Jim Chatto, to head up its winemaking team. It is certain he will make a major impact on its best wines.

A founding member of Australia's First Families of Wine.

McWilliam's Mount Pleasant

Est 1921
Marrowbone Road, Pokolbin, NSW 2320
Open 7 days 10–5
Getting there 2 hours' drive from Sydney CBD
Contact (02) 4998 7505; communications@mcwilliamswines.com.au; www.mcwilliamswinegroup.com
Region Hunter Valley
Lat 32°54'S
Elev 76m
E° Days 1823
Harvest 31 January–11 March

Estate vineyards 85.8ha
Varieties planted Shiraz (48.4), semillon (22.1), chardonnay (9.1), verdelho (2.9), pinot noir (1.8), tyrian (1.5)
Dozens produced NFP
Exports Exports to China and Hong Kong through E&J Gallo (ph) 852 2213 9110; Jonathan.Chang@cjgallo.com Also to all major markets.
Winemaker Phillip Ryan, Scott McWilliam, Corey Ryan

Key wines

Maurice O'Shea Shiraz
How it is made: The grapes come wholly or partly from the Old Hill vineyard, and are destemmed (not crushed) and cold-soaked for 2 days before cultured yeast is added, and a cool fermentation over 12–14 days follows. Matured in a combination of new and second-use French oak barriques for 22 months, with a barrel-by-barrel selection made.

How it tastes: Rich and complex, with powerful blackberry and plum fruit in its youth, progressively becoming more fragrant on the bouquet and showing some earth and leather regional nuances on the palate as it ages, ultimately taking on a silky smoothness. Cellar to 30–40 years from vintage.

Best vintages: 2013, 2011, 2009, 2007, 2005

Lovedale Single Vineyard Hunter Valley Semillon
How it is made: The hand-picked grapes are harvested in the morning, and immediately brought to the winery to be destemmed and crushed. Special drainers designed by Glen McWilliam see only free-run juice taken to be cold-fermented with a special cultured yeast over a period of 3 weeks. After fermentation, the wine is stored cold on lees for a short period of time before being blended, filtered and bottled. The grapes come from the Lovedale Vineyard, which is on sandy flats uniquely suited to semillon, and which was purchased and planted under the direction of Maurice O'Shea in 1946.

How it tastes: Not released until it is at least 5 years old, and with another 15 years to gain even greater depth and complexity, it has intense citrus peel and blossom aromas leading into a palate where lemon, lime and mineral flavours are all on full display. Under screwcap, cellar with confidence to 20 years from vintage.

Best vintages: 2013, 2011, 2009, 2007, 2005

McWilliam's Mount Pleasant

The origins of McWilliam's Mount Pleasant date to 1880, when Charles King planted what is now known as the Old Hill vineyard on some of the best volcanic red soil in the Hunter Valley. In December 1921 it was purchased by John Augustus O'Shea and his French wife Leontine for their son Maurice. It was her influence which had led to Maurice being sent to Montpellier in France to study viticulture and Oenology. He returned to Australia in 1921 and moved to live on the property almost immediately. He renamed the vineyard Mount Pleasant and began to expand it, but it was a slow process, and a universe away from Montpellier.

It is hard to imagine a more difficult time in which to build a business, and in 1932 he sold 50% to McWilliam's. The market of the day was dominated by fortified wine, which O'Shea had no interest in making, and the Great Depression around the world respected no one. The remaining share was purchased by McWilliam's in 1941. Both transactions were welcomed by O'Shea, and he was left in complete control of the winemaking.

Over the 35 years he was winemaker at Mount Pleasant, a constant stream of magnificent white and red wines was produced. It is true that these were all made in small quantities; that these wines represented the pick of the vintage; and that some of his greatest wines were not vinified by O'Shea, but were purchased from other Hunter Valley wineries shortly after vintage and taken to Mount Pleasant for maturation and bottling.

His ability to recognise a great wine immediately after the end of its primary fermentation, coupled with his skill in getting the wine into bottle at the right moment, can be properly understood only with the wisdom of hindsight. Those privileged few who at any time in the last decades of the 20th century have drunk O'Shea wines made in the 1930s and '40s will be only too glad to join in praising one of the four greatest winemakers of the 20th century. One of the greatest wines was the 1937 Mountain A Dry Red, still superb after 40 years.

In 1956 Maurice O'Shea died, and between then and 2013 there were only two long-serving winemakers, first Brian Walsh, and then Phillip Ryan. Since the death of Maurice O'Shea the great strength of McWilliam's has been its large-volume but exceedingly good Elizabeth Semillon and the much smaller volume Single Vineyard Lovedale Semillon, the latter not produced every year. These wines will develop magnificently over 30 years now that McWilliam's uses screwcaps for its wines.

It is hard to deny that for many years after O'Shea's death the Mount Pleasant red wines (all based on shiraz, with a little pinot noir) disappointed as much as they appealed. But since the late 1990s, matters have improved, led by the Maurice O'Shea Shiraz (first made in 1987) and based on the 1880 Old Hill plantings, but with solid support form the Original Vineyard OP & OH Shiraz, OP standing for the Old Paddock planted by O'Shea in 1921/22. The Rosehill Vineyard is on one of the rare patches of red volcanic soil in the area, which it shares with Lake's Folly, directly across the road, and can also produce top-flight shiraz.

The appointment of Jim Chatto as chief winemaker in August 2013 should result in a return to quality of the highest calibre.

A founding member of Australia's First Families of Wine.

Main Ridge Estate

Est 1975
80 William Road, Red Hill, Vic 3937
Open Mon–Fri 12–4, w'ends 12–5
Getting there 1 hour's drive from Melbourne CBD
Contact (03) 5989 2686;
mrestate@mre.com.au;
www.mre.com.au
Region Mornington Peninsula
Lat 38°20′S
Elev 25–250m
E° Days 1428
Harvest 5 March–30 April

Estate vineyards 2.8ha
Varieties planted Pinot noir (1.4), chardonnay (1.2), other (0.2)
Dozens produced 1000 No increase planned.
Exports Wines are not currently exported.
Winemaker Nat White

Key wines

Chardonnay
How it is made: Hand-picked, estate-grown grapes are 100% barrel-fermented in new French oak using natural/indigenous yeasts, full mlf also naturally occurring; then matured for 11 months.

How it tastes: A perfectly composed and balanced mix of white peach, cashew and creamy flavours. Cellar for 7–10 years from vintage.

Best vintages: 2011, 2009, 2008, 2006, 2003

Pinot Noir
How it is made: Uses 6 clones; estate-grown and hand-picked grapes are warm-fermented using natural yeasts and hand pigeage, matured for 18 months in French oak barriques.

How it tastes: The fragrant bouquet introduces a serenely silky and supple mix of gently spiced cherry and plum fruit.

Best vintages: 2011, 2009, 2007, 2004, 2003

Main Ridge Estate

Main Ridge Estate is a diamond in the crown of the Mornington Peninsula, a family-owned business with the sole focus on quality, not quantity. When Nat (formerly a civil engineer) and wife Rosalie White acquired their 5ha property at Red Hill in 1975 the only access from the nearest road was a bush track unsuitable for cars.

So, as well as beginning the slow job of planting the vines by hand, they had to create a dirt road giving access by vehicles. Then, and now, the vineyard is an oasis of green protected by a surrounding forest of massive gum trees that grow on the rich, red volcanic soil which gives rise to the name Red Hill.

During the five years of planting and establishing chardonnay and pinot noir vines, Nat White studied for and obtained his Bachelor of Applied Science (Wine Science) at Charles Sturt University. His civil engineering background had not only made the creation of the access road easy, but also came to the fore with the building of a self-designed winery on the estate in time for the first vintage, in 1980.

When the wines from that vintage went on sale in 1981, they were the first from the Mornington Peninsula. Their quality was immediately obvious, and from that day through to the present they are eagerly sought after, demand exceeding supply.

Visitors to the cellar door, through which much of the wine is sold (the remainder to restaurants), immediately see the attention to detail in every aspect of the estate. The vineyard is immaculately tended by hand, with precise positioning of canes and leaves, bunch-thinning (green harvest) and shoot-thinning done on a vine-by-vine basis. This is necessary to restrict the yield to 2 tonnes per acre (5 tonnes/ha or 32 hectolitres/ha). No grapes are purchased to supplement the estate's production.

The effect of the adjacent lawn and bush garden is heightened by the absence of traffic and of other vineyards. The spotlessly clean and ordered winery completes an idyllic picture. An à la carte Sunday lunch is served throughout the year, using local specialties and fresh vegetables from the estate's organic garden.

Thirty-two years on from 1981, with 94 wineries in the Mornington Peninsula, it is easy to forget how little was known about the very cool climate of Red Hill, and the challenges which Nat and Rosalie had to surmount. The term 'estate' has no legal meaning in Australia (although it does in California), but Main Ridge fulfils every possible requirement, growing all its grapes, making the wine, bottling it, and storing it onsite until sale through the cellar door.

Majella

Est 1969
Lynn Road, Coonawarra, SA 5263
Open 7 days 10–4.30
Getting there 4 hours' drive from Adelaide CBD
Contact (08) 8736 3055; admin@majellawines.com.au; www.majellawines.com.au
Region Coonawarra
Lat 37°18′S
Elev 59m
E° Days 1379
Harvest 11 March–7 May

Estate vineyards 60ha
Varieties planted Cabernet sauvignon (37), shiraz (20), riesling (1.5), merlot (1.5)
Dozens produced 25 000 No increase planned.
Exports To China through Global Fine Wines (ph) 8621 6353 9191; www.global-finewines.com and to Hong Kong through Watson's Wine (ph) 852 2606 8828; info@watsonswine.com. Also to the UK, Canada, Sweden, The Netherlands, Singapore, Malaysia, Thailand, South Korea, Japan, Taiwan and Cambodia.
Winemaker Bruce Gregory

Key wines

Cabernet Sauvignon
How it is made: Primary fermentation takes place with cultured yeasts in both rotary and static stainless steel tanks for 5–7 days, and finished in new and second-use French oak hogsheads, where it remains for 3 months until the completion of mlf. The wine is racked and returned to the same oak for a further 15 months, when final decisions are made on the amount to be bottled under the Cabernet Sauvignon label. Less successful barrels are used in The Musician. Not fined, but coarse earth–filtered. 4900–7400 dozen made.

How it tastes: Deep purple-crimson when young, it is a profound medium- to full-bodied cabernet awash with cassis/blackcurrant, mulberry and Coonawarra earth flavours, the tannins ripe, the oak playing a pure support role. Cellar to 20+ years from vintage.

Best vintages: 2010, 2008, 2005, 2004, 2001

The Malleea (Cabernet Shiraz)
How it is made: A blend of 55% cabernet sauvignon and 45% shiraz, the components are separately fermented in static stainless steel tanks, pumped over twice daily, and then taken to new French oak hogsheads to complete primary and secondary mlf. The two components are kept separate, racked and returned to the same oak for a further 12 months, when a final selection of the best hogsheads are blended, and then returned to oak for an additional 3 months. Not fined, but coarse earth–filtered. 500 dozen made.

How it tastes: The wine has an abundance of supple, sweet cassis and redcurrant fruit (sometimes more chocolatey than savoury), always perfectly weighted, with ripe tannins and totally integrated but positive French oak. Cellar to 25 years from vintage.

Best vintages: 2009, 2008, 2004, 2001, 2000

Majella

The Lynn family have been residents of the Coonawarra district for over four generations, originally as storekeepers, then moving into grazing sheep, gradually increasing the size of their land holdings. The property on which Majella now stands was originally owned by Frank Lynn, and was purchased from him by nephew George in 1960. He and wife Pat Lynn had a merino wool farm 16km away, and acquired the land for raising fat lambs; viticulture was not on the agenda until 1968.

George had been a long-term friend of Eric Brand, who had started his Laira winery, and was selling wine to Hardys. So in that year George's elder son, Brian Lynn, planted a little over 2ha of shiraz, intending to sell the grapes to Brand. It was a logical arrangement, for Brand then lacked the money to plant his own vineyards quickly enough.

So Lynn proceeded to plant 28ha, split between shiraz (60%) and cabernet sauvignon (40%). But just as the vines came into full bearing, the arrangement between Eric Brand and Hardys came to an end. The timing could not have been worse, with little demand for shiraz, and Brian recounts that for several years 30 tonnes of premium shiraz were left to rot on the vine.

Matters improved greatly in 1980 when Wynns Coonawarra Estate began purchasing Majella's grapes, a relationship that continued for two decades, fulfilling the original aim of diversifying the family's still extensive grazing activities. In 1991 that plan gained a further dimension when Majella moved into winemaking, entering into a contract-winemaking agreement with Brand's, bringing the wheel full circle.

Steady increases in the planting of the vineyards were punctuated by the erection of stage 1 of the Majella winery in 1996, stage 2 (the fermentation and barrel storage facility) completed in time for the 1999 vintage. In the meantime, McWilliam's had moved to full ownership of Brand's, so there was no acrimony when Brand's winemaker Bruce Gregory resigned to become full-time winemaker for Majella.

The wines he had made earnt Majella a formidable reputation for its shiraz and cabernet sauvignon, but he pressed Brian Lynn to agree to a super-premium flagship wine. In 1998 the first The Malleea wine (an Indigenous name for green paddock) was made, a cabernet shiraz blend which finished its fermentation and was matured in 100% new French oak. It gained even more praise than the wines made up to that time, and is still seen as one of the benchmark blends of Coonawarra.

At the other end of the spectrum, the first The Musician was made in 2004. Also a cabernet shiraz blend, it is invariably one of the best value red wines on the market. Bruce Gregory's quiet personality is the polar opposite of Brian 'Prof' Lynn's – Prof because he has colourful views on virtually everything and everyone, spoken at high speed. It's a very effective partnership.

Meerea Park

Est 1991
2198 Broke Road, Pokolbin, NSW 2320
Open 7 days 10–5
Getting there 2 hours' drive from
Sydney CBD
Contact (02) 4998 7474;
info@meereapark.com.au;
www.meereapark.com.au
Region Hunter Valley
Lat 32°54′S
Elev 76m
E° Days 1823
Harvest 31 January–11 March

Leased or contracted vineyards 10ha
Varieties planted NFP
Dozens produced 13 000 May increase
to 20 000.
Exports To China through
Jiangsu JinYongDa Trade Co.
(ph) 025 5552 2999; njmora@yahoo.cn
and to Hong Kong through Wines
Connection Limited (ph) 852 2947 7988;
al@wines-connection.com. Also to the
US and Singapore.
Winemaker Rhys Eather

Key wines

Shiraz (regional blend)

How it is made: The grapes are crushed and moved to closed-tank cultured-yeast fermentation with daily pumpovers. The wine spends 12 months in used French and American oak barrels, and is fined and sterile-filtered prior to bottling. 5000 dozen made.

How it tastes: A relatively light-bodied, fresh and direct style, the lowest priced of any Hunter Valley on regular release. The wine inevitably reflects its low price. Cellar to 3 years from vintage.

Best vintages: 2012, 2011, 2010, 2009, 2005

The Aunts Shiraz

How it is made: Here open-vat fermentation of destemmed and crushed grapes takes place with daily pumpovers and hand-plunging. The wine spends 18 months in French (80%) and American (20%) oak, 35% new. It is egg white–fined and sterile-filtered prior to bottling. 2000 dozen made.

How it tastes: Has a juicy, medium-bodied palate, driven by its red cherry and plum fruit, the tannins fine, and the oak totally integrated. Cellar to 15 years from vintage.

Best vintages: 2011, 2010, 2007, 2006, 2005

Meerea Park

One of the most famous mid-19th century vignerons in the Hunter Valley was Alexander Munro. His Bebeah Vineyard was at one stage the largest in New South Wales, his success as a winemaker evidenced by over 2000 awards from wine shows around the world.

By the end of World War I the vineyard had gone, and the winery disappeared stone by stone over the next 40 years. But two of his great-great-grandchildren have brought his memories of his career back to life by establishing Meerea Park. They are brothers Rhys and Garth Eather, the former the winemaker in the partnership. An Oenology graduate from Roseworthy (now part of the Adelaide University), Rhys has undertaken vintages in Italy (Puglia and Piedmont) and France. Here he worked with M. Chapoutier in the northern Rhône Valley, leaving him with a deep and abiding love of Hermitage. Garth manages the administration and sales side of the business, seldom venturing from his office.

The grape of this region is known in Australia as shiraz (or syrah), although until 2010 (when a wine agreement between Australia and the EU was signed) it was called hermitage in the Hunter Valley, Coonawarra and elsewhere – but never in the Barossa Valley.

When the Eathers established their winery, they made a number of decisions. Most important was the freedom to seek outstanding grapes from independent grapegrowers and make individual vineyard wines. They call themselves 'terroirists', and have set up long-term relationships with growers whose grapes are of especially high quality, and where there is special synergy in a given blend, they do not hesitate to create a blend.

Another decision taken at the outset was to create a label for their wines which explicitly recognised their vigneron forefather, Alexander Munro. He had commissioned an ornate drinking fountain and gas street lamp to be made in Scotland and shipped to his town of Singleton in the Upper Hunter Valley. He was Singleton's first mayor, and when he retired he gave the objects to the town, which in turn duly erected them on the main street: it is their image that is reproduced on Meerea Park's labels. The Aunts Shiraz is named after three pioneer women of the Hunter Valley, who established the initial homestead on Meerea in the 1830s. The three women were referred to by the family as the 'Aunts'. The establishment of the homestead coincided with the planting of the first shiraz in the Hunter Valley.

While Rhys Eather's first love is shiraz, with up to six different wines being made in any given vintage, including a co-fermented shiraz viognier, Meerea Park also makes classic Hunter Valley semillon; a Hunter Valley blend of shiraz and pinot noir, made famous between 1925 and 1955 by the legendary winemaker Maurice O'Shea; a semillon sauvignon blanc, the latter component coming from the Adelaide Hills; and small quantities of chardonnay.

The Eathers have been prepared to present blind tastings of their wines matched by the greatest Australian and French examples (Grand Cru White Burgundies, Paul Jaboulet Aîné Hermitage La Chapelle among others), and have emerged with distinction from these comparative tastings.

Moorooduc Estate

Est 1983
501 Derril Road, Moorooduc, Vic 3936
Open Thurs–Mon 11–5
Getting there 1 hour's drive from Melbourne CBD
Contact (03) 5971 8506;
mooroduc@ozemail.com.au;
www.mooroducestate.com.au
Region Mornington Peninsula
Lat 38°20'S
Elev 25–250m
E° Days 1428
Harvest 5 March–30 April

Estate vineyards 5ha
Varieties planted Pinot noir (2.6), chardonnay (2), shiraz (0.4)
Leased or contracted vineyards 7.5ha
Varieties planted Pinot noir (5.5), chardonnay (1), pinot gris (1)
Dozens produced 5500 No increase planned.
Exports To Hong Kong through Boutique Wines (ph) 852 2872 4234; orders@boutiquewines.com.hk. Also to the UK, Singapore, New York and California.
Winemaker Dr Richard McIntyre

Key wines

The Moorooduc Chardonnay

How it is made: Whole-bunch-pressed, the unclarified juice taken directly to barrel for natural primary fermentation and mlf, remaining on lees until ready for the final filtration and fining prior to bottling.

How it tastes: The way the wine is made invests it with highly complex aromas and flavours, with a mix of stone fruit and very different savoury characters sustained by the ample backbone of the wine. Cellar up to 4 years from vintage.

Best vintages: 2011, 2010, 2008, 2006, 2003

The Moorooduc Pinot Noir

How it is made: The whole bunches are first cooled, then destemmed but not crushed, and dropped into 2-tonne open fermenters; after 4–6 days the natural fermentation commences, peaking at 34°C; after 7 days it is complete; pressing follows and the wine is settled for several days before going to French oak for 15 months' maturation. It is neither fined nor filtered.

How it tastes: A deeply coloured wine with aromas including black cherry, plums and spices, the palate long, rich and expressive. Cellar up to 8 years from vintage.

Best vintages: 2010, 2009, 2008, 2006, 2004

Moorooduc Estate

Founded by (now retired) surgeon Dr Richard McIntyre and wife Jill, this is one of the older wineries on the Mornington Peninsula, its name bestowed on the district by Aboriginal people, its meaning lost in the mists of time. Their philosophy is best summarised by the message on the back label of all their wine bottles: 'The fundamental quality and character of fine wines comes from the vineyard where the grapes are grown.' The focus is on simple winemaking techniques for the hand-picked and carefully sorted grapes, notably wild yeast ferments in barrel (chardonnay) and open vat (pinot noir) with natural mlf.

The grapes come from four vineyards in the Moorooduc area: the McIntyre Vineyard (5ha) which is estate-owned, the first vines having been planted in 1983 on the gentle north-facing slope. The surface soil is sandy, the subsoil a mix of clay with veins of sand penetrated by the vines' roots when mature, eliminating the need for irrigation. The nearby Garden Vineyard is leased by Moorooduc Estate, planted to pinot noir and pinot gris.

The Robinson Vineyard is owned by viticulturist Hugh Robinson, who also manages the McIntyre and Garden vineyards. To tighten the bonds further, Moorooduc Estate buys high-quality clonal selection pinot noir and chardonnay and makes single-vineyard wines from some of these grapes. The final twist comes with the Osborn Vineyard, owned and managed by the Osborn family, with advice from Hugh Robinson; the McIntyres buy chardonnay and pinot noir from this productive vineyard, and they form the basis of Moorooduc Estate's Devil Bend Creek wines. This is the basic level; next come Individual Vineyard wines, and, at the top, The Moorooduc Chardonnay and Pinot Noir.

The climate is cool, with a strong maritime cooling effect in summer from the nearby ocean. While the late summer and autumn weather is usually stable, with sunny days and cool nights, the earlier part of the growing cycle sees more rain and higher humidity. Great care has to be taken with the vine canopy; excess shoots are removed early in the growing season. The canopy will be trimmed at least once, and leaf-plucking on the east (morning) side of the canopy is usual, especially for the pinot noir. Any bunch-removal (thinning) will be done at veraison.

The Mornington Peninsula is a place of great beauty, much facing one or other part of the seas which surround it. It is undulating country, with its green grass supporting white-railed horse studs, the paddocks and vineyards regularly broken up by stands of thick eucalypt forest. These areas are now protected by law, and it is very difficult to get approval to remove any trees. All this adds up to a haven for birds, which forces most vineyards to cover the vines with nets once the grapes start to go through veraison.

It is no coincidence that daughter and marketing manager Kate McIntyre (who speaks fluent French) should have obtained her MW (Master of Wine) degree, nor that mother Jill should be a superb chef. When she 'retired' and closed the winery restaurant (other than for special events), it was a cause of considerable regret.

Morris

Est 1859
Mia Mia Road, Rutherglen, Vic 3685
Open Mon–Sat 9–5, Sun 10–5
Getting there 3 hours' drive from
Melbourne CBD
Contact (02) 6026 7303;
cellardoor@morriswines.com;
www.morriswines.com.au
Region Rutherglen
Lat 36°03'S
Elev 170m
E° Days 1591
Harvest 17 February–27 March

Estate vineyards 76.8ha
Varieties planted Brown muscat (24.3),
durif (13.8), cabernet sauvignon (12.6),
muscadelle (9.8), shiraz (6.7), cinsaut
(4.2), touriga (1.5), grenache (0.7), other
varieties (3.3)
Leased or contracted vineyards 12.5ha
Varieties planted NFP
Dozens produced 22 000 May increase
to 30 000.
Exports Wines are not currently
exported to China or Hong Kong;
possibly by 2014. Exports to the UK and
the US.
Winemaker David Morris

Key wines

Durif
How it is made: From estate vines planted in 1920, and, like the Muscat (and other fortified wines), fermented in the 100-year-old open wax-lined concrete fermenters before being aged in French and American oak for 24 months.

How it tastes: It is deeply coloured and full-bodied, with blackberry fruit, and firm tannins. Will cellar for 20 years or more from vintage.

Best vintages: 2013, 2009, 2007, 2002, 2001

Muscat
How it is made: It is released in four levels, with the glorious Old Premium Rare at the top, followed by Cellar Reserve Grand, Classic, and Black Label at the entry level. The wines are made by a solera system, the average age increasing with each level. Once bottled, no further change takes place.

How it tastes: The Old Premium Rare is deep olive-brown in colour; it is so concentrated that the texture is like syrup, the flavours oriental sweet spices, semi-dried raisins and dark chocolate. A tiny sip stays in the mouth for minutes.

Best vintages: NA

Morris

In 1851 a young Bristol bank clerk, George Francis Morris, left England to join those lured to the country by the discovery of gold. His prospecting was not successful, and he soon realised that there was much greater profit to be made by supplying gold miners with all their necessities of life. Within a few years he had made so much money that he was able to return to England with his young wife, and his son, Charles Hugh Morris, was born there in 1859. Later that year George Francis returned to Victoria, and purchased a 100ha property near Rutherglen, planting part to vines.

At first development was slow, but it increased rapidly through the 1870s and 1880s. He built a magnificent two-storey mansion called Fairfield, and the surrounding vineyard grew to over 250ha. Both it and the Fairfield winery were the largest in the southern hemisphere. In 20 years, Fairfield Wines won 425 first prizes at exhibitions in London, Amsterdam, Paris, Calcutta, New Zealand, South Africa, Perth, Melbourne and Sydney.

In 1887, his 28-year-old son, CH Morris, purchased his own land at Mia Mia, 3km east of Fairfield, planting 36ha of shiraz and muscat. In 1897 he built a modest corrugated iron winery which is used to this day, the only significant change being a cellar door, designed by leading architect Robin Boyd, constructed within the winery.

The arrival of phylloxera progressively destroyed all Rutherglen's vineyards, including Fairfield, and GF Morris died in 1910, a broken man, albeit an elderly one. CH Morris, however, had realised that phylloxera did not survive in sandy soil, and in 1908 planted the 120ha Sandhills Vineyard across the Murray River in New South Wales, on the sand which gave the vineyard its name. This provided grapes for the winery, and after World War I, he and his three sons, Charles Tempest, Gerald and Frederick, replanted the Mia Mia vineyard with grafted, phylloxera-resistant vines.

The three brothers took over winemaking after CH Morris's death in 1943, and CT Morris's son, CH 'Mick' Morris, obtained a Bachelor of Science degree from Melbourne University, and thereafter a Diploma in Oenology from Roseworthy Agricultural College. When he returned to the business in 1950, he was the first member of the family to have formal qualifications.

In 1970, the family accepted a generous offer for the business, which passed into corporate ownership, and is now owned by Pernod Ricard. But Mick Morris stayed as winemaker, and in 1993 passed responsibility to son David, the fifth generation. Mick, still hale and hearty, has continued to support David, particularly in blending the magnificent muscats and topaques (muscadelles) which are the heart of the business. The one table wine of (considerable) consequence is the durif, a wine which Mick Morris kept as a single varietal in 1954, even though it was then simply called claret.

In 2003 Morris's range of fortified, table and sparkling wines emulated the success of Fairfield 130 years ago by winning 20 trophies, 80 gold medals and 123 silver and bronze medals. It continues to share the limelight with Chambers Rosewood.

Moss Wood

Est 1969
926 Metricup Road, Wilyabrup, WA 6284
Open By appt
Getting there 3 hours' drive from Perth CBD
Contact (08) 9755 6266; mosswood@mosswood.com.au; www.mosswood.com.au
Region Margaret River
Lat 33°57'S
Elev 40–90m
E° Days 1552
Harvest 26 February–8 April

Estate vineyards 22.84ha
Varieties planted Cabernet sauvignon (10.89), semillon (3.6), chardonnay (2.38), sauvignon blanc (1.98), merlot (1.63), pinot noir (1.55), petit verdot (0.44), cabernet franc (0.37)
Dozens produced 14 000 No increase planned.
Exports To China and Hong Kong through Summergate Fine Wines (ph) toll free 800 820 6929; info@ summergate.com. Also to the UK, the US and other major markets.
Winemaker Clare and Keith Mugford

Key wines

Chardonnay

How it is made: Hand-picked grapes are whole-bunch-pressed and cold-settled in stainless steel tanks until the juice is clear, whereafter cultured yeast initiates fermentation before the fermenting juice is transferred to French oak barrels. When complete, all barrels are pumped to tank and, once blended, the wine is returned to barrel for partial (30%) mlf before bottling in September. 800 dozen made.

How it tastes: Deliberately made in a riper style with white peach, melon, fig and cashew flavours (rather than grapefruit) balanced and lengthened by a line of acidity. Cellar 10–15 years from vintage.

Best vintages: 2010, 2006, 2005, 2003, 2002

Cabernet Sauvignon

How it is made: A cabernet sauvignon–dominant blend, hand-picked and destemmed into small open fermenters with hand-plunging 3 times a day. After 10–14 days on skins, pressed to tank for the mlf, then racked to barrel in May; the components are blended the following January, then returned to barrel for further maturation before being bottled 32–33 months after picking. A small percentage of cabernet franc and petit verdot is included. 2700 dozen made.

How it tastes: Deep purple-crimson colour; a fragrant bouquet, the palate with perfect weight and balance to the blackcurrant fruit on the medium- to full-bodied, yet supple, palate, finishing with appropriate savoury tannins and oak. Cellar to 20 years from vintage.

Best vintages: 2010, 2008, 2005, 2003, 2001

Moss Wood

After briefly toying with the idea of establishing a vineyard in Mount Barker, Perth doctor Bill Pannell switched his attention to Margaret River, and in 1969 spent six months digging holes in paddocks looking for the ideal soil. He found it in a farming property in Wilyabrup, and persuaded the owner, Jack Guthrie, to subdivide his land and sell the block that would become Moss Wood to him and wife Sandra.

A nursery of cabernet sauvignon cuttings was established in the same year, and 2ha of cabernet sauvignon were planted the following year, with the first vintage made in 1973. Pinot noir, semillon and chardonnay followed later in the decade. The wines were made by Bill during his annual holidays, the weekends given over to vineyard work, all involving almost four hours' drive to and from Perth.

When Sandra (and their children) threatened rebellion, Roseworthy graduate (Applied Science in Oenology) Keith Mugford was employed as winemaker prior to the 1979 vintage. By this time the cabernet sauvignon had already achieved recognition as one of Australia's finest examples of the variety. In 1984, Keith and new wife Clare leased the vineyard and winery from the Pannells, and purchased it outright the following year.

With their four children starting to grow up, and Ian Bell appointed as vineyard manager in 1985, and moving to assistant winemaker in 1989, the Mugfords had the opportunity to embark on their postgraduate studies. Clare Mugford studied for and obtained a Graduate Diploma in Wine Business from Adelaide University, and Keith completed a Master of Business Administration from the Australian Graduate School of Management (a joint school of the Universities of Sydney and New South Wales) graduating dux in 2006 and receiving the Integritas Award.

They were also continuously proactively engaged in improving the dry-grown vineyards management, with cover crops, minimal tillage and mulching, also introducing sophisticated trellis systems. In the winery, ways of further improving the quality of already excellent wines were constantly under consideration.

With demand far exceeding supply, forcing prices up and making long-term customers unhappy, the Mugfords purchased the 6.36ha Ribbon Vale Vineyard, which had been established in 1977, just prior to the 2000 vintage, and have since made the Single Vineyard Ribbon Vale wines. Then, in 2006, Ian Bell resigned to work full-time on his Glenmore Vineyard, planted between 1990 and 1995 in Yallingup. Moss Wood buys some of its cabernet sauvignon to make yet another cabernet, blended with cabernet sauvignon from the Montgomery Vineyard in Cowaramup. This wine is called Amy's.

In 2008 the family moved back to Margaret River from Perth, having sold their house there, their two youngest children completing their education at boarding school. The way Moss Wood has been built is testament to the Mugfords' business expertise, and carefully positioned so that it will attract some (or all) of their children to make it their life's work.

Mount Langi Ghiran Vineyards

Est 1969
Warrak Road, Buangor, Vic 3375
Open Mon–Fri 9–5, w'ends 10–5
Getting there 2 hours' drive from Melbourne CBD
Contact (03) 5354 3207; sales@langi.com.au; www.langi.com.au
Region Grampians
Lat 37°17'S
Elev 240–440m
E° Days 1377
Harvest 7 March–14 May

Estate vineyards 74ha
Varieties planted Shiraz (64), riesling (4), cabernet sauvignon (4), pinot gris (2)
Leased or contracted vineyards 20ha
Varieties planted Shiraz
Dozens produced 65 000 No increase planned.
Exports Exports to China through The Wine Republic (ph) 010 5869 7050; info@thewinerepublic.com and to Hong Kong through Northeast Wines & Spirits Ltd (ph) 852 2873 5733; www.northeast.com.hk. Also to all major markets.
Winemaker Kate Petering

Key wines

Cliff Edge Shiraz

How it is made: While cultured yeast is used, the fermentation techniques are complex. Part of the wine is given a short pre-fermentation cold soak before a traditional destem, crush and ferment for 7–10 days with 3–5 punchdowns per day, while 15–20% is fermented as whole bunches, with foot-stomping twice per day and a 5-day fermentation time. Most primary and secondary fermentation is finished in French oak (20% new), and the wine spends 12–15 months in oak before the components are finally blended, and crossflow-filtered before bottling.

How it tastes: A deliciously complex wine, the bouquet and palate singing the same song, with a precocious display of spicy and black pepper the soprano, rich plummy/velvety fruit the bass. Cellar to 15 years from vintage.

Best vintages: 2012, 2010, 2008, 2005, 2004

Langi Shiraz

How it is made: Fermentation is similar to the Cliff Edge, except that the proportion of whole bunches is closer to 80%, some foot-stomped, the other co-fermented with crushed fruit, usually an 8-day process. Fermentation is finished in French oak (50% new). The wine spends 15 months in barrel, and may be racked only once during that time. The wine is not fined, but is crossflow-filtered. 500 dozen made.

How it tastes: Vivid crimson-purple colour when young; the perfumed bouquet is exquisite, with red and black fruits in a swathe of violets and rose petals, then a supremely elegant and intense palate, the finish exceptionally long. Cellar to 25 years from vintage.

Best vintages: 2012, 2010, 2008, 2005, 2004

Mount Langi Ghiran Vineyards

The mountain that is the dramatic backdrop for this great vineyard was named Langi Ghiran by the local Aboriginals, meaning yellow-tailed black cockatoo. Despite its remote and wild location, a vineyard was planted in 1870, and photographs show it as it was until it went out of production in 1920.

No less than four dates (between 1963 and 1971) have been given for the re-establishment of this vineyard by the Frantin family. It is known that shiraz, cabernet sauvignon and riesling were the varieties chosen, and that when the quality of the grapes (sold to other winemakers) became known, it was decided to build a small winery into the side of the hill, using gravity flow for most wine movements.

The quality of the riesling was deplorable, and that of the red wines decidedly variable. Trevor Mast, then winemaker at Best's, was retained as a consultant, and quickly improved the quality of the wines – so much so that he and wife Sandra purchased the property in 1987, he relinquishing his role at Best's.

In 1996 the Rathbone family acquired Yering Station, then little more than a small vineyard and a small building dating from the mid-19th century. More than A$10 million was spent on transforming it to one of the showpieces of the Yarra Valley, with a combined production of Yarrabank sparkling wines and fine table wines thanks to the skill of winemaker Tom Carson.

In 2002 the family took the first step in building a group of top-quality producers from different parts of Australia making wines of distinctively different styles, and purchased Mount Langi Ghiran from the Masts. Dan Buckle was transferred from Yering Station to Langi (as it is known for short) to stand alongside Trevor Mast. With investment in the vineyard and winery alike, and the skill of Dan Buckle, the quality of the wines increased significantly.

Prior to his departure in 2012 to become chief winemaker at Domaine Chandon, Dan Buckle and viticulturist Nathan Scarlett had made two important innovations. The heart of the vineyard is a 6ha block planted in 1963 on the dome of a small hill towards the bottom of the property. Using airborne infrared photography coupled with ground-penetrating radar it has been divided into five blocks, with only the best two used for the limited production of the Langi Shiraz.

Second, they have established several ongoing contracts providing grapes from individual vineyard releases such as Nowhere Creek Shiraz and a tiny annual make of Bradach Pinot Noir. That said, there is considerable diversity with Billi Billi Pinot Grigio, Cliff Edge Pinot Gris (from vines planted in 1994), Cliff Edge Riesling (both dry and sweet) and the three mainstream shiraz releases, with Billi Billi the lowest priced, then Cliff Edge, and Langi at the top. The portfolio is completed by Cliff Edge Cabernet Sauvignon, and sparkling shiraz.

Considerable emphasis is placed on sustainable production practices, with the aim of increasing biodiversity on the large area of forest surrounding the property; sulphur (permitted by all organisations, including biodynamic) is used to control mildew, but no synthetic chemicals are used in insecticides or herbicides. These practices protect these ancient soils, which are rarely found elsewhere in Australia: granitic topsoil eroded from the mountain behind on top of red clay loams. This soil, combined with the cool climate, gives the Mount Langi Ghiran shirazs their distinctive character.

Mount Mary

Est 1971
Coldstream West Road, Lilydale,
Vic 3140
Open Not
Getting there 45 minutes' drive from
Melbourne CBD
Contact (03) 9739 1761;
liz@mountmary.com.au;
www.mountmary.com.au
Region Yarra Valley
Lat 37°42'S
Elev 50–350m
E° Days 1253
Harvest 1 March–25 April

Estate vineyards 15ha
Varieties planted Pinot noir (3),
chardonnay (3), cabernet sauvignon
(2.5), merlot (1.25), cabernet
franc (0.75), sauvignon blanc (0.65),
semillon (0.25), malbec (0.25), petit
verdot (0.25), muscadelle (0.1), other (3)
Dozens produced 4500 No increase
planned.
Exports To China and Hong Kong
through Yu Tai Wine Distribution Pty
Ltd (ph) 86 755 2654 6507; yutai.cn@
gmail.com. Also to the UK, the US,
Denmark, Singapore and South Korea.
Winemaker Sam Middleton

Key wines

Chardonnay

How it is made: The hand-picked grapes are crushed, pressed and 100% barrel-fermented in French oak (25% new) with cultured yeast, lees-stirred for the first 2–3 months of a total of 11 months in oak. A mix of barrique and larger oak formats are used. No mlf takes place, necessitating sterile filtration. 900 dozen made.

How it tastes: Gleaming yellow-green colour, with an aromatic and complex bouquet, varietal fruit in a grapefruit zest/white peach/melon spectrum, its fruit anchored on minerally acidity, oak merely a vehicle. Cellar to 9 years from vintage.

Best vintages: 2012, 2011, 2010, 2006, 2005

Quintet (Cabernet blend)

How it is made: The blend varies from year to year around a 45/30/15/5/5% blend of the 5 varieties (cabernet sauvignon, merlot, cabernet franc, petit verdot and malbec). Cultured yeast is used for the 10–12 days the wine spends on skins. For the first 12 months, part of the wine is matured in large used oak casks of up to 2000 litres; for the second 10 months all of the wine is aged in French oak barriques (30% new). Light egg white–fining and light filtration prior to bottling. 1900 dozen made.

How it tastes: An exercise in harmony and balance from start to finish; its vibrant black- and red-currant fruit rolls out for a seeming eternity on the palate, and on the lingering aftertaste. Builds notes of cedar and cigar box as it ages. Cellar to 20 years from vintage.

Best vintages: 2012, 2010, 2006, 2004, 2000

Mount Mary

Doctors John Middleton and Peter McMahon shared a surgery in Lilydale, and were two of the 20th-century pioneers of the Yarra Valley, helping to bring it back to life after 50 years of inactivity. While they were close friends, forever playing practical jokes on each other, their personalities could not have been more different, Middleton irascible and self-opinionated, McMahon always with a smile on his face and a twinkle in his eye. Both were self-taught winemakers who made wines of the highest quality right from the first vintage, their palates tuned by the great wines of Bordeaux and Burgundy, and the trips they made to those regions.

Middleton began experimental winemaking in the mid-1960s, using grapes grown in the backyard of his house at Chirnside Park (near Lilydale), and began looking for a vineyard site. When he saw the property known as Mount Mary, he instantly recognised its gentle north-facing slope as perfect, and – with wife Marli at his side, as always – immediately purchased it.

By mid-1972 they had planted cabernet sauvignon, merlot, cabernet franc, petit verdot and malbec, the first vineyard to be planted in Australia with these varieties intended for a single Bordeaux blend wine. He also planted pinot noir and chardonnay, the other two varieties. Less felicitous were gewurztraminer and chasselas; these two were, in due course, replaced by sauvignon blanc, semillon and muscadelle to produce a white Bordeaux blend.

He despised shiraz, but his death in 2006 (aged 82) has allowed his son, Dr David Middleton, a veterinarian, and grandson Sam, with a degree in agricultural science, to rethink the issue. For some years they have been developing a Rhône Valley style, based on seven varieties not previously planted at Mount Mary.

John's mailing list brochure, in a small gatefold format, was the ideal soapbox for him to vent his displeasure at the many fools who inhabit the wine planet. He was the living embodiment of Socrates, dissatisfied about everything and anything (including screwcaps, wine shows and, most particularly, wine writers) other than his beloved wines. I didn't have the chance to discuss with him a piece in *The Wine Advocate*, in which Robert Parker dismissed the Mount Mary Quintet as poor-quality Bordeaux and took a thinly veiled swipe at me for praising Mount Mary's wines.

In a sense, however, Parker's criticism is simply validation of the style of wines John Middleton strived to make – and succeeded in making. His quintet and pinot noir have always been elegant and graceful, alcohol in a 12.5–13.5% range, the tannins fine and the oak subtle. Unless you have often tasted these wines, and watched them develop for decades (in the case of Quintet) you could easily walk past them without pausing for thought (or a second taste). Thus they are the antithesis of the style of red wines Parker so admires.

It is true that over the years John Middleton had sometimes failed to meet the lofty expectations he had for his wines, which proved he was a mere mortal, and reinforced that truth by refusing point blank to admit there were occasional imper-fections. David recognised the impact of smoke taint in the bushfire-ravaged 2009 vintage, and used a one-off name (Reflexion) with significantly reduced prices. But in one respect he keeps the fire burning: his father progressively decreased the size of the font in the printed once-a-year newsletter to increase the number and length of his Don Quixote–like diatribes to the point where a magnifying glass was needed. Nothing there has changed.

Oakridge Wines

Est 1978
864 Maroondah Highway, Coldstream, Vic 3770
Open 7 days 10-5
Getting there 1 hour's drive from Melbourne CBD
Contact (03) 9738 9900; info@oakridgewines.com.au; www.oakridgewines.com.au
Region Yarra Valley
Lat 37°42'S
Elev 50–350m
E° Days 1253
Harvest 1 March–25 April

Estate vineyards 9.8ha
Varieties planted Chardonnay (2.8), cabernet sauvignon (2.1), pinot noir (2), shiraz (1.6), merlot (1.2), semillon (0.1)
Leased or contracted vineyards 45ha
Varieties planted Chardonnay (18), pinot noir (13), Bordeaux varieties, predominantly cabernet sauvignon (4.5), shiraz (4), pinot gris (3.5), sauvignon blanc and semillon (1), arneis (1)
Dozens produced 24 000 May increase to 30 000.
Exports To China and Hong Kong through Montrose Fine Wines (ph) 852 2555 8877; www.montrose.com.hk. Also to the UK, the US and other major markets.
Winemaker David Bicknell

Key wines

864 Chardonnay

How it is made: Hand-picked and sorted bunches are chilled in cool rooms overnight before whole-bunch-pressing, the juice transferred directly to 500 litre puncheons (25–30% new) for fermentation at temperatures 20–25°C until completely dry. It remains on yeast less in barrel for 10–11 months, with a monthly topping regime. Prior to bottling the wine is clarified, and has a single filtration to bottle. Approximately 500 dozen made.

How it tastes: Unfailingly very complex, with characters typically found in top-end French white burgundies. The wine has exceptional length, and can be cellared for 10 years from vintage.

Best vintages: 2012, 2011, 2010, 2009, 2006

864 Cabernet Sauvignon

How it is made: Hand-picked and sorted, the bunches chilled overnight before destemming without crushing to fermenters for wild/natural yeast fermentation commencing after a 3–6-day cold soak. Temperatures typically 22–32°C, primary ferment lasting 9–15 days, then macerated for a further 2–4 weeks, for a total time on skins of 28–40 days. The wine is then pressed and allowed to settle for 7 days before transfer to French oak barriques (40% new) where the wine remains in barrel for 14–16 months before a single filtration at bottling. 250 dozen made.

How it tastes: The wine reflects its cool-grown origin, its bouquet with blackcurrant fruit to the fore, the palate bringing fine-grained but persistent tannins into play, supported by cedary French oak. Performs best in the warmer vintages, when it has many of the markers of fine Bordeaux-red wines. Cellar to 40 years from vintage.

Best vintages: 2012, 2010, 2008, 2006, 2005

Oakridge Wines

The Oakridge Wines of today has only two links carried through since its establishment in 1978: its name, and its situation in the Yarra Valley. Even the latter link needs some qualification: it was originally located in the Upper Yarra Valley, in contrast to its present site in the heart of the Lower Yarra Valley in Coldstream.

Its intervening changes in ownership and fluctuating financial fortunes are irrelevant to today's very successful and highly regarded business. The majority ownership is that of the d'Aloisio family, CEO and chief winemaker David Bicknell a minor shareholder. A highly intelligent and sensitive man, he has an excellent palate (and career as a leading wine show judge) and is a skilled and innovative winemaker.

These abilities are reflected in two specific ways: a belief in the special qualities of a single vineyard site with a carefully matched varietal planting, and a winemaking philosophy using an intuitive balance between a non-interventionist approach and careful observation of the critical points of fermentation and/or maturation pathway, intervening decisively where it is needed.

The Oakridge philosophy is expressed thus: 'Each bottle of Oakridge wine holds a memory, each has a unique story that starts in one of our vineyards and ends when you enjoy it. Our wines are fresh, with a purity of flavour and balance. As young wines they are almost seamless – nothing appears out of place. You simply yearn for another glass. With age, our wines retain their freshness and purity but build additional layers of complexity and palate length.'

The mix between owned and contract vineyards allows Oakridge to explore and market the small-volume ultra premium 864 single block (within a single vineyard) series; next comes the Local Vineyard Series, the larger production matched by lower prices; and finally, the Over the Shoulder varietal range, always 100% Yarra Valley, all made at the Oakridge winery, and at prices seldom bettered in the Valley.

The Local Vineyard Series allows customers to compare and contrast wines of a single variety made from vines grown on the hillsides and valleys of both the Lower and Upper Yarra Valley. Indeed, in one respect the wheel has turned full circle, for the red volcanic soils of the Upper Yarra Valley, the first home of Oakridge, have produced some of David Bicknell's most highly praised chardonnays.

The two varieties made at all three price points are chardonnay – undoubtedly Oakridge's strongest wine – and shiraz. Pinot noir features strongly in the Local Vineyard series, and will make its appearance in vintages which favour this demanding variety. Some excellent cabernet sauvignon is made in most vintages, sourced from the Lower Yarra Valley.

In February 2013 it opened the ultimate showcase for its wines: a stylish and airy 50-seat restaurant, with a full high-quality à la carte lunch menu 7 days a week – it is also open for breakfast on Sunday – and a wine list offering back vintages, and wines by the glass. There is, of course, a full range of current release vintage wines.

Paringa Estate

Est 1985
44 Paringa Road, Red Hill South, Vic 3937
Open 7 days 11–5
Getting there 1 hour's drive from Melbourne CBD
Contact (03) 5989 2669; info@paringaestate.com.au; www.paringaestate.com.au
Region Mornington Peninsula
Lat 38°20′S
Elev 25–250m
E° Days 1428
Harvest 5 March–30 April

Estate vineyards 4ha
Varieties planted Pinot noir (1.5), shiraz (1.2), chardonnay (0.8), pinot gris (0.5)
Leased or contracted vineyards 17.2ha
Varieties planted Pinot noir (10.5), chardonnay (5.5), riesling (1.2)
Dozens produced 15 000 No increase planned.
Exports To China through Sourceland Wines Shenzhen Ltd (ph) 86 755 8293 1699; info@sourcelandwines.com and to Hong Kong through Ponti Trading Ltd (ph) 852 2306 9198; stephen.lai@ponti.tdg.com. Also to the UK, Canada, Denmark, Japan, South Korea, Malaysia, Singapore and Ukraine.
Winemaker Lindsay McCall, Craig Thompson

Key wines

The Paringa Single Vineyard Pinot Noir
How it is made: The grapes come from the 25-year-old pinot noir vineyard. The fruit is hand-picked and chilled overnight prior to being destemmed into small open stainless steel fermenters; after 4–5 days' pre-fermentation maceration, wild yeast fermentation is initiated, and followed by a further period of maceration after the ferment is finished. The wine goes through mlf in barrel, and is bottled after 11 months in oak. 250 dozen made.

How it tastes: The wine has a super-fragrant bouquet of black cherries and a dash of French oak; the palate has a magical combination of power with elegance, length with finesse; oak and tannins are an essential part of a beautiful pinot. Cellar to 10+ years from vintage.

Best vintages: 2012, 2010, 2009, 2006, 2004

The Paringa Single Vineyard Shiraz
How it is made: The wine is made in a near-identical fashion to The Paringa Pinot Noir, the only differences being co-fermentation with 5% viognier, and 15–18 months' maturation in barrel, rather than 11 months. 200 dozen made.

How it tastes: The colour is a very deep but vibrant purple-crimson, the bouquet with plum, dark cherry, black pepper and spice, the palate densely packed with fruit, supple tannins and yet managing to have a finely textured palate, with a long, cleansing finish. French oak is a contributor to the overall character of the wine. Cellar to 15–20 years from vintage.

Best vintages: 2012, 2010, 2009, 2007, 2004

Paringa Estate

Would Lindsay McCall have established Paringa Estate if his first occupation had been as a doctor, lawyer or banker, rather than a schoolteacher? We will never know the answer to that question, of course, but I suspect the answer would be yes, and what is more, with greater speed and less financial stress. (The salary of a schoolteacher is far, far less than the earnings of other professionals.)

Lindsay's fascination with wine started as a consumer in the mid-1970s, and in 1984 he took the first step towards his dream of growing and making his own wine with the purchase of a derelict orchard on Paringa Road, Red Hill South. He began planting the following year, but remained a full-time teacher, so progress was slow, even though he worked every possible weekend and through much of the holidays.

Nonetheless, the home vineyard of 2.5ha was fully planted by 1990, and a token crop of 3 tonnes had been produced in 1988. In 1996 he left school-teaching forever, devoting himself full-time to Paringa Estate, having already demonstrated his exceptional skill as a grapegrower and winemaker by winning trophies and gold medals at an astonishing rate in the very influential Australian wine show system.

By 2000 production had risen to 78 tonnes (5500 dozen bottles), and by 2008 had reached 15000–16000 dozen (vintage variation), with no plans to increase that level. Paringa's exalted reputation has been built around its shiraz and pinot noir, which are made in three levels.

The basic range is the Peninsula series, made from estate-managed/leased vineyards at Red Hill plus purchased grapes from other carefully chosen vineyards across other localities on the Peninsula. Next is the Estate series, made from the mature estate-owned or leased vineyards. Since 2008, a single-vineyard chardonnay has been made each year, but with no corresponding shiraz or pinot noir.

Off to one side, as it were, is a riesling from the Thracore Vineyard in Callanan's Road, which has been leased by Paringa Estate since 2003. There is also a limited amount of pinot gris from the home vineyard. Finally, there are three wines made in very small quantities, all coming from the first estate plantings: The Paringa Chardonnay, The Paringa Pinot Noir and The Paringa Shiraz; until 2008, these wines were called 'Reserve'.

There is no question that the small amount made of each of the wines (even the largest volume Peninsula series) has allowed a constant barrel-by-barrel scrutiny, and a ruthless weeding out of the occasional barrel that doesn't come up to the expected standard. None of this would produce the exceptional quality of these wines were it not for the meticulous care of the vineyards, and a vine-by-vine management. The saying 'Great wine is made in the vineyard' is used all too often, but in the case of Paringa Estate, it is fully justified.

Penfolds

Est 1844
Tanunda Road, Nuriootpa, SA 5355
Open 7 days 10–5
Getting there 1 hour's drive from
Adelaide CBD
Contact (08) 8568 9408;
barossa.cellardoor@penfolds.com.au;
www.penfolds.com
Region Barossa Valley
Lat 34°29'S
Elev 274m
E° Days 1571
Harvest 27 February–17 April

Estate vineyards 1800ha
Varieties planted NFP
Dozens produced NFP
Exports To China through ASC Fine
Wines (ph) 8621 3423 9599; www.asc-
wines.com and to Hong Kong through
Jebsens (ph) 852 2923 8777; www.
jebsen.com. Also to all major markets.
Winemaker Peter Gago

Key wines

Grange
How it is made: Shiraz, with a small but variable amount of cabernet sauvignon,
is fermented in stainless steel and open wax-lined concrete vats, both types
with boards that keep the cap (the skins) submerged. The fermenting must is
drained and returned to each vessel during the 6–7-day cultured yeast ferment.
The wine is pressed prior to the end of fermentation and transferred direct to
100% new American oak for 18–20 months' maturation. The wine is not fined,
but has minimal filtration prior to bottling. Released after a further 3 years'
bottle maturation.

How it tastes: The wine has a velvety opulence and obvious oak when young,
and can be enjoyed then, but will gain elegance as the oak is absorbed, and the
black fruits, spice and tannins are harmoniously linked on a palate with a unique
marriage of balance, texture and structure. A 50-year cellaring future has been
proved many times in Penfolds' Rewards of Patience tastings.

Best vintages: 2008, 2006, 2005, 2004, 2001

Yattarna (Chardonnay)
How it is made: Since 2008, largely sourced from Tasmania, 100% barrel-fermented
in French oak (35–50% new, vintage-dependent) and 100% mlf, then 8–9 months in
a very cold cellar with regular lees stirring. No fining, and seldom filtered.

How it tastes: A wine of great purity, intensity and length on the palate, with subtle
flinty notes, acidity not blurred by the mlf. Given the screwcap, will develop for
20+ years, becoming more complex with age.

Best vintages: 2010, 2008, 2006, 2004, 2002

Penfolds

By far the greatest red wine maker in Australia, its brand awareness reaching all corners of the world. When English physician Dr Christopher Rawson Penfold arrived in Adelaide in 1844, he had already purchased a 202ha land grant at Magill on the outskirts of Adelaide at the foot of the Mount Lofty Ranges, and the house he and wife Mary built that year still stands on the same property, as does part of the (now much enlarged) Magill Estate winery.

Like other doctors of his time, notably Dr Henry Lindeman, he was firmly convinced of the medical benefits of moderate wine consumption, as are many doctors who have established wineries in Australia since Dr Max Lake in 1963. Under the direction of Mary Penfold, the wine business flourished, and over the next 100 years grew to be the largest in Australia.

Fortified wine was of major importance in the first half of the 20th century, and in 1950 winemaker Max Schubert was sent to Jerez, Spain, to learn more about making sherry. At the end of his stay in Europe he went to Bordeaux, then leading into the 1950 vintage, and saw red wine pressed straight to barrel prior to the end of fermentation. He had also seen new barrels 'seasoned' by fermentation of low-quality white wine while at Jerez, and was intrigued by the taste of the wine.

When he returned to Australia for the 1951 vintage, he decided to experiment by finishing the fermentation of high-quality shiraz in new American oak. So pleased was he that in 1952 the first commercial vintage of Grange was made. The story between then and 1962, when the outstanding quality and unique style were recognised, is too long to tell, but the might of Penfolds red wines has Grange as its rock of ages. The pre-eminent UK wine writer, Hugh Johnson, once described Grange as 'One of the only true First Growths of the Southern Hemisphere.'

Penfolds has developed a Bin number system for its red wines, so numerous that space does not allow a full list, but Bin 707 Cabernet Sauvignon and Bin 389 Cabernet Shiraz, produced in virtually every vintage, lead the way. Then there are Special Bin releases, only made in perfect vintages, such as Block 42 Cabernet Sauvignon and Bin 60A Coonawarra Cabernet Kalimna Shiraz (the 1962 vintage of this wine is, in my view, the greatest of all Australian red wines made in the 20th century). The roll call of honour continues with St Henri, Magill Estate, RWT Barossa Shiraz and many more, some single-variety, single-vineyard wines, most both vineyard and varietal blends.

In the 1990s Penfolds embarked on a project called 'The White Grange', which resulted in the first vintage of Yattarna Chardonnay (1995), now also supported by annual releases of Reserve Bin A Chardonnay. In all there are 46 separate labels produced by Penfolds covering a price range (in 2013) of $18 to $1000 a bottle, taking in 12 white wines, 29 red wines, and five fortified wines. It has 1800ha of vineyards spread across 16 wine regions, and a large team of winemakers headed by Peter Gago, an utterly brilliant and fiercely loyal presenter of Penfolds' best wines across countless countries and cities, travelling tens of thousands of kilometres each year.

In the years to come, more and more of Penfolds best red wines will be sold in Hong Kong and China.

Petaluma

Est 1976
Spring Gully Road, Piccadilly, SA 5151
Open At Bridgewater Mill, 7 days 10–5
Getting there 25 minutes' drive from Adelaide CBD
Contact (08) 8339 9300; petaluma@petaluma.com.au; www.petaluma.com.au
Region Adelaide Hills
Lat 34°00′S
Elev 496m
E° Days 1359
Harvest 12 March–30 April

Estate vineyards 126.9ha
Varieties planted Petaluma Vineyard (Adelaide Hills) Chardonnay (42), pinot noir (19), sauvignon blanc (17), shiraz (7.5), semillon (4.7), pinot gris (2.2) mourvedre (1), viognier (0.5); **Hanlin Hill Vineyard (Clare Valley)** Riesling (24); **Evans Vineyard (Coonawarra)** Cabernet sauvignon (4.5), merlot (3), shiraz (1), petit verdot (0.5)
Leased or contracted vineyards 166ha
Dozens produced 110 000 May increase to 140 000.
Exports To China and Hong Kong through ASC Fine Wines (ph) 8621 3423 9599; www.asc-wines.com. Also to all major markets.
Winemaker Andrew Hardy, Mike Mudge, Penny Jones

Key wines

Coonawarra (Cabernet blend)
How it is made: Entirely estate-grown; hand-picked and transported to Piccadilly, then destemmed, crushed and chilled before a 5-day cold soak, followed by cultured yeast fermentation, and a post-ferment 2 weeks on skins. Spends 2 years in new French oak, mainly barriques, but moving to some bigger-format barrels. Normally a Cabernet Merlot blend, occasionally with a small percentage of other varieties. Only made in good vintages (thus none in 2009 and 2011). 2000–5000 dozen made.

How it tastes: Offers cassis, red fruits and cedary oak first up, then darker berry characters with fine but persistent tannins on the finish, underpinning its long-term future. Cellar to 12 years from vintage.

Best vintages: 2010, 2008, 2006, 2004, 2002

Hanlin Hill Clare Valley Riesling
How it is made: 100% estate-grown grapes, crushed, pressed and then gravity-settled before being cold-fermented in stainless steel, using cultured yeast, at 10–14°C; sterile-filtered after blending and immediately prior to bottling; usually not fined. 9000–15 000 dozen made.

How it tastes: A distinguished wine with a long pedigree, the lemon blossom fragrance of the bouquet leading into an initial impact of lime and lemon fruit before a burst of minerally acidity takes hold until releasing its grip on the aftertaste, allowing the fruit the last say. Cellar to 15 years from vintage.

Best vintages: 2012, 2011, 2010, 2005, 2002

Petaluma

This is one of the great medium-sized estate-based wineries of Australia, created in the crucible of the formidable intelligence and powerful personality of Brian Croser AO. It was he who devised the concept of distinguished site: a parcel of land, normally but not necessarily small, which could produce grapes of outstanding quality. There were – and are – two caveats: first, the varieties grown on it have to be suited to the climate, and second, calamitous weather, be it bushfire, drought or flood, have to be treated as exceptions to prove the rule.

Croser moved with deliberation in securing estate vineyards that met his high standards. Petaluma was created in 1976, and a spätlese-style riesling from grapes grown by Mitchelton in the Goulburn Valley was made bearing the distinctive yellow label. This was followed by a gewurztraminer (a once-only wine); a chardonnay from Cowra (in New South Wales) followed in 1977.

In 1978 two fundamentally important acquisitions were made: the high-altitude Clare Valley riesling Hanlin Hill Vineyard, which had been planted in 1968, and the Evans Vineyard in Coonawarra, planted to cabernet sauvignon and merlot. The third event was the commencement of the building of the Petaluma winery on Spring Gully Road, Piccadilly. It was the first winery to be built in the conservation-conscious Adelaide Hills. The planting of chardonnay on the adjoining land, to become known as the Tiers Vineyard, followed in 1980 and 1982, with further plantings of chardonnay and pinot noir specifically for sparkling wine, which in due course appeared with the name 'Croser' the main feature of the label.

It was not until 1990 that Petaluma Chardonnay became 100% Piccadilly grown, but it marked the completion of the main framework of the key vineyards. Within a few years Petaluma joined the lists of the Australian Stock Exchange, and in 1994 acquired Mitchelton, next Knappstein (Clare Valley, South Australia), then Smithbrook (Pemberton, Western Australia) and Stonier (Mornington Peninsula, Victoria). It was a grand coalition, and proved irresistible to Lion Nathan, ultimately owned by Japanese brewer Kirin, which made a takeover offer in 2001.

It was opposed by Croser and the Petaluma board, but ultimately succeeded. Croser stayed on as CEO for some years, and after stepping down, remained a consultant for a further time, but no longer has any connection – except for one thing. Lion Nathan has approved the construction of a new winery some distance away, due to be completed in time for the 2015 vintage, and has agreed to sell the existing winery back to the Croser family interests.

The chief winemaker since 2004 has been Andrew Hardy, rightly described as 'known for his elegant winemaking style and engaging manner'. He is not only a gifted winemaker, but one of the nicest men. He is responsible for a portfolio of four sparkling wines, a shiraz, a shiraz viognier, four rieslings, a sauvignon blanc, a pinot gris, two chardonnays, two cabernet sauvignons, a merlot and a cabernet blend – all made from the three cornerstone regions of the Adelaide Hills, Coonawarra and Clare Valley.

And for visitors, the Bridgewater Mill restaurant, housed in an 1860s stone flour mill, is one of Adelaide's best, with an incomparable atmosphere. The slightly controversial White label has replaced the former Bridgewater Mill label, providing a range of varietal wines at lower price points.

Peter Lehmann

Est 1979
Para Road, Tanunda, SA 5352
Open Mon–Fri 9.30–5, w'ends & public hols 10.30–4.30
Getting there 1 hour's drive from Adelaide CBD
Contact (08) 8565 9555; plw@peterlehmannwines.com; www.peterlehmannwines.com
Region Barossa Valley
Lat 34°29′S
Elev 274m
E° Days 1571
Harvest 27 February–17 April

Estate vineyards 45ha
Varieties planted Shiraz (22), cabernet sauvignon (13), merlot (5), grenache (1), semillon (1), other (3)
Leased or contracted vineyards 1195ha
Varieties planted Shiraz (564), cabernet sauvignon (172), semillon (88), chardonnay (70), riesling (65), grenache (58), merlot (56), pinot gris (25), mataro (15), tempranillo (7), other (75)
Dozens produced 750 000 No increase planned.
Exports To China and Hong Kong through ASC Fine Wines (ph) 862 160 561 999 (China); (ph) 852 3923 6720 (Hong Kong); www.asc-wines.com. Also to all major markets.
Winemaker Andrew Wigan, Ian Hongell, Peter Kelly, Tim Dolan

Key wines

Stonewell Shiraz
How it is made: This is the best wine of the vintage, made from very old vines. It spends 2 weeks on skins in the fermenter, part finishing its fermentation in barrel. It spends 14 months in 90% French and 10% American oak hogsheads.

How it tastes: Deep purple-crimson; the aromas and flavours are complex, yet are seamlessly moulded in a supple display of red and black fruits, the tannins also soft, the oak totally integrated and balanced. Cellar to 25 years from vintage.

Best vintages: 2010, 2008, 2006, 2004, 2002

Mentor
How it is made: The blend is typically 70% cabernet sauvignon, 20% shiraz and 10% malbec from the Barossa and Eden valleys. It is macerated and fermented on skins for up to 2 weeks, part finishing its fermentation in 100% French oak hogsheads in which all the wine will be matured for 18 months.

How it tastes: This is a powerful medium- to full-bodied wine with a generous palate of black and red fruits, earth, black olive and cedary oak, finishing with firm tannins. Cellar to 15 years from vintage.

Best vintages: 2010, 2008, 2006, 2004, 2002

Peter Lehmann

Peter Lehmann was the personification of all that is great about the Barossa Valley: its ancient vines, its grapes, and its people who guard those vines. He was born at Angaston in 1930, the son of a Lutheran pastor, and was of fifth-generation Barossan stock. He worked first as a winemaker at Yalumba, where he spent 13 years, then moved to Saltram as chief winemaker in 1960, making a series of great wines.

In 1979 Saltram was acquired by Seagram, then the largest wine company in the world. It was also a time of a large (and still growing) surplus of grapes from the Barossa and Eden valleys, and Peter Lehmann knew he would be directed to terminate a large number of grape purchase agreements entered into by Saltram on the basis of a handshake by Peter Lehmann.

He pre-empted that direction by leaving Saltram and setting up (with major investments by well-resourced financiers) his own company, and honoured all those multi-generation verbal grape purchase agreements ('My word is my bond' was his motto). Various changes in ownership led to Peter Lehmann Wines being listed on the Australian Stock Exchange, and ultimately being acquired – with the Lehmann family's full agreement – by the Swiss/Californian Hess Group in 2002.

Lehmann's 1979 premonition had been proved 100% correct. In 1982 there was a surplus of 10 000 tonnes of red grapes, which led to the removal of 450ha of old, low-yielding vines, and the grafting of grenache and mourvedre to chardonnay. Worse was to follow, with dried shiraz used in muffins (cakes) or carbon-fined to make a neutral white wine for use in cheap casks. In 1987 the South Australian Government introduced a bounty for the removal of vines (the Vine Pull Scheme) and the area of mainly very old vines was reduced by 9%.

By the end of the 1980s Australia's exports had begun to grow, a trickle turning into a flood by the late 1990s. Almost overnight, it seemed, the ancient shiraz and grenache vines, and the grapes they grew, became precious treasures. Now it was time for the grapegrowers to repay Lehmann's loyalty, and they did exactly that.

On 28 June 2013 Peter Lehmann finally succumbed to his longstanding life-threatening illnesses, most due to life-long smoking and near-permanent occupation during vintage of the incoming grape weighbridge, armed with bottles of wine to be shared with every one of the 165 grapegrowers supplying the Peter Lehmann Wine business. His death means the Barossa Valley will have lost one of its greatest-ever vignerons.

For more than 30 years, chief winemaker Andrew Wigan has nurtured the extraordinary range of wines made by the company. Two of his many achievements have been the creation of the Wigan Riesling and Margaret Semillon (the latter named after Peter Lehmann's wife), both wines only released once they are five years old.

Pewsey Vale

Est 1847
**Eden Valley Road, Eden Valley,
SA 5353**
Open By appt
Getting there 1.25 hours' drive from Adelaide CBD
Contact (08) 8561 3200; info@pewseyvale.com; www.pewseyvale.com
Region Eden Valley
Lat 34°35'S
Elev 450m
E° Days 1460
Harvest 20 March–30 April

Estate vineyards 40ha
Varieties planted Riesling
Dozens produced 20 000 No increase planned.
Exports To China through Summergate Fine Wines (ph) toll free 800 820 6929; info@summergate.com and to Hong Kong through Fine Vintage (Far East) Ltd (ph) 852 2896 6108; info@finevintage.com.hk. Also to the UK, the US, Canada, Ireland and Finland.
Winemaker Louisa Rose

Key wines

The Contours Eden Valley Riesling

How it is made: The Contours comes from a single, south-facing (hence coolest) block of vines that was planted in 1965. Hand-picked grapes are destemmed, crushed and immediately separated from the skins via a static drainer; only free-draining juice is used, up to 500 litres per tonne (compared to the usual 700 litres per tonne). From 2011, the wine has been fermented with the yeast indigenous to the vineyard. Bottle aged for 5 years prior to release. 600 dozen made.

How it tastes: When 6 years old has a highly floral lime and apple blossom, the palate driven by lime and lemon juice flavours wrapped around a spine of minerally acidity, toasty aromas to develop in the distant future. Cellar to 25 years from vintage.

Best vintages: 2008, 2007, 2002, 2001, 1997

Eden Valley Riesling

How it is made: This wine is made from grapes planted in the early 1960s, the '80s and the '90s; each block has a slightly different aspect, giving it individual nuances which, when blended, gives rise to a great consistency from vintage to vintage. The only difference (apart from the broader fruit selection) between this and The Contours is that cultured yeast is used for fermentation, the wine is stabilised for heat and cold, and has one filtration prior to bottling. Both this and The Contours are vegan and vegetarian friendly.

How it tastes: Always very elegant and fine at the dawn of its life, with racy acidity threaded through citrus and apple fruit, and driving the length of the palate. Cellar to 15+ years from vintage.

Best vintages: 2013, 2012, 2002, 1999, 1984

Pewsey Vale

Pewsey Vale is a single-vineyard Eden Valley brand with a history dating back to 1847, when the first vines were planted by Joseph Gilbert. The vineyard and winery were visited by the wine journalist Ebenezer Ward in 1862, and a very detailed account appears in his collected articles in *The Vineyards and Orchards of South Australia*, first published in the *Adelaide Advertiser*. The initial plantings were (using the spelling of the time) verdeilho, gouais, riesling, shiraz and carbonet. Gilbert soon realised that verdelho, riesling, shiraz and cabernet sauvignon gave the best results, and so increased their plantings every year.

Ward recounts a tasting in Adelaide when the 1854 riesling was compared with 'some choice (German) Hock, considered to be the best wine of its class ever imported to this colony. The decision was in favour of the colonial product.' In 1862 Gilbert was still busily extending the already large cellars; likewise the vineyard.

But like cool-climate vineyards across the length and breadth of Australia, Pewsey Vale faded away at the end of the 19th century. When Yalumba moved back into the property in 1961, in partnership with Geoffrey Angus Parsons, the proprietor of Pewsey Vale Station, only the history books recorded its prior use as a vineyard. Yalumba correctly foresaw that riesling would be the best-suited variety, and progressively lifted the plantings to 40ha.

In doing so, it chose what it calls the Pewsey Vale clone, thought to have originated from the James Busby collection imported into Australia in the 1830s, and into the Eden Valley in the late 1840s. (Although the Joseph Gilbert vineyard disappeared, other plantings of riesling in the area survived.) Since 2011, the vineyard has been managed biodynamically.

Various other varieties, including cabernet sauvignon and semillon, were trialled, but today the riesling (with additional plantings in the 1980s and 1990s) is the sole variety planted in the vineyard. Yalumba also made history in 1977 when it bottled the riesling of that year under screwcap. Trials before 1977 (in 1969), and history since the late 1990s, fully justified the choice of the closure from a quality (and longevity) viewpoint. However, retailers and consumers rejected the screwcap because it connoted cheapness, and after a few years (including a bizarre time when corks were inserted underneath the screwcap) the experiment was abandoned.

Yalumba did not waver in its faith in the technology, and in the second half of the 1990s quietly put stocks of the Pewsey Vale Contours Riesling (under screwcap) into a maturation reserve scheme, releasing each vintage when five years old, and sweeping all before it on the show circuit.

In 2007, after much experimentation, it also released a 9.5% alc/vol wine modelled on the Mosel (Germany) kabinett. This wine, made in relatively small quantities, is called Prima, and reflects a growing interest in, and appreciation of, this style.

Port Phillip Estate and Kooyong

Est 1987
263 Red Hill Road, Red Hill, Vic 3937
Open 7 days 11–5
Getting there 1 hour's drive from
Melbourne CBD
Contact (03) 5989 4444;
info@portphillipestate.com.au;
www.portphillipestate.com.au
Region Mornington Peninsula
Lat 38°20′S
Elev 25–250m
E° Days 1428
Harvest 5 March–30 April

Estate vineyards 62.3ha
Varieties planted Port Phillip Estate
Pinot noir (10.3), chardonnay (1.8),
shiraz (1.8), sauvignon blanc (0.7);
Kooyong Pinot noir (31), chardonnay
(13.7), pinot gris (3)
Dozens produced 15 000 No increase
planned.
Exports To Hong Kong through Rare
and Fine Wines Limited (ph) +852 2168
6868; enquiry@rarefinewines.com.hk.
Also to all major markets.
Winemaker Sandro Mosele

Key wines

Port Phillip Estate Shiraz
How it is made: The hand-picked grapes are destemmed but not crushed,
moved into the fermenter via escalators to maintain the maximum whole berry
percentage. Depending on the vintage, some whole bunches are retained, and the
wine is fermented in wooden vats and/or open concrete fermenters depending
on vintage conditions. Skin contact ranges between 17 and 30 days, with only
moderate pumpovers and/or hand-plunging. The wine is then matured in used
French oak for 16–18 months. 300 dozen made.

How it tastes: Exceptional purple-crimson colour; always shows sensitive
winemaking, the spicy red cherry and plum fruit supported by subtle French oak
and supple tannins. Cellar to 20 years from vintage.

Best vintages: 2012, 2010, 2008, 2006, 2004

Kooyong Single Vineyard Selection Haven Pinot Noir
How it is made: A largely similar approach to that used with the Port Phillip Estate
Shiraz, except for a lesser period of 12 months' maturation in French oak (15–20%
new). 350 dozen made.

How it tastes: Pure dark fruits are abundant on the bouquet, with Asian spices
and well-handled oak; the palate starts with a refreshing blend of red and dark
fruits and tangy acidity, and then makes way for a rush of firm but fine tannins,
common in top-quality Burgundies, but not in Australia. A pinot built for cellaring
to 15 years or more from vintage.

Best vintages: 2012, 2010, 2006, 2005, 2004

Port Phillip Estate and Kooyong

While these two vineyards are some distance from each other, both are owned by Giorgio Gjergja and wife Dianne, and since November 2009 have been effectively merged at Port Phillip Estate. Giorgio explains, 'I have always had a love of the sea, and a passion for sailing,' and in 1996 he won the Sydney–Hobart Yacht Race, one of the foremost of such events in the world. When he purchased Port Phillip Estate in 2000, he redesigned the label to show the 'Blue Peter' flag used to start yacht races.

In 2004 the Gjergjas purchased Kooyong, and Giorgio decided to sell Ateo, the highly successful electrical manufacturing business he had set up decades earlier. This supplied the money he needed to give the leading Wood Marsh Architecture firm the brief to 'build me a truly outstanding and uncompromisingly architectural landmark, the most exciting new winery in Victoria'.

Over the course of the following three years, the architects did precisely that, designing and supervising the construction of a multi-multi-million-dollar multi-purpose rammed earth building, built deep into the side of the hilltop it occupies. Thus approaching it from Red Hill Road, also on the hilltop, you have no idea how massive it is. Once inside, the panoramic and spectacular view out over the vineyard far below, and the blue water of Western Port Bay in the distance, gives some idea, looking up from the vineyard even more so. It is tailor-made for top-end weddings or special occasion events.

A tasting room, cellar door, and a large restaurant with an exterior deck for outdoor dining if the weather is appropriate, sit on top of a barrel room 5 metres below ground level, with a highly sophisticated bottling line, wine tanks, cellaring space, offices. Also, discreetly separated, there are six luxurious accommodation suites with private decks.

The rammed earth exterior, wide eaves, massively thick walls, solar panels, low-energy lighting and integrated water recycling system all lower the carbon footprint of the building. Moreover, the first stages of winemaking take place at the Kooyong winery, where the greater amount of winery waste is appropriately treated. Sustainable viticulture, and precise attention to canopy management, come as no surprise.

Winemaker Sandro Mosele's first university degree was biological sciences, with honours in genetics. The next step of a PhD didn't appeal, but a holiday looking after a small vineyard did, and Sandro enrolled in Oenology at Charles Sturt University (with credits for all the knowledge he already had), and began making wine at Kooyong, and stayed on board when it was acquired by the Gjergjas, also taking responsibility for Port Phillip Estate.

At Kooyong he produces a range of four single-vineyard block chardonnays and pinot noir, all very different, all reflecting their varying terroir, and all of very high quality; there is also a Kooyong pinot gris. Port Phillip Estate provides a more Catholic selection of sauvignon blanc, rose, shiraz and arneis, plus chardonnay and a distinguished pinot gris, linked by their consistently high quality.

It is an absolute must-visit for any wine/food/lifestyle tourist, but there's no hurry. This will be a landmark for many decades to come.

Rockford

Est 1984
131 Krondorf Road, Tanunda, SA 5352
Open 7 days 11–5
Getting there 1 hour's drive from Adelaide CBD
Contact (08) 8563 2720; info.contact@rockfordwines.com.au; www.rockfordwines.com.au
Region Barossa Valley
Lat 34°29'S
Elev 274m
E° Days 1571
Harvest 27 February–17 April

Leased or contracted vineyards NFP
Varieties planted All grapes purchased through long-term agreements
Dozens produced NFP
Exports To China and Hong Kong through Summergate Fine Wines (ph) toll free 800 820 6929; info@summergate.com. Also to the UK and other major markets.
Winemaker Robert O'Callaghan, Ben Radford

Key wines

Basket Press Shiraz

How it is made: This wine is crafted, not created. The skill is to capture and enhance the fleeting flavours that grapes give from their variety, and extract from the earth, then bottle these as a living record of the vintage they represent. 'My preference is to produce elegant but rich, earthy, soft generous wines that will age – the kind I drank in my youth.' (The words are, of course, not mine, but Rocky's.)

How it tastes: The wine does indeed reflect each vintage, simply because the fermentation technique and oak use is basically the same year after year. Nonetheless, in the best vintages there is another level of superb generosity to the fruit flavours. Cellar to 30 years from vintage.

Best vintages: 2013, 2012, 2010, 2004, 2002

Rifle Range Cabernet Sauvignon

How it is made: Both this wine and the Basket Press are open-fermented for 5–7 days with cultured yeast, pumped over twice a day, then aged in a mix of used French and American oak barrels and vats of various sizes (only 5% new), where it spends 12–24 months. Each grower block or section is aged separately until blending shortly prior to bottling.

How it tastes: A wine of admirable restraint, the bouquet fragrant, the palate focused and linear, tannins, acidity and oak joined seamlessly. Cellar to 25 years from vintage.

Best vintages: 2013, 2012, 2010, 2004, 2002

Rockford

All the clichés come tumbling out when I think about Robert 'Rocky' O'Callaghan. Icon. Rock of Ages. Institution (the man and the winery). Unique. A storyteller beyond compare (in his lyrical and poetic winery newsletters). And most of all, a philosopher.

His grandparents and his parents were Barossa Valley grapegrowers, moving to Rutherglen when his father was appointed manager of Seppelt's vineyards in that region. It was preordained that in 1965 he would become a trainee winemaker at the Seppelt Rutherglen winery.

I cannot help but quote him directly, for he explains his formative years better than I ever could. 'It was a wonderful apprenticeship in the old, ordered, slow and gentle Australian wine trade. The wines I drank, the winemakers from previous generations with whom I associated and everything I absorbed in that period had a major influence on the way Rockford is today. Although I've spent all my life in vineyards and wineries, the pleasure I derive from walking through rows of vines or casks filled with wine has not diminished.'

In the interval between returning from Rutherglen in 1966 and establishing Rockford in 1984, he worked for several long-established wineries in the Barossa Valley, making friends with many of the finest grapegrowers in the region. So by the time he started Rockford he knew exactly what style of wine he wished to make, and precisely which vineyards grew the grapes he needed.

But he had already laid the groundwork for the winery. In 1971 he purchased a 120-year-old stone cottage and outbuildings sitting on 2ha of land in the village of Krondorf. The courtyard-shaped winery which grew from this was slowly built in the same style and with the same materials as the original buildings.

Over the years he collected pieces of old winemaking equipment, including the venerable basket press which gives its name to his most famous wine – this was long before basket presses came back into fashion. It and numerous other pieces of machinery had been discarded by wineries as they modernised. (I can see his lip curl through his bushy red beard.)

So Rockford makes wines not only in truly traditional fashion, but also on the small scale, age and pace as the small patches of his growers' vineyards. When he started making his wines in 1984, he was not in a financial position to buy existing old-vine vineyards, and buying land to plant new vines never crossed his mind.

I imagine he could afford to buy old vineyards now, but I am quite sure he would regard that as treachery. Once again, I have to quote his words if I am to give him the courtesy he deserves: 'Many of the growers have vines that were planted on their own roots, sixty to one hundred years ago. The partnership not only gives Rockford access to exceptional grapes from ancient vines, but also provides consistency and reliability that is not possible from a single vineyard. I have a great deal of respect for the accumulated knowledge, skill and long-term commitment of my growers.'

He has trained some of the very best younger Barossa Valley winemakers, and has a gifted winemaker at his side today – Ben Radford. Where Rockford will go when Rocky joins the pantheon of the greatest winemakers of bygone generations I don't know. But one thing I do know: the cellar door price (as at 2013) of the quite glorious 2012 Basket Press Shiraz will likely be ten times as much as it is today.

Scotchmans Hill

Est 1982
190 Scotchmans Road, Drysdale, Vic 3222
Open 7 days 10.30–5.30
Getting there 1.25 hours' drive from Melbourne CBD
Contact (03) 5251 3176; info@scotchmans.com.au; www.scotchmans.com.au
Region Geelong
Lat 38°09′S
Elev 25–150m
E° Days 1377
Harvest 8 March–21 May

Estate vineyards 47.75ha
Varieties planted Pinot noir (28), sauvignon blanc (8.5), chardonnay (8), shiraz (2.5), riesling (0.75)
Leased or contracted vineyards 74ha
Varieties planted Pinot noir (22), chardonnay (22), shiraz (17.5), sauvignon blanc (6), pinot gris (3), semillon (2), cabernet sauvignon (1), riesling (0.5)
Dozens produced 50 000 No increase planned.
Exports To China and Hong Kong through Watson's Wine (ph) 852 2606 8828; info@watsonswine.com. Also to the UK, Canada, Sweden, Singapore and Dubai.
Winemaker Robin Brockett, Marcus Holt

Key wines

Bellarine Peninsula Pinot Noir
How it is made: The grapes are destemmed, cold-soaked for 5–6 days, followed by a 7-day fermentation in 3-tonne open fermenters, the grapes hand-plunged twice a day. The wine spends 12 months in French oak barriques (30% new), and is lightly fined and filtered. 5000 dozen made.

How it tastes: A full-flavoured wine, with a multi-clone make-up, the dark cherry and plum fruit married well with the French oak and supple tannins. Cellar to 10 years from vintage.

Best vintages: 2012, 2010, 2008, 2007, 2006

Bellarine Peninsula Shiraz
How it is made: Made in similar fashion to the pinot noir, the main difference 33% new French oak barriques, and 16 months' maturation. 3000 dozen made.

How it tastes: Deep purple-crimson in its youth, with a striking vibrancy of flavour to its red and black fruits, with spice and licorice also in play on the long, medium-bodied palate. Cellar to 15 years from vintage.

Best vintages: 2012, 2010, 2008, 2005, 2001

Scotchmans Hill

The genesis of Scotchmans Hill, owned by David and Vivienne Browne, dates back to 1946, when David's father built a holiday cottage at Port Arlington on the tip of the Bellarine Peninsula, joining half a dozen other cottages. Obviously, he developed considerable local knowledge as the years passed, and he was on the spot to buy a 260ha grazing property originally settled by Scottish immigrants in the 1840s, the early years of what was still to be recognised as the state of Victoria.

The hill to which their name was appended was caused by volcanic activity 30 million years ago, which created Port Phillip Bay, Geelong and Mount Bellarine, of which Scotchmans Hill forms part. It enjoys a panoramic view across the Bay to the Melbourne skyline; while the rich black volcanic soil created prime grazing land, it is also a very beautiful property.

The Brownes did not buy the property with the intention of planting vines, but in 1982 they decided to experimentally plant a little under 1ha each of riesling, cabernet sauvignon, gewurztraminer and chardonnay. They were only the second family to plant vines on the Peninsula (which is part of the Geelong region), so there was little or no local experience to draw from.

The first vintage followed in 1986; it and 1987 were contract-made, but in 1988 New Zealand–born, Charles Sturt University–qualified Robin Brockett became the first winemaker, and 'thought he might only stay a couple of years'. He is still there, and has been responsible for making wines of the highest quality, year in, year out, while guiding the business through a long period of sustained growth.

Two strokes of luck became three in 1994, when the nearby National Trust-registered Spray Farm came on the market. Its homestead, built in two stages from 1851, was in a sad state of repair, and its restoration was both lengthy and expensive. It was a labour of love, and formed an integral part of the business, but in 2010 it was sold, Scotchmans Hill securing a lease-back of the vineyard.

Three strokes became four in October 2012, when the former Pettavel winery was purchased by a group of investors. The Brownes have taken a long-term lease of the winery, which they have renamed The Hill. Taking advantage of its location on the edge of the Great Ocean Road, it is the new home for Scotchmans Hill's concerts, functions, weddings and events, with Peter Rowland Catering also a partner.

It will also house bottled wine stocks, packaging materials and so forth, freeing up space in the main winery, which was built in 1998 with groundbreaking technology using an insulated concrete sandwich wall system. The two generations of the Browne family involved in this very successful business will no doubt say you create your own luck, and I would not argue with that. It has always been driven hard, and many of its moves have been in front of the field.

The kaleidoscopic array of 40 different wines is tangible evidence of that success. All the major varieties and blends are represented, reaching as far away as New Zealand (pinot gris and pinot noir), the Clare Valley, Adelaide Hills, McLaren Vale and Adelaide (a super zone) and, closer to home, the Mornington Peninsula. On home base, there are labels covering numerous varieties at all price points. The cellar door is located in the small cottage at the entrance of the Scotchmans Hill property, where the full range of the estate-grown wines, including the Single Vineyard and Cornelius wines, are offered for tasting.

Seppelt

Est 1865
36 Cemetery Road, Great Western, Vic 3377
Open 7 days 10–5
Getting there 2.5 hours' drive from Melbourne CBD
Contact (03) 5361 2239; cellardoor.seppelt@seppelt.com.au; www.seppelt.com.au
Region Grampians
Lat 37°17'S
Elev 240–440m
E° Days 1377
Harvest 7 March–14 May

Estate vineyards 595ha
Varieties planted Shiraz (280), chardonnay (170), pinot noir (48), riesling (35), cabernet sauvignon (20), grenache (15), pinot meunier (12), mourvedre (12), pinot gris (3)
Leased or contracted vineyards 189ha
Varieties planted Shiraz (155), cabernet sauvignon (20), chardonnay (7.5), pinot noir (4.5), pinot meunier (2)
Dozens produced NFP
Exports No significant exports to China and Hong Kong. Exports to the UK and the US.
Winemaker Adam Carnaby, Melanie Chester

Key wines

St Peters Shiraz

How it is made: Takes its name from the shiraz planted in 1923 adjacent to the winery. It is the flagship table wine of Seppelt, and is hand-picked; most is destemmed (not crushed) but with some whole bunch inclusion, spending 10–12 days on skins, before 14 months in French oak, 40% new.

How it tastes: Deeply coloured, the aromas and flavours are of blackberry, licorice, spice and black pepper; the concentration coming from the old vines gives the wine its medium to full body and the ability to absorb the oak; the tannins are never aggressive or dry, hence no fining is needed. Cellar for 30 years or more, but drink whenever you wish.

Best vintages: 2012, 2010, 2008, 2004, 2002

Salinger

How it is made: It is a blend of 60% pinot noir, 30% chardonnay and 10% pinot meunier, and at least 85% of the grapes come from the Henty Vincyard. It is fermented with special cultured yeast, and 60–70% undergoes mlf. The blend is finalised by June of the year of vintage, and is then tiraged to bottle for its second fermentation, and spends 3 years on yeast lees before disgorgement.

How it tastes: The mlf creates an extra layer of complexity without leading to any loss of the finesse and purity of the Henty fruit, 3 years on lees adding notes of brioche. Running through the bouquet and palate are lemon, citrus blossom and white stone fruit flavours with perfectly balanced, refreshing acidity on the finish and aftertaste. Cellar to 4 years from release.

Best vintages: 2012, 2011, 2008, 2006, 2004

Seppelt

Few wineries in Australia have a history as rich as that of Seppelt, born in the days of the gold rush of the 1850s. Not only was there a mass exodus from the cities of Sydney and Melbourne, but would-be miners came from as far as China, the United States and France. Thus in 1853, 20-year-old Anne Marie Blampied and her 15-year-old brother Emile ran away from their home in Lorraine, France, and went first to the town of Beechworth, where Anne Marie met and married Jean Pierre Trouette, a Frenchman from Tarbes.

The three realised there was more money to be made by selling food and provisions to miners than in the very risky business of gold prospecting. They then moved to the epicentre of the gold rush at Great Western, Ballarat not far away, and planted a market garden and vines. At the same time brothers Joseph and Henry Best moved to nearby Ararat, and adopted the same approach, establishing a butcher shop and planting vines in 1862, four years after Trouette and Blampied had established their St Peter's Vineyard.

When the gold ran out, Joseph Best employed out-of-work miners to tunnel through the soft, decomposed granite under his substantial winery, creating the famous drives akin to the limestone cellars of Champagne, and providing perfect conditions for storing bottled wine and large casks and vats of maturing wine. Best died intestate in 1887, and the winery and vineyards were acquired by businessman Hans Irvine for £12 000, a large sum in those days. Irvine sponsored Charles Pierlot, a champagne-maker from Rheims, and began a major expansion of the vineyards.

In 1891 he planted 21ha of a variety he believed to be chardonnay – it was in fact ondenc, which became known as Irvine's White. In 1892 he built large new red-brick cellars, and the cellars had a capacity of 1.35 million litres, the drives 1.7km long.

In 1902 Irvine and Benno Seppelt met, and came to an agreement that if Irvine ever wished to sell the business it would be offered to Seppelt, and in 1918 this came to pass. In 1932 one of the greatest Australian winemakers, Colin Preece, was put in charge. Over the next 31 years he made a series of magnificent and long-lived red table wines in addition to sparkling white and red wines. The first vintage of Moyston Claret was made in 1952, followed by Chalambar in 1953. These were complex blends of different varieties and regions owned by Seppelt.

In 1964 Seppelt planted the first vines on its 94ha Drumborg Vineyard in the Henty region, the coolest on the Australian mainland, specifically for high-quality base wine for sparkling wine, but also riesling, chardonnay, pinot gris and pinot noir for table wine, ultimately leading to the first vintage of Salinger (1983). Its chardonnay and riesling are of outstanding quality, and very long-lived.

In 2007 Seppeltsfield, originally the parent company of Seppelt Great Western, was sold, leaving Seppelt as a high-quality producer of Victorian table wines and sparkling wines, with Show Sparkling Shiraz – traditional method, and 9 years on lees – a personal favourite.

This to one side, Seppelt has the good fortune to be able to choose 40% of the grapes it grows for its own label wines in the Grampians, Henty, Heathcote and Bendigo regions. The remainder of the grapes are used by other brands in the Treasury Wine Estates portfolio.

Seppeltsfield

Est 1851
Seppeltsfield Road, Seppeltsfield via Nuriootpa, SA 5355
Open 7 days 10.30–5
Getting there 1 hour's drive from Adelaide CBD
Contact (08) 8568 6200; cellarsales@seppeltsfield.com.au; www.seppeltsfield.com.au
Region Barossa Valley
Lat 34°29′S
Elev 274m
E° Days 1571
Harvest 27 February–17 April

Estate vineyards 170ha
Varieties planted Predominantly shiraz, with lesser amounts of grenache and mourvedre.
Dozens produced 10 000 May increase to 20 000.
Exports To Hong Kong through Grand Vintage (ph) 852 2521 2628; info@grand-vintage.com.
Winemaker Fiona Donald

Key wines

100 Year Old Para Vintage Tawny
How it is made: This unique wine is a blend of grenache, mourvedre and shiraz, partially fermented before the fortifying spirit is added, taking the alcohol to 17%. As it goes through the next 60 years, the changes of age take place at different rates, before achieving balance. Alcohol increases most rapidly, from 17% to 24% alc/vol, over the first 20 years. The baume (sugar) increases from 6 to 12.5 baume over the first 60 years, then to 14 baume over the final 40 years, and acidity increases from 4 g/l to 9.5 g/l during the first 40 years. The most visible change is from deep purple-red in its first few years to dark mahogany with an olive-green at 100 years.

How it tastes: The wine is so viscous it doesn't pour, just oozes out of the bottle, thickly coating the sides of the glass, slowly separating into retreating separate streams, creating an effect like marble. The hyper-intense flavours of raisin, burnt toffee and plum pudding search out every nook and cranny of your mouth, the aftertaste lingering for an impossibly long time. Should be served in a tiny glass, and micro-sipped.

Best vintages: 1913, 1912, 1911, 1910, 1909

Barossa Shiraz and Shiraz Touriga Grenache
How they are made: These two wines are made in the same way, using a self-cultured yeast, and placed in the open fermenters of the gravity-flow winery, with a minimum of 7 days on skins, then 12–14 months in French oak barriques and hogsheads (10–20% new), racked and returned at least once during the maturation. No filtration, light egg white–fining if required. 400 dozen of each made.

How they taste: Even in the ultimately challenging vintage of 2011, these wines have great flavour and balance, the shiraz with spicy plum and blackberry fruit with supple tannins, the shiraz blend with bright, spicy red fruits, the medium-bodied palate sustained by fine tannins. Cellar to 20 years from vintage.

Best vintages: 2013, 2012, 2011, 2010

Seppeltsfield

So rich is the history of Seppeltsfield that it is impossible to do justice to it in 100 pages, let alone one. Six generations, each with multiple members, guided the business between 1851 and 1985. A mausoleum was built on the top of a hill on the property which houses the remains of 28 members of the family born between 1852 and 1922, and who died between 1913 and 2001.

The founder of the business was Joseph Seppelt, who was born in Silesia in 1813, and became head of a profitable tobacco and snuff company at the age of 20. Sensing the religious troubles in Silesia, he decided to sell the company and migrate to Brazil, but at the last moment impending revolution there led to a change of plans and his ultimate arrival (via two years in Adelaide) in the Barossa Valley in 1852.

He was a focal point for the increase in vineyards from 31ha in 1856 to 2400ha in 1867, the year in which he completed the first stage of today's winery. In 1868 he retired, saying to his 21-year-old son Benno Seppelt, 'Make of this what you will.' He died one month later. Benno and his wife Sophie had amazing energy, having 16 children, twice doubling the size of the winery by 1877, growing the estate vineyards to 225ha, building a port cellar in 1878 in which Benno marked the best two hogsheads (500 litres each) and stipulated that the wine could not be sold until it was 100 years old. The company respected that command, and it was not until 1978 that the first 100 Year Old Para Liqueur was sold, and every year hogsheads are laid down for their turn in 100 years' time.

In 1888 Benno built the gravity-flow winery, on a series of terraces down the side of a long hill. It was the largest and most advanced of its type in the world, but was decommissioned in the 1980s due to the need for restoration. It was fully recommissioned prior to the 2010 vintage.

The third, fourth and fifth generations all contributed to the growth of the company, but the next visionary was Karl Seppelt (a graduate of Roseworthy Agricultural College). In 1964 he identified the coolest area on the Australian mainland as Drumborg in the Henty region, and pioneered viticulture there; in 1965 he identified and planted the first vines in the region now known as Padthaway.

Then came a series of corporate takeovers which resulted in then owner Foster's selling the Seppeltsfield brand (but not Seppelt), the winery, adjoining vineyard (but not the cool region vineyards) and wine stock to The Seppeltsfield Estate Trust in 2007. Viticultural magnate (and one time Seppelt sparkling winemaker) Warren Randall became the CEO, and between 2009 and 2013 built his shareholding from 50% to 90%. Nathan Waks, former principal cellist of the Sydney Symphony Orchestra, and major Barossa vigneron Carl Lindner both have minority shareholdings.

These changes led to the expenditure of the $1 million needed to bring the magnificent winery back into production for both high-quality red table and fortified wines, and to bring back to life the numerous heritage-listed houses, offices, workshops (including a full-time cooper on site) and storage buildings. A large tasting room is another feature, all set in immaculate, park-like grounds. For any first-time visitor to the Barossa Valley, their tour must start or finish here (or both).

Seville Estate

Est 1970
65 Linwood Road, Seville, Vic 3139
Open 7 days 10–5
Getting there 55 minutes' drive from Melbourne CBD
Contact (03) 5964 2622;
wine@sevilleestate.com.au;
www.sevilleestate.com.au
Region Yarra Valley
Lat 37°42'S
Elev 50–350m
E° Days 1253
Harvest 1 March–25 April

Estate vineyards 8.4ha
Varieties planted Pinot noir (3), shiraz (2.2), chardonnay (2.1), cabernet sauvignon (0.7), riesling (0.4)
Dozens produced 7000 May increase to 10 000.
Exports To China and Hong Kong through Origin Star (ph) 61 3 9988 2763; Estelle@originstar.com.au.
Winemaker Dylan McMahon

Key wines

Old Vine Reserve Shiraz

How it is made: The grapes come from the best of the vines planted in 1972. The grapes are largely destemmed, but with some whole bunch inclusion in the small open fermenter; hand-plunged and basket-pressed, then spends 12 months in French oak (20% new). Usually neither filtered nor fined. 110 dozen made.

How it tastes: Deeply coloured, and remarkably concentrated and powerful, with spice and cracked pepper running through the deep black cherry fruit. Cellar to 25 years from vintage.

Best vintages: 2013, 2012, 2010, 2004, 2001

Old Vine Reserve Cabernet Sauvignon

How it is made: In very similar fashion to the shiraz, likewise coming from the best vines from the 1972 plantings. No whole bunches are included in the ferment, which is initiated by wild yeast (as it is for the shiraz). 90 dozen made.

How it tastes: Not made every vintage, but when it is, a particularly rich and generous wine, with an abundance of blackcurrant fruit, ripe tannins and integrated oak. Cellar to 30 years from vintage.

Best vintages: 2012, 2010, 2006, 2003, 2001

Seville Estate

Lilydale general practitioner the late Peter McMahon, and wife Margaret, purchased the beautiful property on which Seville Estate now stands in 1970. It is on the deep red volcanic soil of the Upper Yarra Valley, with a mix of gentle and steep slopes. Some of the records suggest the first vines were planted that year, others point to 1972.

What is not in doubt is the eclectic range of varieties planted – eclectic by the standards of the day, at least. Peter McMahon's close friend and fellow GP, the late John Middleton of Mount Mary, was vociferous in his disregard for riesling and shiraz, yet these two were major successes for Seville Estate from the outset.

Cabernet sauvignon was another bold choice: this part of the Yarra Valley is cooler and wetter than the Lower Yarra Valley, and given the climate of the 1970s and '80s, achieving full ripeness could be a major challenge. The final two varieties, chardonnay and pinot noir, were – and are – eminently suited and, with the shiraz, are the heart of the business. Moreover, when Yeringberg pulled out its shiraz in 1981 because there was no demand for the variety, Peter McMahon stuck to his guns, and was duly rewarded, for it remains a benchmark for cool-climate shiraz.

Peter McMahon was the first vigneron of note to plant vines on the red soils, and thus to confront the issues caused by the vigour of the growth. The solution was some radical surgery, and the installation of a T-trellis to open up the canopy to much more sunlight penetration, achieving a natural balance. The 'Young' vines, planted in 1996, use a contemporary vertical shoot position (VSP), a more efficient way of achieving the same outcome.

When running the vineyard and cellar door ceased to be a labour of love, after 26 years, a partnership associated with Brokenwood acquired a controlling interest. When the logistics of long-distance management became obvious, Graham and Margaret Van Der Meulen fulfilled a long-term wish to own and run a cool-climate vineyard and bought Seville Estate in December 2005.

They have a range of qualifications – Margaret with a Masters Degree in Wine Science and Viticulture from the University of Melbourne, and also a Certificate III in Commercial Cookery – and also have Peter and Margaret McMahon's grandson, Dylan McMahon, as their winemaker.

Dylan not only has a Bachelor of Wine Science from Charles Sturt University, but has worked vintages in Alsace (Hugel & Fils 2002 and Paul Blanck 2003) and in Burgundy (Jean-Claude Boisset 2008).

The wines come in four ranges: Dr McMahon Shiraz at the top; then Old Vine Reserve Shiraz, Cabernet Sauvignon, Chardonnay and Pinot Noir; next Estate Riesling, Chardonnay, Pinot Noir, Shiraz and Blanc de Blanc; and at the bottom, the Barber range of Fume Blanc, Chardonnay, Rose, Pinot Noir and Shiraz. The estate-grown top end provides wines of great quality, and the Barber wines (from contract and estate-grown grapes) are impressive value for money.

Given that the vineyard is on the red soils of the cooler Upper Yarra Valley, it is not surprising that the finest, most elegant, wines are chardonnay and pinot noir. The chardonnay is one of many examples which make the Yarra Valley one of the top four regions for chardonnay. The special quality of the region's chardonnays is the length of the palate, reducing the need for much oak influence. What is surprising is the quality of the Reserve cabernet sauvignon; shiraz has, of course, long proved its suitability in cool climates such as this.

Shaw + Smith

Est 1989
136 Jones Road, Balhannah, SA 5242
Open 7 days 11–5
Getting there 30 minutes' drive from Adelaide CBD
Contact (08) 8398 0500; info@shawandsmith.com; www.shawandsmith.com
Region Adelaide Hills
Lat 34°00'S
Elev 496m
E° Days 1359
Harvest 12 March–30 April

Estate vineyards 83ha
Varieties planted Sauvignon blanc (42), chardonnay (21), pinot noir (15), shiraz (5)
Dozens produced NFP
Exports To China and Hong Kong through Links Concept Company Limited (ph) 852 2802 2818; marketing@linksconcept.com. Also to the UK, the US and other major markets.
Winemaker Martin Shaw, Adam Wadewitz

Key wines

M3 Chardonnay

How it is made: The grapes are hand-picked, sorted and whole-bunch-pressed direct to barrel with no settling, wild yeast fermentation, and matured for 9 months in French oak (30% new) on lees, with partial mlf. The wine is filtered but not fined prior to bottling.

How it tastes: This is a very elegant and finely structured wine, with white stone fruit, melon and grapefruit flavours, the acidity perfectly balanced, the oak restrained. Cellar to 8 years from vintage.

Best vintages: 2013, 2012, 2010, 2006, 2002

Shiraz

How it is made: The grapes are hand-picked, crushed, and undergo a pre-fermentation cold soak in both open and closed fermenters, spending 15–20 days on skins in total. The wine spends 15 months in French oak (30% new) and is filtered, but not fined, prior to being bottled.

How it tastes: A very consistent high-quality medium-bodied wine from vintage to vintage, notable for its balance of red and black fruits, ripe, almost silky, tannins and perfectly integrated French oak. Cellar 15–20 years from vintage.

Best vintages: 2013, 2012, 2009, 2007, 2006

Shaw + Smith

It is not often that one can say a new winery was bound to succeed, but the credentials of cousins Martin Shaw and Michael Hill Smith made success certain for this venture. Michael Hill Smith comes from a distinguished winemaking family in South Australia. He was the first Australian to be made a Master of Wine and has always been at the forefront of Australia's presence overseas as an international wine judge, and long-term wine consultant to Singapore Airlines. His contribution to both the domestic and international success of the wine industry was recognised in 2008 when he was made a Member of the Order of Australia.

Martin Shaw graduated in Oenology from Roseworthy Agricultural College (now part of Adelaide University) in 1981, and worked with Brian Croser at Petaluma for eight years before setting up a 'Flying Winemaker' network in France, Chile, Spain and New Zealand while also joining forces with Michael Hill Smith to found Shaw + Smith in 1989. Shaw continues to consult to wineries in Australia and overseas.

Their business plan was as successful as it was simple. For the first five years they purchased Adelaide Hills grapes and made the wine at Petaluma winery, thus avoiding capital expenditure and allowing them to concentrate on brand-building and marketing.

In 1994 they purchased their first property, at Woodside, naming it M3 Vineyard to reflect Michael's brother Matthew Hill Smith's involvement as a financial partner in the business. Here they close-planted chardonnay (the primary source of their high-quality M3 Chardonnay) and sauvignon blanc (the latter regarded as one of Australia's best, and a major contributor to cash flow each year).

The 46ha property at Balhannah was acquired in 1999. The following year the winery and adjacent cellar door were built on the idyllic site, with green lawn stretching down to an expansive lake teeming with bird life. Extensive use of glass maximises the impact of the beauty of the development and its inspired architecture. In the same year, sauvignon blanc, shiraz, pinot noir and riesling were planted, on the free-draining sandy loam over red clay and underlying quartzite and shale.

In 2012 they had the opportunity to acquire a 20ha vineyard at Lenswood, planted in 1999 primarily to chardonnay and pinot noir, with some sauvignon blanc. The property is undulating, with some very steep slopes rising to 500m – compared to the 420m of the other two vineyards.

Between 2002 and 2009 the winery was enhanced by a high-speed bottling line and large underground, temperature-controlled facilities for receiving and pressing grapes. From being totally dependent on others, they now grow 75% of their grape requirements, and can provide winemaking services to others.

They also put in place wide-ranging environmental practices, using biological controls wherever possible in the vineyards, minimising the use of insecticides, eliminating herbicides, and using seaweed fertilisers (not synthetics) where required. They have cut water use to 45% of the industry average, with only rainwater used in the winery, and water recycled where possible. Greenhouse gas emissions are monitored and reported to help build future protocols for their management. In 2013 they purchased an important, mature vineyard in the south of Tasmania which will be developed as a separate, stand-alone venture.

Stanton & Killeen Wines

Est 1875
440 Jacks Road, Murray Valley
Highway, Rutherglen, Vic 3685
Open Mon–Sat 9–5, Sun 10–5
Getting there 3 hours' drive from
Melbourne CBD
Contact (02) 6032 9457;
wine@stantonandkilleenwines.com.au;
www.stantonandkilleenwines.com.au
Region Rutherglen
Lat 36°03′S
Elev 170m
E° Days 1591
Harvest 17 February–27 March

Estate vineyards 38ha
Varieties planted Brown muscat (13),
shiraz (7), durif (4), muscadelle (4), plus
small plantings of a further 10 varieties
including tinta roriz, tinta barocca,
touriga, tinta cao (10)
Dozens produced 20 000 No increase
planned.
Exports No exports to China and Hong
Kong at present.
Winemaker Brendan Heath, Simon
Killeen

Key wines

Durif

How it is made: The grape is a cross between syrah (shiraz) and peloursin, bred
in France by Dr Durif in 1880; the wine is conventionally crushed and fermented,
but then spends 2 years in new and used oak during which time the formidable
tannins are given space to sufficiently soften.

How it tastes: Deeply coloured, the wine has a mix of plum and more earthy
flavours which speak of both its place of origin and its variety. Cellar to 15 years
from vintage.

Best vintages: 2009, 2006, 2005, 2004, 2002

Vintage Fortified

How it is made: Australia can no longer use the word 'port', so simply uses the
expression 'vintage fortified', sometimes coupled with the word 'red'.

How it tastes: The wine has true vintage port characters (the inclusion of shiraz
doesn't diminish its impact), with spicy dark cherry fruits and a lively, high-quality
finish, the fortifying spirit not obvious. Cellar to 25+ years.

Best vintages: 2010, 2009, 2005, 2004, 2002

Stanton & Killeen Wines

Seven generations of the Stanton family have been involved in this emblematic business, with up to three generations working together at the one time. The story starts with the arrival in Australia in the 1850s of Timothy Stanton (1803–96) and son John Lewis Stanton (1845–1925), lured from East Anglia in England by the gold rush. They soon decided that farming, and winemaking, would provide greater financial rewards, and in 1875 the first vintage of Stanton Wines was made, in a red gum slab winery on property still owned by the family.

When phylloxera struck the vineyard, Timothy's grandson John Richard Stanton (1872–1955) replanted the vineyard, but when his son Charles 'Jack' Stanton (1895–1989) returned safely from World War I, his father bought him a parcel of farming land that had once been a vineyard (abandoned after phylloxera) and had concrete vats and tanks still in place from an onsite winery built in the 1890s – but with no walls or roof remaining. Jack soon built a new winery using second-hand materials from the defunct Great Southern Gold Mine.

In 1948 the manager of the Rutherglen Viticultural Research Station, Norman Killeen (1919–2004), married Jack's daughter Joan. Norman left the Research Station in 1953 and joined his father-in-law as a business partner. Ironically, booming wool and food prices led them to reduce the size of the vineyard to focus on the farming potential of the 360ha property. By the 1960s the Australian wine industry had begun to change for the better, and the focus changed permanently. Norm (as he was known) had an agricultural science degree and much practical knowledge of winemaking, so in 1967 took over as winemaker of the newly christened Stanton & Killeen Wines. Plantings recommenced the following year.

In 1977 a second property 1km away from the 'home' Moodemere vineyard was purchased; named Quandong after the 1875 winery, it has the most highly regarded red loam soil of the region. Two years later an insulated building for barrel and bottle storage was added, and the winery itself was progressively updated. In 1986 a new cellar door replaced the tin shed which had served the purpose until then.

Sixth generation Chris Killeen (1954–2007) took over winemaking responsibilities in 1980, and initiated the planting of traditional Portuguese varieties of tinta roriz, tinta barocca, touriga and tinta cao. In due course he used these to make vintage port in the Portuguese style, with a lower baume level (thus less sweet) than traditional Australian vintage ports. He also lifted the quality of the table wines (mainly red) and the regional specialties of muscat and topaque (formerly called Tokay).

Tragically, Chris did not enjoy the longevity of his Stanton or Killeen progenitors, succumbing to cancer, but leaving a reputation second to none. His son Simon (born 1986), the seventh generation of this winemaking family, has gained praise for his dry red table wine made from the Portuguese varieties, working alongside chief winemaker Brendan Heath. Simon has named his red wine The Prince in honour of his father, who was named 'The Prince of Port' by his fellow Rutherglen vignerons. However, durif and shiraz are the leading red table wines here, as they are throughout the region.

Stefano Lubiana

Est 1990
60 Rowbottoms Road, Granton, Tas 7030
Open Thurs–Mon 11–3 (closed July and some public hols)
Getting there 20 minutes' drive from Hobart CBD
Contact (03) 6263 7457; wine@slw.com.au; www.slw.com.au
Region Southern Tasmania
Lat 42°53′S
Elev 55m
E° Days 1195
Harvest 3 April–26 May

Estate vineyards 24.5ha
Varieties planted Pinot noir (13), chardonnay (4.6), riesling (2.3), merlot (1.6), pinot gris (1.4), sauvignon blanc (1.3), other (0.3)
Dozens produced NFP
Exports To China through Pran Cellar Australia (ph) 86 21 5178 0108; tina@cellaraustralia.com. Also to the UK, Japan and Singapore.
Winemaker Steve Lubiana

Key wines

Estate Pinot Noir
How it is made: Is open-fermented in a mix of stainless steel and oak vats using indigenous (wild) yeasts, hand-plunged, with 20% whole bunches; there is both pre- and post-ferment maceration, and the wine spends 14–15 months in French oak (25% new).

How it tastes: Deliciously fresh fruit aromas and flavours range through cherry and plum fruit, with silky tannins and great length; new oak can sometimes intrude when the wine is young. Cellar to 12 years from vintage.

Best vintages: 2012, 2009, 2008, 2005, 1998

Vintage Brut
How it is made: Made using the traditional method; in other words, the second fermentation takes place in the bottle that is ultimately disgorged and sold. The Vintage Brut is a blend of 60% chardonnay and 40% pinot noir, not taken through mlf, but spends 8 years on lees prior to disgorgement.

How it tastes: Bright, pale straw-green, excellent mousse; strong toasty/brioche aromas, layers of fruit flavour, with some pinot influence evident. Surprising freshness continues long after the wine is disgorged. Cellar to 12 years from release.

Best vintages: 2004, 2003, 1999, 1998, 1995

Stefano Lubiana

Stefano (always called Steve) Lubiana is a fifth-generation winemaker, who began his career in the hot South Australian Riverland region. He and wife Monique moved in 1990 to one of the coolest parts of Australia: Southern Tasmania. His aim was to make high-quality sparkling wine. They purchased a beautiful property on the banks of the Derwent River, and in 1991 planted the first 2.5ha of their current 24.5ha estate vineyard. In 1998 they began organic management of the vines, and thereafter moved to full biodynamic growing.

This conversion was founded on the family's perception of their property as a place of wild beauty, refreshed by the world's cleanest air and embellished by rare gifts: ancient soils, endless clear skies, and the maritime influences of the vast Southern Ocean.

In the early years, Steve Lubiana offered specialised contract winemaking services for other local wineries wishing to make sparkling wine from their own grapes, but as the reputation and size of the Lubiana production grew, he became less dependent on the cash flow earned by contract winemaking, and now is entirely committed to only making the Lubiana wines, both table and sparkling.

In 2012 Steve and Monique commenced an ambitious building program in two parts. The first was a new cellar-door tasting facility, a biodynamic interpretation centre and a 40-seat restaurant. The second was the construction of a vaulted-ceiling underground barrel hall, which will deliver enhanced wine quality through an energy-efficient and humidified environment: the temperature will remain at 14°C throughout the year.

The biodynamic approach includes miniature sheep grazing in the vineyard throughout the year; they are too small to reach up to the grape bunches or any part of the vine canopy in the growing season. The new restaurant will also use herbs and vegetables grown in an expanded biodynamic garden.

Steve Lubiana is not only a skilled winemaker, but is also constantly thinking about new approaches to and ways of making his wines, especially the pinot noir, which is now his most important wine: over half the vineyard is planted to this variety. Thus in 2008 he made three special pinot noirs: the first was a winemaking experiment, with the wine remaining in the fermenter in contact with the grape skins for 146 days (compared to a normal 30 days) before being pressed.

The second and third experiments involved separate blocks in the vineyard, with vines of different ages and different clones; 25% new oak was used for one wine, 75% new oak for the other. One wine was closed with a screwcap, the other with Diam cork. Sufficient stocks of the three wines have been retained to allow repeated comparative tastings over future years as the wines mature.

The lesson from the experiments, but also from the 2009 and '10 vintages, is that even in Tasmania – with its generally favourable environment for pinot noir – the winemaker (here Steve Lubiana) has to respond proactively to the differences in the composition of the grapes (however slight) from year to year.

Stonier Wines

Est 1978
Cnr Thompson's Lane/Frankston-Flinders Road, Merricks, Vic 3916
Open 7 days 11–5
Getting there 1 hour's drive from Melbourne CBD
Contact (03) 5989 8300; stonier@stonier.com.au; www.stonier.com.au
Region Mornington Peninsula
Lat 38°20'S
Elev 25–250m
E° Days 1428
Harvest 5 March–30 April

Estate vineyards 17ha
Varieties planted Chardonnay (8.5), pinot noir (8.5)
Leased or contracted vineyards 92.6ha
Varieties planted Pinot noir (52), chardonnay (40.6)
Dozens produced 25 000 May increase to 40 000.
Exports To China and Hong Kong through ASC Fine Wines (ph) 8621 3423 9599; www.asc-wines.com. Also to most major markets.
Winemaker Michael Symons

Key wines

Reserve Chardonnay
How it is made: Hand-picked and whole-bunch-pressed, the grapes coming from 2 or 3 of the best estate vineyards, cultured yeast added before going to French oak puncheons and barriques (25% new, previously 35%) for primary fermentation and mlf (previously 100% went through mlf, but now 30–80% does). Racked and blended in November, then returned to barrel until late April. Not fined, but crossflow-filtered. 700–1400 dozen made.

How it tastes: A vibrant and juicy wine, the tangy, concise and focused palate with grapefruit and white peach running through to the long finish, the oak restrained and integrated. Cellar to 10 years from vintage.

Best vintages: 2013, 2011, 2010, 2009, 2005

Reserve Pinot Noir
How it is made: A blend of 6 vineyards, 3 from Merricks and 3 from the cooler Red Hill/Main Ridge areas. Hand-picked and destemmed except for 2–5% whole bunches, each component separately fermented in 1–3-tonne fermenters, with some pre-fermentation cold soak. Light hand-plunging, with temperatures up to 32°C; total time on skins 18–30 days, then 13–14 months in French oak barriques (25% new). Not fined, but crossflow-filtered. 450–1400 dozen made.

How it tastes: Varies with vintage climate, with perfumed red fruits and spices in the cooler vintages, black cherry and plum joining the red fruits in the majority of years, forest floor and fine tannins adding to flavour and texture complexity. Cellar to 8 years from vintage.

Best vintages: 2012, 2010, 2009, 2007, 2005

Stonier Wines

The Stonier family, headed by patriarch Brian Stonier AO, was one of the pioneers of the Mornington Peninsula, planting chardonnay at Merricks in 1978. Pinot noir followed in 1982, the same year that produced the first Stonier wine (chardonnay). In 1986 the first Stonier pinot noir was released, and by 1988 plantings had increased to 6ha.

In 1991 a new winery was completed, designed by noted Melbourne architect Daryl Jackson, and opened by then Governor of Victoria, Dr David McCaughey. In my *1992 Pocket Guide to the Wines of Australia and New Zealand*, I commented that it had become the Mornington Peninsula's largest producer (with 5000 dozen bottles) and was 'set to become known throughout Australia', giving it an AA rating (the highest possible under the system I then used). The first Stonier Reserve wines were made in the exceptional 1992 vintage, and released in 1993. The following year Stonier did some trailblazing by winning two trophies at the Royal Adelaide Wine Show, for Best Pinot Noir and Best Varietal Red Wine of Show, with its 1993 Reserve Pinot Noir.

This success led Petaluma, headed by Brian Croser, to negotiate a friendly acquisition of Stonier, leaving Brian Stonier to continue to guide the business, and also leaving winemaker Tod Dexter in place. The Petaluma strategy of assembling a group of complementary wineries in Pemberton, the Goulburn Valley, Clare Valley, Mornington Peninsula, Adelaide Hills and Coonawarra was so tempting that in 2001 Lion Nathan made a takeover offer for Petaluma (then a listed company) which ultimately succeeded.

Lion Nathan, a New Zealand liquor group in turn owned by Kirin of Japan, has proved to be a largely hands-off owner, also bringing St Hallett into the fold, and supporting the desire of all the wineries in the group to make the best wines possible.

While Stonier has resolutely (and in my opinion, very wisely) limited its portfolio to chardonnay and pinot noir for both table and sparkling wines, its production has steadily grown to encompass a two-tier structure, with a series of limited-production, single-vineyard and reserve wines at the top, and a Mornington Peninsula chardonnay and pinot noir made from contract-grown grapes sourced from all parts of the Peninsula. Thus the chardonnay may have components from as many as 14 different vineyards.

Stonier has also benefited from stable, long-serving winemaking teams headed by Tod Dexter, then Geraldine McFaul, and now Mike Symons (appointed in 2009). The result has been a style as consistent as it is elegant, its ability to stand up with cool-climate pinot noirs from around the world demonstrated by its annual SIPNOT blind tasting of 12 highly rated wines from Burgundy, Oregon, New Zealand and elsewhere in Australia. It is presented to an audience of 160 covering media, winemakers and – predominantly – lovers of pinot noir, who cheerfully pay for a seat at the event.

This may be one of the most senior wineries on the Mornington Peninsula, but that does not stop it moving with the times. It has embarked on a serious sustainability program that touches on all aspects of its operations. It is one of the few wineries in Australia to measure its carbon footprint in detail, using the officially recognised system of WFA; it is steadily reducing its consumption of electricity; it uses rainwater, collected from the winery roof, for rinsing and washing in the winery, as well as supplying the winery in general; it has created a balanced ecosystem in the vineyard by strategic planting of cover crops and reduction of sprays; and has reduced its need to irrigate. None of this has in any way affected (other than beneficially) the quality of its wines.

Summerfield

Est 1979
5967 Stawell-Avoca Road, Moonambel, Vic 3478
Open 7 days 10–5
Getting there 2.25 hours' drive from Melbourne CBD
Contact (03) 5467 2264; info@summerfieldwines.com; www.summerfieldwines.com
Region Pyrenees
Lat 37°05'S
Elev 220–375m
E° Days 1440
Harvest 24 February–14 April

Estate vineyards 14ha
Varieties planted Shiraz (8.3), cabernet sauvignon (2.6), merlot (2.4), sauvignon blanc (0.7)
Leased or contracted vineyards 20ha
Varieties planted Shiraz (15), cabernet sauvignon (5)
Dozens produced 10 000 No increase planned.
Exports To China through Sulu Wines (ph) 0061 39602 2348; sarah@suluwines.com.au.
Winemaker Mark Summerfield

Key wines

Reserve Shiraz and Reserve Cabernet Sauvignon

How they are made: The making regime for these two wines is the same. Fruit is hand-picked early in the morning to keep the grapes cool, and thus achieve a slow start to fermentation with cultured yeast. The grapes are mainly destemmed, resulting in a large number of whole berries in the ferment. The mlf is initiated halfway through the fermentation process; immediately the fermentation is completed, the wines are basket-pressed and allowed to partially clear overnight before being taken to American oak puncheons (30% new), where they spend the next 18 months. The wines are not fined, but are lightly filtered. 300–600 dozen made.

How they taste: The Reserve Shiraz, always with deep, clear purple-crimson in its youth, has a rich and voluptuous display of black cherries, spice and licorice, the oak adding vanilla to the mix. Cellar to 30 years from vintage. The Reserve Cabernet Sauvignon is deeply coloured, the wine has good varietal character from the outset to the finish, blackcurrant fruit balanced and complexed by ripe, earthy tannins and vanillan oak. Cellar to 30 years from vintage.

Best vintages: 2011, 2009, 2008, 2005, 2000

Summerfield

The Summerfield family has lived in the Pyrenees region, and specifically in the Moonambel district, for 140 years. Ian Summerfield's parents owned and ran the Moonambel General Store for 45 years, and Ian worked there until it was sold in 1962. He then joined his brother Russell in running the family's grazing property, although it was a difficult time for graziers, so much so that Ian was happy to sell a section of the property in the mid-1960s to local earth mover Wal Henning. He had the equipment and general knowledge to begin the development of a substantial vineyard (in 1969), which was sold in 1972 to wealthy Californian businessman and grapegrower John Goelet – and which was to become Taltarni.

In 1970 Ian Summerfield planted 4ha of vines (mainly shiraz), intending to sell the grapes to his neighbour Taltarni. When the building of its winery took longer than expected, the grapes went to Seppelt, a win/win outcome, for former Seppelt winemaker and viticulturist Leo Hurley gave him much useful viticultural advice.

By 1979 Ian Summerfield had decided to take the next step and begin making his own wine. Dominique Portet, Taltarni winemaker, and Leo Hurley both gave assistance, but wine quality was variable until Victorian State Government oenologist Drew Noon came on the scene. He led to a transformation in the small winery prior to the 1988 vintage; all the old oak and wine in storage was disposed of, replaced by a refrigeration plant and new American oak barrels and vats.

Quality soared, and son Craig (known as Jo) graduated with a degree in Oenology from Roseworthy (now Adelaide University). Events then moved quickly: Jo became interested in the opportunities for winemaking in China (long before most others), and married Cui We, CW for short, in 2002. Tragically, he lost a short battle with cancer in June 2006.

In the meantime, responsibility for winemaking at Summerfield had been passed on by father Ian to youngest son Mark, with Ian returning to his first love, the vineyard. He had overseen the planting of a further 10ha of vines by the early 2000s, and also secured contract growers for substantial amounts of shiraz and cabernet sauvignon.

Since 1990 the style of Summerfield's shiraz and cabernet sauvignon has been very consistent, the focus on richness and plentiful but soft tannins. Subject to the occasional challenge of nature, the quality of the wines has risen, as the vines have grown older and Mark Summerfield's experience has grown year by year. Even the extremely difficult 2011 vintage, with incessant rain, failed to impinge on the quality of the wines.

American oak, and substantial levels of alcohol, remain the foundation stones of the shiraz and cabernet sauvignon, which are Summerfield's most important wines. They may not please the personal tastes of some, but they appeal greatly to the loyal clientele Summerfield enjoys in Australia and China.

Visitors to the winery (and region) can stay at one of five fully equipped studio apartments or one Winemakers Apartment, a substantial contribution to quality accommodation not widely available in the region.

Tahbilk

Est 1860
Goulburn Valley Highway, Tabilk, Vic 3608
Open Mon–Sat 9–5, Sun 11–5
Getting there 1.5 hours' drive from Melbourne CBD
Contact (03) 5794 2555; admin@tahbilk.com.au; www.tahbilk.com.au
Region Nagambie Lakes
Lat 36°42′S
Elev 130–200m
E° Days 1534
Harvest 22 February–8 April

Estate vineyards 224.7ha
Varieties planted Marsanne (38.5), shiraz (34.4), sauvignon blanc (30.7), cabernet sauvignon (26.6), chardonnay (22.4), viognier (21.4), merlot (13.8), semillon (12.9), riesling (9.1), verdelho (4), roussanne (2.9), cabernet franc (2.4), grenache (1.9), mourvedre (1.8), savagnin (1.3), tempranillo (0.6)
Dozens produced 120 000 May increase to 135 000.
Exports To China through Longfellows (Shanghai) Trading Co. Ltd (ph) 8621 5058 8537; info@longfellows.com.cn. Also to the UK, the US and other major markets.
Winemaker Alister Purbrick, Neil Larson, Alan George

Key wines

Shiraz and Cabernet Sauvignon

How they are made: Both wines are made in the same way, using similar techniques to those of 50 years ago, although some of the equipment is new, such as the membrane (bag) press. The grapes are crushed and destemmed, and the must is pumped into casks in the original 1860 and 1875 cellars. Those casks are made of Polish or French oak, the majority being well over 100 years old, some 150 years old. Cultured yeasts are added, and the fermentation takes 7–10 days to complete. When complete, the wine is pressed, the skins removed, the casks cleaned, and the wine returned for 18 months' maturation in the same casks, the cellars at a natural year-round temperature of 15–16°C. The wine is then filtered and bottled, and matured in bottle for a further 12–18 months prior to labelling and release.

How they taste: The wines are very deliberately made using the philosophy and methods developed by Eric Purbrick, placing maximum emphasis on the interaction in the vineyard of the variety, the soil/terroir and the climate. New oak plays little or no role, and while strict attention to detail is of fundamental importance, this is a form of natural winemaking. The resultant wines are medium- to full-bodied, deeply coloured, and age with grace over many decades.

Best vintages: 2013, 2009, 2008, 2007, 2002

Tahbilk

Tahbilk is a magical combination of unique history, unsurpassed beauty, triumph over adversity, a proud lineage of family ownership, and estate-grown wines that are of high quality and speak clearly of their place of origin. If I had to choose one destination for a first-time visitor to an Australian winery, it would be Tahbilk.

The establishment date of 1860 saw the commencement – and completion – of the underground cellar and original winery building, and the planting of 25ha of vines, increased to 80ha the following year. In 1875, the 'new cellar', running at right angles to the 1860 cellar, was excavated. In 1882, the four-storey tower that is depicted on the wine labels of today was built; the first level was used for winemaking until the 1940s.

The arrival of phylloxera in the 1880s, the departure of key managers, and the ownership of the property by an uninterested English family, led to a period of near neglect. But in 1925 Reginald Purbrick purchased Chateau Tahbilk (as it was then known), intending to remove the vines and close the winery, then subdivide the property into dairy farms (something he knew a lot about, having sold his milk business to Nestlé for a large sum).

But he was persuaded that the winery and vineyards could be rehabilitated, and in 1929 his son, Eric, despite having just been called to the Bar of Inner Temple in London, decided he would accept the task of rehabilitation. He was a man of immense charm and erudition, and I count it my good fortune that I came to know him quite well in his later years.

Eric's son John became involved in the business, especially the large pastoral side, but the true mantle passed to grandson Alister, who graduated in oenology, and returned to the winery as the first formally qualified winemaker. Alister has proved to be a great deal more than just a winemaker, accelerating the regeneration of the business, serving with distinction on a number of wine industry boards, and driving the formation of the First Families of Wine. His daughter Hayley (of the fifth generation) joined Tahbilk in 2010 to manage the Wine Club and tourism operations.

The tourism side has involved the development of boardwalks and small boat access to the series of lagoons forming part of the large Goulburn River (which runs through the property) system, a capacious restaurant overlooking the lagoon part of the development. It goes alongside an in-depth commitment to the environment which made the business carbon neutral by 2012.

Red wines – notably shiraz and cabernet sauvignon – are produced at a number of levels. The 1860 Vines Shiraz seldom exceeded 200 dozen bottles, but a freak frost killed 40% in 2007, reducing the current production to between 100 and 150 dozen bottles. Next are the Eric Stevens Purbrick Shiraz (from 75–80-year-old vines) and the Eric Stevens Purbrick Cabernet Sauvignon (from vines dating back to 1949). The heart of the winery is the varietal shiraz and cabernet sauvignon, which are also made from vines many decades old.

The other unique wine is the 1927 Vines Marsanne, from the block planted in that year, and believed to be the largest single planting of vines as old as these.

A founding member of Australia's First Families of Wine.

Tamar Ridge

Est 1994
653 Auburn Road, Kayena, Tas 7270
Open 7 days 9–5
Getting there 40 minutes' drive from
Launceston CBD
Contact (03) 6394 1114;
info@brownbrothers.com.au;
www.brownbrothers.com.au
Region Northern Tasmania
Lat 41°27′S
Elev 81m
E° Days 1208
Harvest 11 March–10 May

Estate vineyards 303ha
Varieties planted Pinot noir (123.9),
chardonnay (68.6), sauvignon blanc
(48.2), pinot gris (35.3), riesling (21.2),
gewurztraminer (2.9), savagnin (1.5),
merlot (1.4)
Dozens produced 56 000 May increase
to 65 000.
Exports No exports to China as yet.
Exports to other major markets.
Winemaker Tom Ravech

Key wines

Pinot Noir
How it is made: Hand-picked, destemmed into open 5-tonne fermenters and then
a period of cold maceration before the must is warmed for a natural (indigenous)
yeast fermentation, peaking at 30°C. Hand-plunged up to 6 times per day, basket-
pressed when dry, and racked to oak after 48 hours' settling, with mlf occurring
in barrel the following spring. Maturation for 12 months in 20% new oak, and
minimum filtration prior to bottling. 5000 dozen made.

How it tastes: Strong colour; a powerful pinot noir, anchored on ripe plum fruit at
perfect ripeness around 13.5 baume; the structure is provided by foresty tannins,
and the wine deserves to be cellared for 9 years from vintage.

Best vintages: 2012, 2009, 2007, 2005, 2002

Riesling
How it is made: The techniques used are precisely the same as for 95% of Australia's
overall riesling production, the whole emphasis on protecting the expression
of the variety and the terroir on which it is grown: neutral cultured yeast, cool
fermentation in stainless steel, sterile filtration prior to bottling within 6 months
of vintage. 1300 dozen made.

How it tastes: Riesling is one of the outstanding wines of Tasmania, on a par with
chardonnay, and with only sparkling and pinot noir in front of it. The bouquet
and palate are led by lime, green apple and mineral characters when the wine is
first released, gaining depth with age, even to some notes of honey and toast. The
high natural acidity guarantees a long life in the manner of German Rheingau dry
rieslings. Cellar to 20 years from vintage.

Best vintages: 2012, 2009, 2008, 2004, 2000

Tamar Ridge

Tamar Ridge has lived in the fast lane since it was established by Josef Chromy in 1994. In 2003 it was purchased by Tasmanian timber company Gunns Limited, and entered a period of hectic growth, with Tasmanian veteran winemaker (and viticulturist) Dr Andrew Pirie working in tandem with one of Australia's foremost viticultural consultants, Dr Richard Smart. Smart has consultancies in many parts of the world, his reputation as high internationally as it is in Australia.

Dr Smart oversaw the rapid expansion of its home Kayena Vineyard to 135ha and the White Hills property to 83ha. It took another major step in 2005 with the acquisition of the Coombend property on the east coast, with 160ha of both young and mature vineyards.

Back at Kayena home base, Dr Pirie ran a A$1.9 million micro-vinification winery offering courses for PhD students, research into clonal variations and vine canopy trials. All this investment came about because Gunns Limited's controversial CEO, John Gay, was a wine enthusiast; when Gunns' attempts to get approval for a major wood pulp mill were thwarted, he was replaced as CEO. Gunns' financial problems grew rapidly, and the new management saw wine as irrelevant to the core business of the company – Victoria's Brown Brothers purchased Tamar Ridge in August 2010 for a reported A$32.5 million.

In 2012 neighbouring Freycinet purchased a 42ha portion of the Coombend property, and in June 2013 Treasury Wine Estates announced that it had purchased the White Hills Vineyard. The monies thus raised reduced the debt Brown Brothers had accrued to buy Tamar Ridge, but were in no way forced sales, and still leave room for growth of the business.

The demand for Tasmanian grapes outstrips supply, and its harvest dates show no sign of global warming. As is the case in Burgundy, and many other parts of Europe, warming by 1.5°C would (on balance) be an advantage. Given its southerly location, and its air conditioning from the Southern Ocean stretching between the Antarctic and Tasmania, it has little to fear over the next 50+ years. In the shorter term, Brown Brothers intends to increase production by 9000 dozen bottles in 2014.

Notwithstanding the sale of the 82.9ha White Hills Vineyard to Treasury Wine Estates, Tamar Ridge is still the largest holder of Tasmanian vineyards, with just over 303ha. Moreover, it has 124ha of the key variety, pinot noir, 20% of the state total, and 69ha of chardonnay, representing 21%. It has 31% of the sauvignon blanc, 29% of the pinot gris and 20% of the riesling. The one variety which might possibly be of interest in the future is shiraz. It indirectly raises the question of global warming. So far, there has been little or no trend to earlier picking dates, but if there were to be, it would most likely result in a net benefit over the next 40+ years.

Tapanappa

Est 2002
PO Box 174, Crafers, SA 5152
Open Not
Getting there NA
Contact 0419 843 751;
wine@tapanappawines.com.au;
www.tapanappawines.com.au
Region South Australia (Piccadilly Valley)
Lat 35°00′S
Elev 450–600m
E° Days 1359
Harvest 12 March–30 April

Estate vineyards 7ha
Varieties planted Whalebone Vineyard Cabernet sauvignon (5), merlot (1), cabernet franc (1)
Leased or contracted vineyards 9ha
Varieties planted Tiers Vineyard Chardonnay (4); Foggy Hill Vineyard Pinot noir (4); Daosa Vineyard Shiraz (1)
Dozens produced 4350 May increase to 6000.
Exports To China and Hong Kong through Jebsens (ph) 852 2923 8777; www.jebsen.com. Also to the UK, France, the UAE, Thailand, Macau, Denmark, Sweden and Canada.
Winemaker Brian Croser

Key wines

Whalebone Vineyard Merlot Cabernet Franc
How it is made: The 60/40% blend is cold-soaked for 4 days prior to fermentation commencing, hand-plunged with a peak of 32°C, then macerated for 7 days post-fermentation; thereafter it spends 20 months in French oak (30% new) before being bottled unfiltered. 450 dozen made.

How it tastes: Vivid purple-crimson, the medium-bodied palate is exceptionally supple and smooth, the tannins are silky and fine. Cellar to 15 years from vintage.

Best vintages: 2013, 2012, 2010, 2009, 2008

Foggy Hill Vineyard Pinot Noir
How it is made: Is hand-picked and chilled to 5°C over 24 hours in a cold store, then crushed and partially destemmed into 1-tonne open fermenters, with 8% stalks retained. The must cold-macerates for 3 days before vineyard-selected yeast initiates fermentation, which peaks at 35°C. The time on skins is 20 days, and the wine is then gravity-transferred to French oak barriques, 30% new, for 10–12 months prior to bottling.

How it tastes: Strong, clear and deep colour; a thoroughly serious pinot noir, with a fragrant bouquet followed by a black cherry and plum palate with excellent texture and structure; tannins and oak are woven through the mid-palate and into the finish. Cellar to 9 years.

Best vintages: 2013, 2012, 2010, 2009, 2008

Tapanappa

Tapanappa has a diverse but very distinguished trio of owners: the Croser family, headed by Brian Croser AO (formerly of Petaluma); Jean-Charles Cazes of Château Lynch-Bages in Pauillac, Bordeaux; and Société Jacques Bollinger, the parent company of Champagne Bollinger.

Brian Croser is arguably the most experienced and influential member of every part of the Australian wine landscape: shaping industry politics, directing research, providing important consultancy advice, wine show judging at the highest level, establishing Petaluma in 1976, and now Tapanappa. He is forbiddingly intelligent, and one of the lasting legacies of that intelligence will be his concept of 'distinguished sites'. It is a recognition that Australia may have the equivalent of the terroir of Grand Cru Burgundy and First Growth Bordeaux, but does not have a structure to formally delineate the boundaries of those parcels of land.

It is this that has driven the partnership's selection of the very different vineyard sites. The first is the Tiers Vineyard in the Piccadilly Valley, high in the Adelaide Hills (450–600m), planted by the Croser family in 1979, and the first to be established in the Adelaide Hills in the 20th century. The second-coolest and -wettest location in South Australia, it has a climate identical to the southern end of Burgundy's Côte de Beaune. It is thus ideally suited to chardonnay, planted on soil derived from a 1.6-billion-year-old geological stratum.

Close-planting, and the replacement of part of the vineyard in 2003 with new Dijon clones at an even higher density (4444 vines/ha, compared to 3175 vines/ha for the original 33-year-old vines) has given an extra dimension of complexity.

The second site is the Whalebone Vineyard, planted in 1974, acquired in 2002, immediately after the formation of the Tapanappa partnership, and taking its new name from the discovery of a 35-million-year-old whale skeleton in a limestone cave beneath the vineyard. Although only 20km north of Coonawarra, it is in the Wrattonbully region, with a slightly cooler climate that that of Coonawarra, and the underlying limestone is more than 30 million years older than that of Coonawarra.

Croser became acquainted with the vineyard in 1980 when helping make the cabernet sauvignon of its first vintage: shiraz, and cabernet franc, were also part of the original plantings, since joined by merlot. There are now two wines: Cabernet Shiraz and Merlot Cabernet Franc.

The third site is by far the most recent, and is a prime example of the short time-frame often at play in Australia. When the Croser family purchased the Maylands Farm at Parawa, on the extreme southern tip of the Fleurieu Peninsula, in 2003, it was for the sole purpose of growing the finest fat lambs. But climbing the north-facing slopes once the property was theirs led Croser to investigate the climatic data. To his surprise, the data showed that Parawa was nearly as cool as the Piccadilly Valley; indeed, Parawa has lower maximum daytime temperatures than Piccadilly, the extreme maritime influence making the nights warmer.

The result? Within months, Dijon clones of pinot noir had been close-planted on 2ha (4444 vines/ha), followed by a further 2ha in 2006. It's an entirely new site for pinot noir, a long distance from other vineyards, and even further from the Adelaide Hills, the main South Australian region for the variety. The only comparable region is Mount Gambier, 480km to the south-east.

TarraWarra Estate

Est 1983
311 Healesville-Yarra Glen Road,
Yarra Glen, Vic 3775
Open Tues–Sun 11–5
Getting there 55 minutes' drive from
Melbourne CBD
Contact (03) 5962 3311;
enq@tarrawarra.com.au;
www.tarrawarra.com.au
Region Yarra Valley
Lat 37°42′S
Elev 50–350m
E° Days 1253
Harvest 1 March–25 April

Estate vineyards 28.8ha
Varieties planted Pinot noir (14.9),
chardonnay (9), shiraz (1.6),
merlot (1.1), nebbiolo (0.9),
barbera (0.9), roussanne (0.2),
marsanne (0.1), viognier (0.1)
Dozens produced 15 000 No increase
planned.
Exports To China and Hong Kong direct
from winery on demand.
Winemaker Clare Halloran

Key wines

Reserve Chardonnay

How it is made: A hand-picked mix of four clones, all highly regarded: Mendoza, P58, and Dijon 76 and 78, predominantly from the 1983 plantings. The wine is fermented in a mix of French oak barriques and puncheons (25% new), spending 11 months in oak without racking until bottling. The mlf is prevented, and there are no acid additions or fining, just crossflow-filtration.

How it tastes: A wine of fragrance, finesse and purity, with the hallmark length of all Yarra Valley chardonnays, fruit – not oak – the key to its flavours. Cellar to 10 years from vintage.

Best vintages: 2011, 2010, 2008, 2005, 2002

Reserve Pinot Noir

How it is made: Hand-picked at 12.5 to 13 baume, with a blend of clone MV6 planted 1983, and clone D5V12 planted in1989. Destemmed into open pots with cultured yeast, pressed at dryness to a mix of French oak barriques and puncheons (25% new); 11 months in barrel, not fined, but crossflow-filtered.

How it tastes: A restrained dark cherry, earth and mineral bouquet is reticent when young; the palate follows suit, slow to reveal fine dark fruits and enticing Asian spices, ultimately long and expansive. Cellar to 10 years from vintage.

Best vintages: 2012, 2010, 2008, 2006, 2004

TarraWarra Estate

Right from the outset, TarraWarra Estate was destined to be one of the Yarra Valley's showpieces. It was established on a 400ha holding of prime Yarra Valley real estate by Marc Besen AO and wife Eva, also AO. They were (and are) sufficiently wealthy to build a winery of the daunting size and taste of many wineries built in the Napa Valley over the past 30 years.

But the Besens are owners of a magnificent art collection, and are classical music lovers able to travel to Europe every year for the major concert events. Not for them the ostentatious displays of wealth: the winery and restaurant nestle into the side of a hill, and their house is well hidden from prying eyes.

The art gallery building (opened in December 2003) adjacent to the restaurant was built without regard to cost, and – given its size – can be seen as you drive in the gate further down the hill. But even here, that hillside seems to shrink the size of the building; only inside do you fully appreciate its space, and why it was chosen to display the Archibald Prize paintings in 2012, one of the premier art events each year in Australia.

The same ethos marks the naturally well-equipped winery, and the immaculately tended vines. Vineyard manager Stuart Sissins studied agricultural science at tertiary level, and has the care of the large herd of cattle as well as the 29ha of estate vineyards.

He and winemaker Clare Halloran have worked together since they both arrived in 1996, and have progressively moved the care of the vines to a sustainable organic status with a balanced ecosystem. Clare Halloran has gone down a similar route in the winery, with a series of innovative steps to reduce electricity consumption and recycle water until it is ultimately used for irrigation or garden watering.

Except in disastrous vintages (2009 bushfires and smoke), all the wines are made from estate-grown grapes, with the lion's share given to chardonnay and pinot noir, which in the best vintages will be made in four tiers. The base is Estate Pinot Noir and Chardonnay made from different blocks across the vineyards. Next are four single-block wines, H-Block Pinot Noir, J-Block Shiraz, K-Block Merlot and Viognier Marsanne Roussanne.

The key wines are the Reserve Pinot Noir and Chardonnay, made from the best parcels across the vineyard, unless the vintage allows for micro quantities of two icon wines, MDB Chardonnay and MDB Pinot Noir, named for father Marc and son Daniel.

Thomas Wines

Est 1997
c/- The Small Winemakers Centre,
McDonalds Road, Pokolbin, NSW 2321
Open 7 days 10–5
Getting there 2 hours' drive from
Sydney CBD
Contact 0418 456 853;
sales@thomaswines.com.au;
www.thomaswines.com.au
Region Hunter Valley
Lat 32°54′S
Elev 76m
E° Days 1823
Harvest 31 January–11 March

Leased or contracted vineyards 21.6ha
Varieties planted Shiraz (12.8),
semillon (8.8)
Dozens produced 8000 May increase
to 12 000.
Exports Nil so far, but in discussions
which may lead to exports to Hong
Kong and/or China in the future.
Winemaker Andrew Thomas,
Phil Le Messurier

Key wines

Braemore Semillon
How it is made: The grapes come from one of the great Hunter Valley semillon vineyards (planted in 1969), owned and managed by the hugely experienced Ken Bray, the alcohol typically 10.5% alc/vol, its natural acidity one of the reasons for a life span of 20 years or more, its longevity guaranteed by the screwcap.

How it tastes: Vibrant lemon and lime characters fill the bouquet and palate, ranging from juice, zest from the skin, and crushed lemon leaf. Cellar 10–15 years from vintage.

Best vintages: 2013, 2009, 2007, 2006, 2002

Kiss Shiraz
How it is made: The grapes come from the Pokolbin Estate vineyard (planted in 1969), are hand-picked, cold-soaked for 48 hours, fermented on skins for about 7 days, then matured for 16 months in French oak barriques. After bottling, the wine – at the upper level of medium-bodied – is cellared for 10 months prior to release.

How it tastes: While 'Kiss' stands for 'Keep it simple, stupid', the wine has a sophisticated bouquet with red fruits, violets and Asian spices; the medium-bodied palate has excellent texture and structure, and well-balanced oak. Cellar to 30 years from vintage.

Best vintages: 2011, 2009, 2007, 2005, 2003

Thomas Wines

Andrew Thomas was born with wine in his blood. His parents had been vignerons in McLaren Vale for many years, establishing Fernhill Winery, and thereafter Wayne Thomas Wines. Universally known by his nickname, Thommo, he graduated in Oenology from Roseworthy Agricultural College (now part of Adelaide University) in 1987, and began his career with Tyrrell's in the Hunter Valley.

Over the next 13 years he was mentored by industry veteran (and icon) Murray Tyrrell. Under Tyrrell's tutelage he gained a deep understanding of the Hunter Valley's two great wines: semillon and shiraz. This covered the finer nuances of the all-important decisions on the timing of harvest; fermentation and maturation methods; and the timing of bottling.

Although he may not have realised at the time how important the matching of variety and soil was, he gained extensive knowledge of the best vineyards in the Hunter Valley. The core of this was the sandy flat soils, deposited by ancient and long-gone rivers, on which the greatest semillon grapes were grown, with some vines more than 100 years old. Likewise, the well-drained red volcanic soils scattered through the Valley produced the best shiraz.

Another side to his education was gained by vintages in the Sonoma Valley, California (1988), in Tuscany and Piedmont, Italy (1991), and in Aix-en-Provence, southern France (1995). Until these experiences, his intention had been to go back to the family winery in McLaren Vale, but he found the attraction of the unique quality and style of Hunter semillon and of shiraz too strong to turn his back on.

So in 1997 he established Thomas Wines, and for three years built the business from a small base until he was able to leave Tyrrell's and the financial security he had through his salary as winemaker there. But he could not afford to buy land and establish his own vineyards, so used all his experience in identifying the best grapegrowers, and setting up long-term agreements to buy their grapes.

He was also able to become contract winemaker for a number of well-known small wineries; his exceptional skill as a winemaker had resulted in numerous trophies and gold medals from the annual Hunter Valley Wine Show (and other shows). Many of the outstanding wines he makes for his own business are from single vineyards, successfully reflecting the special qualities of those vineyards.

The success he has had with his own label has had two immediate consequences. First, he has scaled back the amount of contract work, but continued to work with two high-quality businesses, McLeish Estate and Pokolbin Estate. He has also been able to lease the James Estate winery on Hermitage Road for his exclusive use. In the longer term, he should be able to buy or erect his own winery, and cement his access by ownership or lease of his own vineyards. An admirable aim, but whether it would lead in due course to a measurable increase in quality is open to doubt.

Torbreck Vintners

Est 1994
Roennfeldt Road, Marananga, SA 5352
Open 7 days 10–6
Getting there 1 hour's drive from Adelaide CBD
Contact (08) 8562 4155; cellardoor@torbreck.com; www.torbreck.com
Region Barossa Valley
Lat 34°29'S
Elev 274m
E° Days 1571
Harvest 27 February–17 April
Estate vineyards 49ha
Varieties planted Shiraz (24), grenache (14.9), cabernet sauvignon (3.5), mourvedre (2.9), roussanne (2.4), viognier (0.9), marsanne (0.4)
Leased or contracted vineyards 53.2ha
Varieties planted Shiraz (38.5), grenache (5.7), semillon (4.5), mourvedre (1.7), viognier (1.6), cabernet sauvignon (1.2)
Dozens produced 70 000 May increase to 100 000.
Exports To China and Hong Kong through Links Concept Company Limited (ph) 852 2802 2818; marketing@linksconcept.com. Also to the UK, the US and other major markets.
Winemaker Craig Isbel

Key wines

The Laird

How it is made: The grapes come from a single 2ha block of dry-grown shiraz planted in 1958, meticulously hand-tended by owner Malcolm Seppelt. The grapes are hand-picked and are placed in open-top fermenters, the juice pumped over twice daily. When fermentation is virtually complete, the wine is transferred to the most expensive French oak barriques (100% new). The barrels spend 36 months in a temperature-controlled stone shed, the wine then being bottled without fining or filtration. 400 dozen made.

How it tastes: Deep crimson-purple, the bouquet signalling the blackest of black fruits, licorice and spice arriving in continuous waves on the palate, the oak embedded in the fruit, the tannins an almost velvety backdrop. The overall impact is akin to a vinous black hole in space when the wine is young, but will progressively reveal more of itself as the decades go by. Cellar to 50 years from vintage.

Best vintages: 2012, 2010, 2008, 2006, 2005

RunRig

How it is made: Until The Laird came along, RunRig was the King of the Torbreck wines. It comes from 8 vineyards in 6 districts spread across the Valley, and harvest can take a month to complete. If only for this reason, each parcel is separately fermented and matured, allowing final blending choices to be left until the end of the 30-month maturation in a mix of new and used French oak. It is neither fined nor filtered, and only racked once during its time in oak. 1500 dozen made.

How it tastes: The full-bodied palate is immensely rich, yet supple and velvety, the fragrant red and black fruits effortlessly flowing through the length of the palate and into the lingering aftertaste; the oak and tannins are seamlessly welded into the fruit. Cellar to 30 years from vintage.

Best vintages: 2012, 2010, 2009, 2006, 2002

Torbreck Vintners

Torbreck founder David Powell intended to follow in the footsteps of his chartered accountant father, setting course for an economics degree from Adelaide University. Happily, an uncle introduced him to the world of wine, and it didn't take long for him to abandon a career in bean counting, even if he took a circuitous path into winemaking.

Casual summer jobs in the Barossa Valley were punctuated by (Australian) winter trips to the best wine regions of Europe (with a detour to Scotland to earn money as a lumberjack), and vintage employment in Italy, and later to California. Returning to the Barossa Valley, he had the great good fortune to secure a job at Rockford, and tutelage from Rocky O'Callaghan.

The pieces of the jigsaw puzzle began to fall into place. His overseas travel and O'Callaghan's abiding commitment to the multi-generational Barossa grapegrowers made Powell keenly aware of the priceless resource of the very old vines in the Barossa. Ironically, this coincided with the South Australian government's Vine Pull Scheme, designed to address a decade-long surplus of red grapes in the Barossa Valley.

In some instances growers had simply abandoned part or all of their vineyards, accepting the bounty paid by the state, but not actually removing the vines. Powell picked the blocks with the greatest potential (often the oldest vines) and in his spare time began the slow process of nursing them back to health with a share-farming arrangement with the owners. This gave him access to some of the very best vineyards in the Barossa Valley.

This process began in 1992, and in 1994 he purchased a 12ha property at Marananga which he called Torbreck, the name of the Scottish forest he had worked in. In 1995 he crushed 3 tonnes of old vine shiraz in the shed on the property, and Torbreck was on the way to becoming the phenomenon it is today.

In June 2003, at the conclusion of vintage, a lovingly restored settlers' hut on the property was opened (seven days a week). Land acquired from a next-door neighbour now has a new winery and administration facility erected on it. A state-of-the-art bottling line means every step in the winemaking process is completed onsite.

In the same year, divorce proceedings led to his loss of control of the business, although he retained a minority stake. In 2008 the very wealthy Californian vigneron Peter Kight purchased 100% of Torbreck, and retained the services of Powell under a five-year service agreement. Unexpectedly, Kight chose not to renew the agreement when it expired in August 2013, with accusation and counter-accusation making headlines in wine media.

Obviously, this was a personal disaster for Powell, and a risk for Kight. While Craig Isbel had been hired by Powell in 2006 (two years before Kight arrived) and has had executive responsibility for the winemaking and viticulture for much of that time, Powell – a skilled marketer – has been the face of Torbreck since the outset.

In all there are 20 wines in the Torbreck range, with Woodcutters white and red blends the entry point, all the way up to The Laird, one of Australia's most exclusive and expensive red wines. Along the way there are unexpected wines such as the Natural Wine Grenache, with no additions of any kind; The Bothie, a sweet dessert wine; Cuvee Juveniles, after the famous Paris wine bar; and The Loon, a co-fermented shiraz and marsanne.

Turkey Flat

Est 1865
Bethany Road, Tanunda, SA 5352
Open 7 days 11–5
Getting there 1 hour's drive from Adelaide CBD
Contact (08) 8563 2851l; info@turkeyflat.com.au; www.turkeyflat.com.au
Region Barossa Valley
Lat 34°29'S
Elev 274m
E° Days 1571
Harvest 27 February–17 April

Estate vineyards 36.8ha
Varieties planted Shiraz (17.1), grenache (8.1), mourvedre (3.7), cabernet sauvignon (3.6), marsanne (2.2), viognier (1), roussanne (0.6), dolcetto (0.5)
Dozens produced 26 500 No increase planned.
Exports Exports to China and Hong Kong through Watson's Wine (ph) 852 2606 8828; info@watsonswine.com, also in China through Ruby Red Fine Wine (ph) 8621 6234 2249; info@ rubyred.com.cn. Also to the UK, the US and other major markets.
Winemaker Mark Bulman

Key wines

Shiraz
How it is made: The grapes are open-fermented, with a period of cold maceration prior to fermentation starting, using a mix of submerged cap and pumpover techniques. The wine then spends 22 months in French oak hogsheads (30% new).

How it tastes: While full-flavoured, it always has a degree of elegance to its red and black fruit flavours; fine tannins and subtle oak add to the presentation of a wine that might be thought to come from a cooler climate. Cellar to 20+ years from vintage.

Best vintages: 2012, 2010, 2006, 2002, 2001

Butchers Block Red (Shiraz Grenache Mourvedre)
How it is made: The percentage of the 3 varieties varies according to the vintage, but shiraz is always the dominant variety. Fermentation is similar to that of the shiraz, the main difference coming with maturation; little or no new oak is used, and the wine spends 14 months in oak.

How it tastes: Has the drive, focus and intensity often missing from this Barossa blend; once it has spent a few years in bottle, a spicy fragrance comes to the fore, reminiscent of the red wines of the southern Rhône Valley. Cellar up to 20 years from vintage.

Best vintages: 2012, 2010, 2009, 2006, 2003

Turkey Flat

While the Turkey Flat winery was not built, nor the first wines made, until 1990, its vineyard roots go back to 1847, when Silesian refugee Johann Frederick August Fiedler planted shiraz vines on the soils. In 1865 the Schulz family acquired the property and its vines, and continued to tend the ancient vineyard; it also developed a thriving butcher's business (hence Butchers Block red blend). The name Turkey Flat was given to the vineyard early on due to the large flocks of native bush turkeys (Australian bustards) in the area.

The winery is situated on the property planted by Fiedler (known as Section One) in the nearby Bethany township, and the restored bluestone butcher's shop is now the cellar door and private tasting room for the business.

Turkey Flat wines are made from four individual vineyard estates. The original Section One vineyard has the shiraz, and also grenache, mourvedre, roussanne and viognier, the last two recent plantings. The second vineyard is a 3.6ha block grown on the banks of Bethany Creek, surrounded by ancient gum trees. The third vineyard is Menge Road, where shiraz, cabernet sauvignon, grenache and dolcetto vines are grown specifically for Turkey Flat's rose. The Butcher's Block blend of shiraz, grenache and mourvedre comes from the Stonewell Vineyard (not the site of the original butcher's shop) on a unique combination of terra rossa over an underlying limestone base.

The vineyards are normally dry-grown, with supplementary water used (if available) in drought years. The yield of shiraz is as little as 2 tonnes/ha (0.8 tonnes/acre or 13 hectolitres/ha) to a still-modest 10 tonnes/ha for rose. Canopy management involves controlling shoot growth as well as shoot and grape bunch removal, practices common in cool regions, but less frequently encountered in the Barossa Valley. Organic practices are in place, certification to come.

In 2013, fourth-generation family member Christie Schulz became the sole proprietor and CEO of the business. She was born into an Adelaide medical dynasty, her father the fourth generation to practise medicine in South Australia. However, she forged her own career at the South Australian School of Art, majoring in photography, thereafter pursuing a career in professional photography, spilling over into retail management with major name clothing companies, and also managing to become involved in sales of Seppelt and Yalumba wines. She hopes that her three sons will one day join her in the company.

All of the wines are made at the Bethany Road winery, a purpose-designed and -built facility, handling all aspects of wine production from fermentation through to eventual bottling. A climate-controlled barrel hall is a feature of what is a carefully managed winery. It is also able to make full use of the differing characters the vineyards offer, reflecting the general move in the direction of single-vineyard bottlings.

Tyrrell's

Est 1858
Broke Road, Pokolbin, NSW 2321
Open Mon–Sat 8.30–5, Sun 10–4
Getting there 2 hours' drive from
Sydney CBD
Contact (02) 4993 7000;
tyrrells@tyrrells.com.au;
www.tyrrells.com.au
Region Hunter Valley
Lat 32°54′S
Elev 76m
E° Days 1823
Harvest 31 January–11 March
Estate vineyards 126ha
Varieties planted Shiraz (61),
chardonnay (36), semillon (24),
pinot noir (5)

Leased or contracted vineyards 212ha
Varieties planted Shiraz (130), semillon
(27), chardonnay (20), verdelho (20),
sauvignon blanc (15)
Dozens produced 415 000 No increase
planned.
Exports To China through
Shanghai Torres Wine Trading (ph)
8621 6267 7979; alberto@torres.com.cn
and to Hong Kong through Edrington
Hong Kong Ltd (ph) 852 2831 7222;
sales@edrington.com.hk. Also to all
major markets.
Winemaker Andrew Spinaze, Mark
Richardson

Key wines

Vat 1 Hunter Semillon
How it is made: Sourced from vineyards dating back to 1923. The clear juice is fermented with specially selected cultured yeast in stainless steel closed tanks at 18°C, and is bottled within 5 months of vintage. It is not released until it is 5 years old, screwcaps having eliminated the 30% loss of (oxidised) wine that occurred with high-quality corks. 2500 dozen made.

How it tastes: The low alcohol (10.5% alc/vol average) and high natural acidity are the foundation for the slow development of the wine, the obvious minerally acidity of its youth being gradually surrounded by nuances of lemon, honey and lightly browned toast. Cellar to 15+ years from vintage.

Best vintages: 2013, 2009, 2006, 2005, 2004

Vat 9 Hunter Shiraz
How it is made: The grapes are estate-grown on the red volcanic clay. The grapes are crushed and fermented in wax-lined open-top concrete vats with hand-plunging, pumpover and rack-and-return (running juice off to another vessel, then pumping it back over the skins) for 7 days at 24°C. Matured in 2700-litre French oak casks, mostly new, for 15 months. Not fined, and only lightly filtered. 1500 dozen made.

How it tastes: The elegant medium-bodied palate reflects the moderate alcohol (around 13% alc/vol) but the wine has all the intensity and length to support extended cellaring, during which time the primary red and black fruit flavours will gain nuances of polished leather, sweet earth and spice, tannins and oak not assertive at any stage of its development. Cellar to 30+ years from vintage.

Best vintages: 2010, 2009, 2007, 2006, 2004

Tyrrell's

When 23-year-old Edward Tyrrell successfully applied for a 134ha land grant in 1858, he had no idea that it contained some of the finest red basalt soil in the district, with a limestone subsoil. First Edward Tyrrell had to clear – by hand – the ironbark gum trees which forested the land, and then work up the soil for planting.

He produced his first vintage in 1864 from the first few acres of vines. By 1870 he had planted 12ha of vines, half to aucerot, and the rest to semillon and shiraz. In the meantime he had built (in 1858) the one-room slab hut which stands diminutively but proudly in the forecourt of today's winery complex, a building beyond price. The first stage of the winery was completed just in time for the 1864 vintage; it, too, stands today at the core of the subsequent extensions, most of which look to be very nearly as old.

The second of the 10 children of Edward and his wife Susan (née Hungerford), Edward George Young Tyrrell, was born in 1871. He and his youngest brother, Avery, were to assume responsibility for the vineyard and winery following the ill health of their father in 1888. Edward George (known to all as Dan, and eventually as Uncle Dan) assumed that responsibility immediately, although he was only 15 years old. His ensuing 70 vintages as a winemaker certainly stand as an Australian record, and can have few parallels in wine history.

Dan Tyrrell died of a heart attack at the age of 88 in April 1959, and Murray Tyrrell – who had spent several years in the winery after World War II learning the trade – came back from his cattle business to take over Tyrrell's Ashmans Winery. Even at this time, virtually all Tyrrell's wine was sold in bulk.

Hail destroyed the harvest in 1959 and 1961, so 1962 was the first year nature gave Murray a chance, and he took it with both hands. Vat 5 of 1962 won a gold medal at the Sydney Wine Show, and the ensuing publicity allowed Murray Tyrrell to rapidly change the nature of the business, bottling and labelling all the wine with the Tyrrell name and logo.

After his death in 2000, son Bruce Tyrrell took over management of what was by then a very large and successful business. He was responsible for the business, focusing on its premium, super-premium and ultra-premium wines, led by a magnificent portfolio of single-vineyard semillons released when five–six years old, and the Winemaker's Selection Four Acres Shiraz, a single-vineyard wine made from estate vines planted in 1879.

Tyrrell's also makes the Old Patch Shiraz from the Stevens Vineyards shiraz planted in 1867; Johnno's Vineyard Semillon and Johnno's Vineyard Shiraz from vines planted in 1908; and HVD Semillon and HVD Chardonnay from vines also planted in 1908. Vat 47 Chardonnay, the first chardonnay to be sold and labelled as such in the Hunter Valley, in 1971, is another flagship. The fifth generation, of Chris (assistant winemaker), brother Johnno and sister Jane, is now actively involved in the business.

A founding member of Australia's First Families of Wine.

Vasse Felix

Est 1967
Cnr Tom Cullity Drive/Caves Road,
Cowaramup, WA 6284
Open 7 days 10–5
Getting there 2.75 hours' drive from
Perth CBD
Contact (08) 9756 5000;
info@vassefelix.com.au;
www.vassefelix.com.au
Region Margaret River
Lat 33°57'S
Elev 40–90m
E° Days 1552
Harvest 26 February–8 April

Estate vineyards 233ha
Varieties planted 48ha in Wilyabrup,
35ha in Karridale and 150ha in
Carbunup: semillon, sauvignon
blanc, chardonnay, shiraz, cabernet
sauvignon, malbec, petit verdot,
cabernet franc, merlot
Dozens produced 150 000 No increase
planned.
Exports To China through
Shanghai Torres Wine Trading (ph)
8621 6267 7979; alberto@torres.com.cn
and to Hong Kong through Watson's
Wine (ph) 852 3521 6274; info@
watsonswine.com. Also to the UK, the
US, Canada and numerous others.
Winemaker Virginia Willcock

Key wines

Estate Cabernet Sauvignon
How it is made: Always includes up to 14% of malbec, petit verdot and cabernet
franc, fermented separately and spending up to 30 days on skins. It is then pressed
to French oak (50% new, the remainder 1–4 years old), where it spends 18 months.

How it tastes: Redcurrant, blackcurrant and savoury black olive fruit flavours drive
the long and powerful palate, firm tannins providing the structure for ageing.
Cellar to 15 years from vintage.

Best vintages: 2010, 2009, 2008, 2007, 2004

Heytesbury Chardonnay
How it is made: Top-performing clones provide the foundation of the wines;
then wild yeast fermentation of cloudy juice in new (70%) and used French oak,
followed by 9 months lees-stirring and maturation in the same barrels. Has had
outstanding show success.

How it tastes: This is an exceptional wine, combining elegance and complexity,
power and great length, and poise, with perfect balance between stone fruit, oak
and acidity. Cellar 10 years from vintage.

Best vintages: 2012, 2011, 2010, 2009, 2008

Vasse Felix

When Perth cardiologist Dr Tom Cullity made the five-hour drive down to the Margaret River region and after a year-long search chose a property in the Wilyabrup district to plant cabernet sauvignon and riesling, he could not have imagined where his pioneering gamble would lead. The year was 1967, and he paid $185 for the 3.2ha block, spending each weekend living in a galvanised iron shed, which in 1971 became a primitive winery. That first vintage was a disaster, but the 1972 riesling won a gold medal at the Royal Perth Show, and the path was set.

Cullity had been drawn to the Margaret River by a paper written in 1965 by research scientist Dr John Gladstones, who might fairly be regarded as the father of the region, who recognised the similarity of the climate to that of Bordeaux. Two other Perth doctors, Dr Bill Pannell and Dr Kevin Cullen, were also keen observers, the former establishing Moss Wood in 1969, the latter establishing Cullen Wines in 1971. These three (and thereafter others) chose Wilyabrup, today regarded as the foremost of the six unofficial subregions delineated by Dr John Gladstones in 1999, and especially suited to cabernet sauvignon and cabernet blends, sauvignon blanc and semillon blends, plus the ubiquitous chardonnay.

In 1987 Vasse Felix was acquired by the Holmes à Court family, having already established its reputation as one of Margaret River's – and Australia's – best wineries. Over the ensuing years, the business has grown exponentially, with a new winery entirely separate from the cellar door and restaurant (still on the site of the original winery), and the development of 232ha of vineyards in three different subregions.

This large financial investment has had a single purpose: to make the best possible wines regardless of cost. That said, the business acumen of the Holmes à Court family – with second generation Paul at the helm of Vasse Felix – demands that the winery's production is profitable.

This has been achieved in a number of ways. The wines are released in a three-tier price structure: at the bottom are the Classic White and Red blends; next, the Estate varietals; and at the top Heytesbury red, a cabernet sauvignon-dominant blend, and Heytesbury Chardonnay.

Since 2006 all the wines have been made under the control of senior winemaker Virginia Willcock, whose skill and dedication resulted in her being named as *Gourmet Traveller Wine Magazine*'s Australian Winemaker of the Year in 2012.

She has maximised the potential of the estate vineyards with organic and sustainable viticulture, focusing on soil biology and environmental health, and an understanding of every block in each of the three vineyards. In Wilyabrup, the 48ha are principally planted to cabernet sauvignon and chardonnay, with small sections of semillon, sauvignon blanc, shiraz, malbec and petit verdot. In the southerly and cooler Karridale area, the 35ha are planted to chardonnay, sauvignon blanc and semillon. In the warmer, more northerly Carbunup district, the 150ha are planted to all varieties, and provide much of the grapes used in the high-volume Classic Range.

Voyager Estate

Est 1978
Lot 1 Stevens Road, Margaret River, WA 6285
Open 7 days 10–5
Getting there 3 hours' drive from Perth CBD
Contact (08) 9757 6354; wineroom@voyagerestate.com.au; www.voyagerestate.com.au
Region Margaret River
Lat 33°57'S
Elev 40–90m
E° Days 1552
Harvest 26 February–8 April

Estate vineyards 110ha
Varieties planted Cabernet sauvignon (26.6), chardonnay (20.6), sauvignon blanc (20.6), shiraz (17.1) semillon (12.8), chenin blanc (5.2), merlot (4.7), viognier (1.2), petit verdot (1), grenache (0.2)
Dozens produced 40 000 May increase to 50 000.
Exports To China through East Meets West Wines (ph) 021 6282 4966; info@emw-wines.com and to Hong Kong through Watson's Wine (ph) 852 2606 8828; info@watsonswine.com. Also to the UK, Canada, Singapore, Japan, the Philippines and Indonesia.
Winemaker Steve James, Travis Lemm

Key wines

Chardonnay
How it is made: The best of the Dijon clones 95, 96, 76 and the so-called Gin Gin clone are harvested for this wine. The hand-picked grapes are cooled overnight, whole-bunch-pressed and taken to barrel for fermentation (35% wild yeast), the barriques from the very best makers. The oak (25% new), and one-third of the wine going through mlf, builds great complexity in the 9 months of maturation. 3750 dozen made.

How it tastes: A highly expressive, totally harmonious bouquet and palate has a core of grapefruit/citrus/white peach fruit, some cashew notes from the oak and mlf, but does not lose purity and is given structure by the minerally acidity. Cellar to 10 years from vintage.

Best vintages: 2012, 2010, 2009, 2005, 2001

Cabernet Sauvignon Merlot
How it is made: Typically a blend of around 85% cabernet sauvignon, 13% merlot and 2% petit verdot. Hand-picked bunches are destemmed, with each lot (linked to vineyard blocks) separately fermented with maceration for 12–26 days before being pressed and matured for 18 months in 50% new and 50% 2-year-old French oak. 3250 dozen made.

How it tastes: Deeply coloured, the bouquet is exceptionally complex, with layers of both dark and red fruits, cedar and some black olive aromas, the palate providing a replay but notable for its seamless integration of fruit, tannins and oak. Cellar to 15 years from vintage.

Best vintages: 2012, 2010, 2006, 2004, 2002

Voyager Estate

Mining barons Lang Hancock and Peter Wright formed a partnership which was to provide untold wealth for Australia as the iron ore deposits they discovered were mined, and the Pilbara turned to red treasure, sold to China at prices neither could have foreseen.

The Hancock fortune has brought highly public bitterness to his heirs, but the death first of Peter Wright and more recently of his son Michael Wright have left their heirs proud. Michael Wright spent the last 20 years of his life creating Voyager Estate, instilling in all those who are involved with it a fierce desire to make its wines equal to the best in the world.

Daughter Alex Burt (née Wright) now heads – and leads – the winery, and is very much of the view that there is no honour in being second-best. Michael Wright used to insist on blind tastings of Voyager's varietal wines alongside wines recognised as benchmarks of excellence. This tasting format is not unique to Voyager Estate, but it has been used many times with journalists, sommeliers and retailers. Each time Voyager Estate has emerged with great distinction, fully supporting Michael Wright's vision.

That vision began in 1991, when he purchased a vineyard planted in 1978 by state viticulturist Peter Gherardi, together with a modest winery. It is situated in what I have long described as a golden triangle, encompassing Voyager Estate, Leeuwin Estate and Cape Mentelle, three of the nine Margaret River wineries profiled in this book. The region's contribution of almost 10% of Australia's top 100 wineries reflects not only the quality of its wines, but also its disproportionately small overall production.

Voyager Estate's success has been due to many things, but first and foremost a near-obsessive focus on its vineyards. Within each of the vineyard blocks the aim is to leave the same number of buds on each vine during pruning, the same number of shoots in spring as the seasonal growth starts, and the same number of bunches to harvest in autumn. The even ripening so achieved delivers a pure expression of the character of the block at optimal ripeness.

Year on year, a precise understanding of the performance of each block builds a body of knowledge which is used throughout the growing season, and, most importantly, at the moment when the grapes should be picked. There is also an ongoing program of clonal selection trials to optimise the future performance of each of the vineyard blocks, and a strong move to sustainable organic farming.

All this has led to an unusual appointment: of one person – Steve James – as manager of winemaking and viticulture. It puts flesh on the bones of the statement that great wine is made in the vineyard. More than 60 people are employed on Voyager Estate to maximise the special quality of the Estate. The Cape Dutch architecture, landscaped gardens, modern winery, great tasting facilities, and an award-winning 90-seat restaurant make this a must-see destination.

Wendouree

Est 1895
Wendouree Road, Clare, SA 5453
Open Not
Getting there NA
Contact (08) 8842 2896
Region Clare Valley
Lat 33°50'S
Elev 398m
E° Days 1493
Harvest 14 February–24 March

Estate vineyards 9.73ha
Varieties planted Shiraz, 3.88ha planted 1893–1920, 1.33ha planted 1997–98; cabernet sauvignon, 1.59ha planted 1920–95, 0.58ha planted 2002–03; malbec, 1.55ha planted 1898, 1929 and 1989; mataro (mourvedre), 0.35ha planted 1919–20, 0.25ha planted 2005; muscat of Alexandria, 0.2ha planted 1940
Dozens produced 2000 No increase planned.
Exports Wines are not currently exported.
Winemaker Tony Brady

Key wines

Shiraz and Cabernet Malbec

How they are made: All the wines are made in the same way today as they have been over the last 100 years, the only exception being a move from American to French oak (a modest amount new). The grapes are hand-picked, crushed and destemmed, open-fermented and hand-plunged. They are then placed in the 120-year-old basket press, the wine thereafter spending 12 months in barrel before being lightly filtered and bottled.

How they taste: The wines are medium- to full-bodied, such differences as there are due to the weather through the growing season, but always offer an extraordinary combination of weight and elegance, once described by Douglas Seabrook as 'delicately big'. The flavours are of black fruits, the malbec blend adding notes of plum. Cellar to 40 years from vintage.

Best vintages: 2013, 2012, 2008, 2006, 2002

Wendouree

This is an utterly irreplaceable treasure in the heart of all that is best about small family-owned and -run Australian wineries. Luckily its owners, Tony and Lita Brady, see themselves as custodians for life, not unlike the monks of the abbeys in Burgundy who nurtured the greatest vineyards of that region.

Thus, without any fanfare, they extended the plantings between 1997 and 2005 by 2.16ha hectares. These micro plantings have to be put first in the context of total vineyard plantings of 9.73ha, and second with the knowledge that, in Tony Brady's words, 'There is no plan to increase our production, and the plantings are for future replacement ... wine made from these vines is not used in any of our current releases.'

The chain of ownership began in 1893 when Alfred Percy Birks planted 1.3ha of shiraz. Roly Birks, Alfred's son, took over winemaking in 1917 due to the ill health of his father, and made 53 vintages before thinking of retirement in 1970. Early in the piece, he embarked on a planting program which added 3.96ha to the vineyard. Shiraz has always been the most important planting. But Roly Birks clearly saw the future when he added 0.64ha of cabernet sauvignon, 0.77ha of malbec, and 0.35ha of mataro (mourvedre), also in 1919–20.

The wine he made, half dry red and half port, was initially sold in hogsheads to hotels in Port Pirie and Adelaide, taken there by Roly Birks in his truck. After World War II, beer was rationed, and wine filled the gap. Later, in the 1950s, the leading Melbourne wine merchant, WJ Seabrook and Son, became a major client, buying red wine in barrel, maturing and bottling it with the Wendouree name on the label; a specialty was the Pressings Red.

Roly Birks' attempt to retire in 1970 was thwarted by an unscrupulous buyer who failed to pay the purchase price. When all seemed lost, in 1974 Sydney businessman Max Liberman purchased the business from the mortgagee of the buyer and installed Adelaide lawyer and son-in-law Tony Brady and wife Lita (Max's daughter) as managers. Tony and Lita have cherished and protected Wendouree as if they were Roly's children, and he died knowing his winery was in the safest possible hands.

The demand for Wendouree's wines since 1975 was exacerbated by the low prices. All wine was (and is) sold by mail list (no email, no website, no cellar door), and it is nigh on impossible for a would-be new customer to get on the list, let alone receive any wine. The five wines every year are 500 dozen bottles each of Shiraz, Cabernet Malbec and Shiraz Mataro; 250 dozen bottles each of Cabernet Sauvignon and Malbec; and 250 dozen bottles of Shiraz Malbec when the crush (and quality) permits.

The monastic feel is enhanced if you are lucky enough to receive an invitation to come to the winery. Little has changed since 1893 in the stone winery. Two railway lines run down its centre, and the 120-year-old basket press (with some of the design characteristics of a champagne press – wide but relatively shallow) an integral part of the winemaking process. In 2013 the steel rails had to be re-laid, as the press had had a nasty habit of running off those rails when full of grapes.

The wines of Wendouree may or may not be the greatest in Australia, but no others have as much heart, soul and terroir in their make-up.

West Cape Howe Wines

Est 1997
Lot 14923 Muir Highway, Mount Barker, WA 6324
Open 7 days 10–5
Getting there 3.75 hours' drive from Perth CBD
Contact (08) 9892 1444; info@wchowe.com.au; www.westcapehowewines.com.au
Region Mount Barker
Lat 34°36′S
Elev 180–255m
E° Days 1548
Harvest 28 February–16 April

Estate vineyards 409ha
Varieties planted Langton (100ha, Mount Barker) sauvignon blanc (22), shiraz (21), chardonnay (18), cabernet sauvignon (16), semillon (12), riesling (11); **Landsdale** (60ha, Mount Barker) **Jindawarra** (39ha, Margaret River) and **Russell Road** (210ha, Frankland River)
Dozens produced 40 000 May increase to 65 000.
Exports To Hong Kong through Boutique Wines (ph) 852 2525 3031; sales@boutiquewines.com.hk. Also to the UK, the US, Denmark, Singapore, Japan, South Korea and Thailand.
Winemaker Gavin Berry, Dave Cleary, Andrew Siddell

Key wines

Two Steps Shiraz

How it is made: Sourced from the Mount Barker and Frankland River subregions, the components separately wild yeast-fermented, with a pre-ferment cold soak for 3 days, then moderate fermentation temperatures for 10–15 days on skins. Regular pumpovers and rack-and-return, then matured for up to 18 months in French oak (25% new); minimal fining, but is filtered prior to bottling. 1250 dozen made.

How it tastes: Purple-crimson in its youth, it is medium-bodied, with spicy/savoury black fruits lingering on the finish and aftertaste, the role of oak and tannins precisely calibrated. Cellar to 15 years from vintage.

Best vintages: 2011, 2010, 2009, 2008, 2004

Book Ends Cabernet Sauvignon

How it is made: The grapes are sourced from Mount Barker and are fermented with cultured yeast at mild fermentation temperatures for 12–18 days; as for the shiraz, regular pumpovers, aeration and rack-and-return to maximise colour, flavour and density; the wine spends 15–18 months in French oak (35% new) and is filtered, but only lightly fined, prior to bottling. 2000 dozen made.

How it tastes: Vivid crimson-purple in its youth, and at the end of its 18 months' maturation is vibrantly fresh, with redcurrant and cherry fruit supported by cedary oak and silky tannins. Drink now or cellar to 20 years from vintage.

Best vintages: 2011, 2010, 2009, 2008, 2004

West Cape Howe Wines

The timeline for the West Cape Howe of today starts either in 1988 when Brendon and Kylie Smith purchased the Landsdale property in Mount Barker, and planted 60ha of vines, or 1997, when viticulturist Rob Quenby (and backers) purchased a share of the vineyard. In 1999 the Smiths built the the West Cape Howe winery in Denmark as a contract winemaking facility with a small (2ha) vineyard for the West Cape Howe label.

In 2001, Quenby (and backers) purchased 50% of the West Cape Howe business, and in 2004 the Smiths sold the other 50% share to Gavin Berry (up to that point senior winemaker at Plantagenet) and the Quenby interests. In 2005 the Landsdale Vineyard was sold to Great Southern Plantations, but part of the grape production was sold under contract to West Cape Howe.

In 2010 the minnow swallowed the whale when West Cape Howe purchased the Langton Vineyard (with some of the oldest plantings in the Great Southern) and the modern 7700-tonne Goundrey winery from Accolade. Three other vineyards included in the purchase have since been sold, as has the Denmark winery (renamed Willoughby Park by its purchaser).

The game of musical chairs continued when a new group of partners (with the West Cape Howe partners themselves part of the new group) purchased three vineyards from the receivers of Great Southern Plantations. Those vineyards are Jindawarra in Margaret River, Russell Road in Frankland River, and the Landsdale vineyard, where the game began. The grapes from these vineyards are sold to wineries throughout the south-west of Western Australia.

The management team at West Cape Howe has accumulated decades of hands-on experience in grapegrowing and winemaking in the region. Gavin Berry is the managing director and chief winemaker, supported by senior winemaker Andrew Siddle, who had significant international (France and California) and domestic (Barossa Valley and Margaret River) experience before his appointment as senior winemaker in 1998.

Rob Quenby began his career with broad-acre farming in Western Australia before moving into viticulture in 1991, and uses organic methods wherever possible. There is also a strong sales and marketing team in place.

In the middle of the fast-moving development of West Cape Howe, the consistent quality, and exceptional value for money, of the wines have been remarkable. The quality has been reflected in the number of trophies and gold medals won in important Australian wine shows, and the consistently favourable reviews of the wines by critics.

If, as seems very likely, demand for the wines (especially from Hong Kong and China) increases, West Cape Howe has an exceptional portfolio of vineyards under its control able to supply high-quality grapes for increased production. What is more, only half the capacity of the former Goundrey Winery is being utilised at this stage. With both the vineyard and winery infrastructure in place already, increased production will not require significantly increased working capital.

Throw in unpolluted environment, and West Cape Howe is in a great place.

Wirra Wirra

Est 1894
McMurtrie Road, McLaren Vale, SA 5171
Open Mon–Sat 10–5, Sun & public hols 11–5
Getting there 40 minutes' drive from Adelaide CBD
Contact (08) 8323 8414; info@wirra.com.au; www.wirrawirra.com
Region McLaren Vale
Lat 34°14′S
Elev 50–200m
E° Days 1680
Harvest 14 February–14 April
Estate vineyards 48.8ha
Varieties planted Cabernet sauvignon (17.1), shiraz (14.9), sauvignon blanc (7.3), viognier (4), semillon (2), mourvedre (1), touriga (1), tempranillo (1), grenache (0.5)

Leased or contracted vineyards 239.5ha
Varieties planted Shiraz (96), cabernet sauvignon (76), grenache (17), merlot (13), chardonnay (12), riesling (6), sauvignon blanc (6), semillon (4), frontignac (3.5), petit verdot (3), mourvedre (1), touriga (1), tempranillo (1)
Dozens produced 180 000 No increase planned.
Exports To China through Aussino (ph) 020-3887 9081; gzo@aussino.net and to Hong Kong through Kedington Wines (Far East) Co. Ltd (ph) 852 2898 9323; info@kedwines.com. Also to the UK, the US and other major markets.
Winemaker Paul Smith, Paul Carpenter

Key wines

Church Block Cabernet Sauvignon Shiraz Merlot
How it is made: A multi-district McLaren Vale blend of 45% each of cabernet sauvignon and shiraz, and 10% merlot, the precise percentages varying from vintage to vintage. After controlled fermentation (25–28°C) it is basket-pressed to French (70%) and American (30%) oak (10–15% new) for 15 months.

How it tastes: The wine is medium-bodied, supple and smooth, driven by its luscious berry fruits; while it can be cellared for 10 or more years, it is always enjoyable when released.

Best vintages: 2010, 2006, 2005, 2004, 2002

RSW Shiraz
How it is made: Named after Robert Strangways Wigley, and sourced from estate-grown and contracted shiraz from low-yielding vines 40–65 years old, picked, fermented and matured in small batches. After 19 months in 100% French oak (40% new), the best barrels are selected for this icon wine.

How it tastes: It is profoundly fragrant and flavoured, with black fruits, bitter chocolate and spice spearing through the long palate. Cellar for 20 years.

Best vintages: 2010, 2006, 2005, 2004, 2002

Wirra Wirra

Wirra Wirra was founded by Robert Strangways Wigley, born in 1864, who studied law and architecture, and played cricket for South Australia. He was the first of two wonderfully eccentric owners of Wirra Wirra (an Aboriginal name meaning 'among the gum trees'). He was a skilled horseman, riding his horse into the hallowed precincts of the Adelaide Town Hall, and towing a meat pie cart down the main street of Adelaide. His wealthy family banished him to McLaren Vale in 1893, and the following year he planted the vineyard.

In 1903 Thomas Hardy, one of the most important vignerons in South Australia, was reported as saying, 'Of all those he ever had under him, no town man worked harder than Mr Bob Wigley, who was at Bankside [the Hardy winery of the time] for 18 months learning winemaking.' Wigley then purchased a 100ha property, planting 40ha of vines, and built a large and fully equipped winery. He had a strong export business with the leading Burgoynes of London shippers.

He died in 1924, and his family sold all but the winery and 2.8ha of surrounding vines, which were left to his foreman Jack Sparrow: he lost interest, and by 1969 the winery was derelict, with only its walls left standing, and the vineyard was only marginally better.

In 1969, cousins Greg and Roger Trott, both living and working in McLaren Vale, purchased the property from Jack Sparrow's son. Roger was an accountant, and Greg – one of the all-time great eccentrics – had represented growers selling to the local co-operative winery, becoming (in his words) 'familiar with the rudiments of winemaking'. It was typical that he would purchase beams for the mezzanine floor from the Pine Street Methodist Church in Adelaide. (Methodists don't drink any form of alcohol.)

Wigley could play cricket well; Trott (as he was affectionately known) was a cricket tragic, who loved the game but couldn't play it. He had a wonderful sense of humour, but had a habit of disappearing if he sensed a difficult wine business decision had to be taken. He commissioned a massive post and rail fence (called Stonehenge), salvaged a three-quarter tonne bell from a wreckers' yard and installed it on the top of the cellars, and had a *trebuchet* (a mediaeval siege machine, for throwing large objects over castle walls) built. He was loved by all and sundry, and when he died on 5 March 2005, after a heroic battle with cancer, there was barely a person in the Australian wine industry with dry eyes.

But his memory will be forever maintained not only because of his personality and love of life, but also through a very successful winery and wine business. It has a highly skilled and utterly dedicated winemaking team; it is seriously committed to virtually all the best environmental programs and protocols, ranging from biodynamic farming to major water conservation initiatives and practices, to the National Packaging Covenant to minimise carbon footprint and environmental impact through recycling and minimising non-essential material use.

It has grown from a standing start to its position as one of Australia's best middle-sized wineries in 40 years, highly regarded by its peers and customers alike, the quality of its wines impeccable.

Wolf Blass

Est 1966
Bilyara Vineyards, 97 Sturt Highway, Nuriootpa, SA 5355
Open Mon-Fri 9-5, w'ends & public hols 10-5
Getting there 1 hour's drive from Adelaide CBD
Contact (08) 8568 7311; visitorcentre@wolfblass.com.au; www.wolfblasswines.com.au
Region Barossa Valley
Lat 34°29'S
Elev 274m
E° Days 1571
Harvest 27 February-17 April

Estate vineyards NFP
Varieties planted As with other wineries that are part of a much larger wine business under single ownership, vineyard resources are shared across all brands in the group.
Dozens produced NFP
Exports To China through ASC Fine Wines (ph) 8621 3423 9599; www.asc-wines.com and to Hong Kong through Watson's Wine (ph) 852 3521 6274; info@watsonswine.com. Also to all major markets.
Winemaker Chris Hatcher (Chief), Matt O'Leary, Marie Clay

Key wines

Platinum Label Barossa Shiraz
How it is made: Individual parcels are destemmed to 8-tonne open fermenters inoculated with cultured yeast, the temperature peaking at 28°C, with plunging and pumpover used; 12-20 days on skins, then pressed to 100% French oak barriques (70-90% new), matured for 20-22 months, and finally blended just prior to bottling. Egg white-fined, but not filtered.

How it tastes: Deeply coloured, and full to the brim with lavish and supremely concentrated black fruits, quality oak and ripe, supple tannins on the saturated finish. Leave for 5 years, and cellar to 25 years from vintage.

Best vintages: 2010, 2008, 2006, 2004, 2002

Black Label Cabernet Shiraz Malbec
How it is made: A blend of predominantly cabernet sauvignon and shiraz, with a little malbec included (less than 10%). In very similar fashion to Platinum, except for the use of some additional 18-tonne static fermenters, and pressed before dryness to complete primary fermentation in 75% French/25% American oak (50-70% new), with a mix of barriques and hogsheads. The exact timing and ultimate blending varies from year to year.

How it tastes: Deep, dense colour; the bouquet and palate overflow with blackberry, plum and licorice fruit, the integration with the high-toned oak achieved through final fermentation in barrel. Carries its substantial alcohol with perceptive ease. Approachable when young, but cellar to 20 years from vintage.

Best vintages: 2010, 2009, 2005, 2004, 2002

Wolf Blass

Wolf Blass, the 27-year-old from Germany, already successful; Wolf Blass the winemaker; Wolf Blass the entrepreneur; Wolf Blass, marketing genius; Wolf Blass the man with the bright bow tie; Wolf Blass, his winemaking guru John Glaetzer at his side for over 25 years; Wolf Blass, winner of more trophies and gold medals than any other Australian winemaker, past or present; Wolf Blass, lover of women, race horses and luxurious motor vehicles; Wolf Blass, founder of the $1 million charity Wolf Blass Wine Foundation, supporting the industry which has given him so much, and vice versa; Wolf Blass AM, 'Why did they take so long to give it to me?'; Wolf Blass, still perpetual motion after 79 years, his English as strangled as it was when he arrived in 1961 to make sparkling wines for Kaiser Stuhl; Wolf Blass, who has had more books written about him than Max Schubert, the last written by Liz Johnston and published in 2009, and by far the best, *Wolf Blass: Behind the Bow Tie.*

In 1966 Blass makes 250 dozen bottles of red wine, having registered the name Bilyara, an Aboriginal word for 'eaglehawk', and offers consultancy winemaking services to a number of significant South Australian wineries. Between 1969 and 1973 he was senior winemaker for Tolley, Scott and Tolley, resigning after being told to cease making wine.

In 1973 he started Wolf Blass Wines International with a bank overdraft, and a tin shed sitting on 1.6ha of land. The following year he won the all-important Jimmy Watson Trophy at the Royal Melbourne Wine Show for his first vintage, and set a record (never since equalled) by winning the same trophy in 1975 and 1976 (for different red wines). Equally, if not more, extraordinary, was his achievement in winning the Royal Adelaide's Montgomery Trophy for six consecutive years from 1978 to 1983. This achievement will, quite certainly, never be repeated.

In 1984 his company joined the lists of the Australian Stock Exchange, raising $15.2 million, and leaving Blass with 60% of the capital. By 1990 Blass had won 2575 awards, including 135 trophies and 712 gold medals. The following year saw the merger of Wolf Blass and Mildara Wines, with a market capitalisation of $125 million, and Blass as its Deputy Chairman.

In 1996 Foster's acquired Mildara Blass for $560 million (its net assets); in 2000 the name was changed to Beringer Blass Wine Estates, reflecting the $2.6 billion purchase of Foster's by Californian Beringer Wine. In 2005 all of the Foster's wine assets were transferred to the newly incorporated stand-alone company Treasury Wine Estates (TWE). TWE has 19 of Australia's best known and most valuable brands, led by Penfolds, with Wolf Blass and Beringer next, then Rosemount Estate, Lindemans, Wynns Coonawarra Estate and Yellowglen, Australia's largest producer of sparkling wines.

The constant, unchanged, marketing signatures of Wolf Blass wines have been the coloured labels: Red Label at the bottom, then Yellow, then Gold, next White, for mature re-release wines, then Grey, followed by the most famous Black Label, and ultimately Platinum. All the red wines from Gold upwards are rich, fleshy and round in the mouth, generous fruit complemented by equally lavish high-quality oak.

Will there ever be another man able to equal what Wolf Blass has achieved? The answer is no, absolutely not.

Woodlands

Est 1973
3948 Caves Road, Wilyabrup, WA 6284
Open 7 days 10–5
Getting there 3 hours' drive from Perth CBD
Contact (08) 9755 6226; mail@woodlandswines.com; www.woodlandswines.com
Region Margaret River
Lat 33°57'S
Elev 40–90m
E° Days 1552
Harvest 26 February–8 April

Estate vineyards 19.7ha
Varieties planted Cabernet sauvignon (10.8), merlot (3.7), malbec (2.1), cabernet franc (1.1), petit verdot (1), chardonnay (0.8), pinot noir (0.2)
Leased or contracted vineyards NFP
Dozens produced 12 500 May increase to 15 000.
Exports To China through Wollemi (Shanghai) International Trading Limited (ph) 8621 6299 3611; wollemiwines@gmail.com. Also to the UK, Indonesia, Japan, Malaysia and Singapore.
Winemaker Stuart and Andrew Watson

Key wines

Margaret (Reserve Cabernet Merlot Malbec)
How it is made: The wine is sorted berry by berry on the new vibrating sorting tables used in Bordeaux, then fermented with cultured yeast for 30 days' total maceration; it then spends 18 months in tight-grain French oak barrels, and is sterile-filtered prior to bottling. 2000 dozen made.

How it tastes: The wine manages to combine complexity with harmony, elegance with intensity, length with finesse; there is a core of red and black berry fruits; tannins and oak are balanced and totally integrated. Cellar to 20 years from vintage.

Best vintages: 2012, 2011, 2008, 2004, 2001

Cabernet Sauvignon
How it is made: Based on the 2.8ha of plantings of cabernet in 1973 and '75. Each batch is hand-picked, destemmed on a sorting table, and fermented either in small open fermenters or small closed fermenters, maceration lasting for a total of 45 days. Matured in French oak barrels (100% new) for 21 months before being lightly filtered. 1000 dozen made.

How it tastes: Deeply coloured, with a medium- to full-bodied palate, ultra-rich and velvety in some vintages, slightly more restrained in others, but with blackberry, plum and ripe tannins almost always present. Cellar to 25 years from vintage.

Best vintages: 2012, 2011, 2008, 2004, 2001

Woodlands

David and Heather Watson began the development of Woodlands in 1973 with the planting of 1.2ha of cabernet sauvignon on the south-facing slope of the estate vineyards. In 1975 two further plots of 0.4ha each were planted: one near the top of the slope, the other near the bottom, and the first block of malbec (0.2ha), was followed in 1976 by cabernet franc (also 0.2ha). In 1985 another plot of cabernet sauvignon (0.8ha) was planted, bringing the total of these original plots to 3.2ha. They receive the greatest number of sunlight hours at Woodlands, but their east-west row orientation, coupled with the south-facing slope, means they are always picked last.

The '73 and '75 plantings gave rise to the first vintage in '79, the wine made by self-trained David Watson, but with encouragement by David Gregg, then Vasse Felix's winemaker. It and the 1980 vintage were 100% cabernet sauvignons.

From 1981 onwards a small percentage (3–8%) of malbec was blended with the cabernet sauvignon, which is only ever produced from the original plantings. Both the 1981 (a bolt from the blue when it won a trophy at the 1982 National Wine Show in Canberra) and 1982 were superb wines, still vibrant and full of fruit 25 years later. The wine was made each year up to 1987, but for a variety of reasons no wine was made in 1988, and from 1989 onwards almost all the grapes were sold (at high prices), keeping enough to make 100 dozen bottles a year under various labels.

Full production recommenced in 2001, the signature wine a cabernet sauvignon from the plantings dating back to 1973 (each year the wine has the name of a family relation). Next is Margaret (the name remaining the same each year) from north-facing blocks, a cabernet blend containing a limited amount of merlot and malbec. This cabernet-based trio has the larger-volume Margaret River Cabernet Merlot at its base.

Off to one side, as it were, are the intermittent releases of around 300 bottles of Reserve de la Cave wines, notably malbec, cabernet franc and pinot noir from the oldest vines, wines of exceptional depth and opulence. Emily is a blend of cabernet franc merlot malbec cabernet sauvignon petit verdot (the blend percentages varying from year to year) from the best rows of each variety on the north-facing slope of the winery, produced in larger, though still limited, quantities. Finally, Chloe chardonnay is always sourced from a 0.8ha block on the south-facing slope, producing 300 dozen bottles a year.

The resumption of winemaking on a full scale marked the arrival of sons Stuart (born 1978) as winemaker, and Andrew (born 1981) on the management/marketing side. It also marked two wholly remarkable blind tastings in 2006 and 2007. The format was essentially the same: the five First Growth Bordeauxs and the so-called Super Seconds matched against an equal number of the best Margaret River cabernet blends, the vintages 2002 for the first, 2003 for the second tasting.

It took a great deal of courage to stage the events; all those attending were wine professionals, but on each occasion Woodlands was in the top five of the 21 wines presented, standing its ground against the First Growths.

Wynns Coonawarra Estate

Est 1897
Memorial Drive, Coonawarra, SA 5263
Open 7 days 10–5
Getting there 4 hours' drive from Adelaide CBD
Contact (08) 8736 2225; cellardoor@wynns.com.au; www.wynns.com.au
Region Coonawarra
Lat 37°18′S
Elev 59m
E° Days 1379
Harvest 11 March–7 May

Estate vineyards NFP
Varieties planted As with other wineries that are part of a much larger wine business under single ownership, vineyard resources are shared across all brands in the group.
Dozens produced NFP
Exports To China and Hong Kong through Jebsens (ph) 852 2923 8777; www.jebsen.com. Also to all major markets.
Winemaker Sue Hodder, Luke Skeer, Sarah Pidgeon

Key wines

Black Label Cabernet Sauvignon

How it is made: The grapes are a selection of up to 80 different parcels taken from up to 30 different vineyard blocks with an average age of 35 years. Three different types of fermenters are used, with 7–12 days on skins, maceration techniques varying with the vineyard source and vintage conditions. Matured for 12–18 months in new and used French oak hogsheads and barriques from 8 coopers selected to match fruit and oak. Occasionally a light egg white fining is used just prior to bottling.

How it tastes: Has intense blackcurrant fruit, with nuances of mulberry, spice and earth to its medium-bodied palate, the tannins ripe and balanced, the oak well integrated. Cellar to 20 years from vintage.

Best vintages: 2010, 2009, 2006, 2005, 2001

John Riddoch Cabernet Sauvignon

How it is made: A selection of the best grapes of each vintage in which the wine is made. The destemmed grapes are open-fermented using wild or cultured yeasts for each lot. The separate parcels are racked three times before the final assemblage (blend) is carried out after 15–20 months in predominantly new French oak hogsheads and barriques.

How it tastes: A spectacularly rich and concentrated wine, with multiple layers of black fruits, tannins and French oak. While needing a minimum of 10 years, it is well balanced from the word go, moderate alcohol levels part of the picture. Cellar to 40 years from vintage.

Best vintages: 2010, 2008, 2006, 2005, 2004

Wynns Coonawarra Estate

If ever the saying 'Truth can be stranger than fiction' needed to be proved, go no further than the waxing and waning of the fortunes of Coonawarra as a region and of what since 1951 has been called Wynns Coonawarra Estate.

The story begins with Scotsmen John Riddoch (who made a fortune selling necessities to gold miners in Victoria) and gardener William Wilson (who intuitively recognised the quality of Coonawarra's terra rossa soil for fruit trees and grapevines). Riddoch had arrived in 1861, and over the next 20 years amassed 51,400ha of freehold, 180km² of leasehold, and a flock of 160,000 sheep.

In 1890, acting on Wilson's advice, he formed the Penola Fruit Colony, subdividing 464ha of terra rossa soil into 4ha blocks and selling these at $50/ha, payable by instalments, with interest at 5%; he subsequently added a further 330ha, also in 4ha lots. Riddoch himself planted 52ha of shiraz and cabernet sauvignon, and smaller amounts of pinot noir and malbec.

He agreed to purchase all the grapes produced, and in 1891 began the construction of the striking stone wine cellars (shown on the labels of every Wynns Coonawarra wine), and continued on undaunted by the Great Australian bank crash of 1893. In 1898 he employed winemaker Ewen McBain, a Roseworthy Agricultural College gold medallist and assistant South Australian government viticulturist.

The quality of the wine was praised, but Riddoch was unable to find markets for the production, and when he died in 1909, his family had no desire to continue the business, and as the legendary Bill Redman said, 'From 1910 to 1950 you can write failure across the face of Coonawarra.' He alone continued to make wine, but all that Riddoch's winery made was brandy, after it was purchased by Adelaide brandy maker Milne & Co. in 1917.

Even the 1946 acquisition of the winery and estate vineyards by Woodley Wines did not guarantee a future. Both winery and vineyards were badly run down, and Woodley only proceeded with the purchase on the basis of Bill and son Owen Redman's agreement to rehabilitate the winery and recommence red winemaking.

Five years later the business was offered for sale as a going concern, and in the face of his own expert wine advisers not to proceed, David Wynn agreed to the purchase, on 19 July 1951. He immediately commissioned Adelaide artist Richard Beck to create the Wynns Coonawarra Estate label, and sent winemaker Ian Hickinbotham to make the first two vintages – 1952 and 1953 Claret.

The Estate has passed through a number of corporate ownerships, culminating in that of Treasury Wine Estates in 2005. While some owners have been more committed than others, a long series of investments sees Wynns Coonawarra Estate as the undisputed king of Coonawarra, owning approximately 70% of the total vineyards planted on the unique terra rossa soil. Those investments include the winemaking legacy of John Wade (creator of the first John Riddoch Cabernet Sauvignon in 1982); a new small-scale winery within the larger winery, dedicated to small batch production of top-quality wines, being built in 2008; the equivalent expenditure being made in rehabilitating the oldest vines, and replanting cabernet sauvignon and shiraz on prime soil, replacing riesling; and the partnership between senior winemaker Sue Hodder and viticulturist Allen Jenkins.

Yabby Lake Vineyard

Est 1998
86–112 Tuerong Road, Tuerong, Vic 3937
Open 7 days 10–5
Getting there 1 hour's drive from Melbourne CBD
Contact (03) 5974 3729; info@yabbylake.com; www.yabbylake.com
Region Mornington Peninsula
Lat 38°20′S
Elev 25–250m
E° Days 1428
Harvest 5 March–30 April
Estate vineyards 79ha
Varieties planted Yabby Lake Vineyard Pinot noir (21), chardonnay (12), pinot gris (6), shiraz (1); **Red Hill Vineyard** Chardonnay (1.5), pinot gris (1), pinot noir (0.5), sauvignon blanc (0.5), gewurztraminer (0.5); **Heathcote Estate** Shiraz (33), grenache (2)
Leased or contracted vineyards 8ha
Varieties planted Barrymore Vineyard Pinot noir (3), pinot gris (3), chardonnay (1), sauvignon blanc (1)
Dozens produced 3500 plus an additional 5000 dozen under Heathcote Estate. No increase planned.
Exports To China through Yabby Lake China (ph) 8620 2264 6835; erin@yabbylake.com and to Hong Kong through Altaya Wines Limited (ph) 852 2523 1945; info@altayawines.com. Also to the UK, Canada and Sweden.
Winemaker Tom Carson, Chris Forge

Key wines

Yabby Lake Single Vineyard Pinot Noir
How it is made: The grapes are hand-picked, with each parcel handled separately in the winery. Destemmed into open fermenters for a 3–4-day cold soak, with some whole bunches. Once the fermentation starts, hand-plunged up to 3 times per day, with a maximum temperature of 32°C. The wine spends around 2 weeks on skins (vintage dependent), whereafter it is pressed to 500-litre French oak puncheons for mlf and 10–11 months' maturation. The wine is not fined, and only lightly filtered.

How it tastes: Bright and clear colour; a fragrant, perfumed cherry blossom bouquet is followed by an elegant red-berried palate in the cooler years, black cherry in the warmer years; the tannins are silky but sustained, the French oak held in restraint. A wine of length and finesse. Cellar to 12 years from vintage.

Best vintages: 2012, 2010, 2008, 2006, 2005

Heathcote Estate Single Vineyard Shiraz
How it is made: Grapes from the 5 separate blocks on the vineyard are hand-picked and handled separately in the winery, creating more than a dozen unique batches of wine. The grapes are fermented in a combination of open and closed fermenters, mostly destemmed, but with some whole bunches. At the end of fermentation the wines are pressed and taken immediately to French oak hogsheads (20% new) for mlf and maturation for between 15 and 17 months.

How it tastes: Good depth and hue; a perfumed bouquet leads into a seamless, fluid palate driven by dark berry fruits with obvious spice nuances, and quality French oak in support. Cellar to 20 years from vintage.

Best vintages: 2012, 2011, 2010, 2006, 2004

Yabby Lake Vineyard

This winery – named after the indigenous freshwater crayfish, *Cheerax destructor*, found in rivers, ponds, dams and lakes over the eastern half of Australia – has come a long way in a short time. The Kirby family had owned land in the Mornington Peninsula for decades prior to their 1992 decision to plant 4ha of vines around their house in Red Hill. Even then this was just a small step; the grapes were sold, and it was not until 1997 that renowned viticulturist Keith Harris came on board to guide the search for prime viticultural land.

That search led to the choice of a substantial property in the Moorooduc area, and to the progressive planting of today's 40ha of vines, which are exclusively used to make the Yabby Lake branded wines. The grapes from the Red Hill vineyard, and from the leased Barrymore Vineyard adjacent to the Yabby Lake vineyard at Tuerong, are only used in the less expensive Red Claw wines.

One year later, in 1998, Robert and Mem Kirby purchased a property on the 500-million-year-old red Cambrian soil of Heathcote, thus creating Heathcote Estate. It was a deliberate strategy to grow and make a wine very different from those of the Mornington Peninsula. (There are an increasing number of wineries on the Peninsula making shiraz, but it is very different from that of Heathcote.)

In the early years of Yabby Lake, Larry McKenna, a former Australian winemaker but long-term pinot noir specialist in the Martinborough region of New Zealand, provided consultancy advice, working in tandem with Keith Harris. In 2004 Tod Dexter, a veteran of the Mornington Peninsula, was appointed winemaker, and steered the business until 2008. In that year, Tom Carson was appointed chief winemaker and general manager, with Tod moving on to concentrate on his own brand.

Carson had graduated in Oenology from what is now Adelaide University in 1991, working at Tim Knappstein in the Clare Valley between then and 1992, moving to the Yarra Valley to work at Coldstream Hills over 1993 and 1994 with (now) wife Nadege Sune. Between 1996 and 2008 he was chief winemaker at Yering Station, making a string of outstanding wines, so when he moved to Yabby Lake, Robert and Mem Kirby had no hesitation in handing the keys to – and responsibility for – Yabby Lake to their children Nina and Clark.

Tom Carson has intimate knowledge of the great wines of Burgundy and the Rhône Valley; he was Dux of the Len Evans Tutorial in 2002, and has an utterly exceptional palate. He was the youngest person (by well over 10 years) to be appointed Chairman of the Royal National Canberra Wine Show, and regards it as his ongoing responsibility to make ever-better wines at Yabby Lake and Heathcote Estate.

On the other side of the fence, as it were, the Kirby family's long position as major shareholder in the film and entertainment distribution company, Village Roadshow Limited, has given Yabby Lake a unique footing in China. Its distribution there is by a company that is majority-owned by a very well connected and equally wealthy Chinese businessman; this has led to cellar doors in Guangzhou, Yangjiang, Zengcheng, Conghua, Qingyuan, Jiujiang and Fogang.

One way or another, it's a story with a long way still to go.

Yalumba

Est 1849
Eden Valley Road, Angaston, SA 5353
Open 7 days 10–5
Getting there 1.25 hours' drive from Adelaide CBD
Contact (08) 8561 3200; info@yalumba.com; www.yalumba.com
Region Eden Valley
Lat 34°35′S
Elev 450m
E° Days 1460
Harvest 20 March–30 April

Estate vineyards 121ha
Varieties planted Barossa Valley Shiraz (30), cabernet sauvignon (20), grenache (14); **Coonawarra** Cabernet sauvignon (32); **Wrattonbully** Cabernet sauvignon (10), viognier (5)
Dozens produced 590 000 No increase planned.
Exports To China through Summergate Fine Wines (ph) toll free 800 820 6929; info@summergate.com and to Hong Kong through Fine Vintage (Far East) Ltd (ph) 852 2896 6108; info@finevintage.com.hk. Also to the UK, the US, Canada, Ireland and Finland.
Winemaker Louisa Rose (Chief), Peter Gambetta, Kevin Glastonbury

Key wines

The Virgilius Eden Valley Viognier
How it is made: Hand-picked grapes are whole-bunch-pressed directly to mature French oak barriques. The wine is fermented by various species of yeast indigenous to the vineyard, each yeast playing a small and subtly different role in the development of the wine, creating layers of richness, complexity, texture and flavour. After fermentation, it is aged on lees with stirring for 10 months. 650 dozen made.

How it tastes: By some distance Australia's greatest example of viognier, the colour gleaming green, the palate elegant, the mouthfeel superb, with mandarin, peach and apricot in a silken web of citrussy acidity. Cellar to 8 years from vintage.

Best vintages: 2010, 2008, 2007, 2006, 2003

The Signature (Cabernet Shiraz)
How it is made: Typically 55% cabernet and 45% shiraz (the cabernet always over 50%) from the Barossa and Eden valleys. Natural yeasts slowly initiate the fermentation, and cultured yeasts are added when the fermentation has progressed about halfway. Total fermentation is about 10 days. All individual blocks are kept separate until blending 12 months after vintage, ultimately bottled after having spent 20 months in American, French and Hungarian hogsheads (30% new). Minimal filtration; both this and The Virgilius are vegan and vegetarian friendly. 3500 dozen made.

How it tastes: Deep in colour, and medium- to full-bodied, with blackberry and blackcurrant fruit easily absorbing the oak in which it was matured; additional bottle age prior to release allows the tannins to soften somewhat and integrate well. Cellar to 25 years from vintage.

Best vintages: 2010, 2005, 2004, 1996, 1992

Yalumba

Yalumba is the chief brand name of Samuel Smith & Sons, the corporate name honouring a remarkable family history. Samuel Smith was clearly no ordinary man: he was 35, with a wife, five children and a successful career as a brewer when he decided to leave the security and comfort of England to make a new home in Australia. Evidently he was then of modest means, for on his arrival in South Australia he moved to Angaston, which was then being created by George Fife Angas. He worked for Angas by day establishing gardens and orchards; by night he began the establishment of a small vineyard on the 12ha of land he had purchased and called Yalumba, an Aboriginal word meaning 'all the country around'.

In 1852 Smith and his 15-year-old son followed the rest of Australia's male population to the Victorian goldfields. After sinking 15 barren shafts, they struck gold on the 16th attempt and returned to Angaston with enough money to purchase a further 32ha, a plough, two horses and a harness, and some money left in the bank to finance the erection of a new house and wine cellars. By the time Smith died in 1889 Yalumba was a thriving business, with markets established both in Australia and England, and medals in international shows and exhibitions to its credit. In 1903 the vintage produced 810 000 litres, and Yalumba was established as one of the principal producers in the region. Samuel's son Sidney built upon the base his father had left, building the imposing two-storey winery and clock tower of blue marble that stand today as part of the vast complex of buildings set in the spacious grounds.

Expansion continued steadily through the first decades of the 20th century; Yalumba was primarily a fortified wine producer, but was making limited quantities of white and red table wine. However, Sidney Hill Smith was responsible for introducing riesling into the Eden Valley, and employed German-trained Rudi Kronberger as winemaker. Kronberger made some remarkable rieslings, introducing early bottling 20 years before it became common practice.

In 1972, after 30 years at the helm, Wyndham Hill Smith handed over the role of managing director to his nephew, Mark Hill Smith, and in due course Mark's cousin (and Wyndham's son) Robert Hill Smith became managing director. He has been an inspired CEO, steering the company through difficult financial days in the early to mid-1980s, selling the fortified wine business at precisely the right time and certainly for the right price, setting the stage for the vibrant company of the 21st century. As well as its highly successful Pewsey Vale, Heggies Vineyard and Hill Smith Estate, anchored in the hills of the Eden Valley, there is also the very large Oxford Landing brand at Qualco, with 260ha in production. Other vineyard holdings are 150ha in the Eden Valley; 35ha in Coonawarra; 170ha in Wrattonbully, for the Smith & Hooper brand; 50ha at Angaston; 70ha in the Barossa Valley proper; and 24ha in Tasmania, for the Jansz Tasmania sparkling wine. Oxford Landing has given Yalumba the critical mass to enable it to develop a wide range of premium, super-premium and ultra-premium wines, sold throughout the world. It also has a major and very successful import business under the Negociants title, and also distributes some leading Australian brands, as does Samuel Smith & Son.

A founding member of Australia's First Families of Wine.

Yarra Yering

Est 1969
Briarty Road, Coldstream, Vic 3770
Open 7 days 10–5
Getting there 1 hour's drive from Melbourne CBD
Contact (03) 5964 9267; www.yarrayering.com
Region Yarra Valley
Lat 37°42'S
Elev 50–350m
E° Days 1253
Harvest 1 March–25 April
Estate vineyards 24.09ha
Varieties planted Shiraz (8.84), cabernet sauvignon (7.75), pinot noir (2.1), merlot (1.5), chardonnay (1.4), malbec (1.2), petit verdot (0.3), Portuguese varieties (predominantly touriga naçional and tinta cão) (1)
Dozens produced 4500 No increase planned.
Exports To China through Kerry Wines (ph) 8621 6032 2999; info.PRC@kerrywines.com and to Hong Kong through Watson's Wine (ph) 852 2606 8828; info@watsonswine.com. Also to the UK, the US, Sweden, Denmark, Singapore, Taiwan, Malaysia, the United Arab Emirates and Indonesia.
Winemaker Paul Bridgeman

Key wines

Dry Red No. 1
How it is made: An estate-grown blend, with cabernet sauvignon dominant, and smaller amounts of merlot, malbec and petit verdot separately picked and separately fermented in ultra-small half-tonne fermenters. Part is given a short 5–7-day ferment, part a longer period (up to 21 days) using a mix of crushed and entire berries, plus stalk inclusion. The wine is pressed and then spends 18–20 months in 100% new French oak barriques, and is neither fined nor filtered. 1100 dozen made.

How it tastes: Magnificent deep, purple-crimson; while medium-bodied and seldom exceeding 13.5% alcohol, has exceptional intensity to its blackcurrant fruit, neatly framed by cedary oak and firm but fine tannins. Cellar to 30+ years from vintage.

Best vintages: 2012, 2010, 2008, 2005, 2004

Dry Red No. 2
How it is made: While the percentage of shiraz is even higher than that of the cabernet sauvignon in Dry Red No. 1, inter-planted viognier and marsanne (and the possibility of mourvedre) are co-fermented using a similar mix of crushed, entire berries and stalks, the only significant difference being a limitation of 33% new French oak. 1100 dozen made.

How it tastes: Superb colour, although sometimes not quite as deep as No. 1; the bouquet is positively perfumed, and the fruit flavours in the mouth have an extra degree of vibrancy, both spice and pepper adding yet further interest, the tannins silky. Cellar to 30+ years from vintage.

Best vintages: 2012, 2010, 2008, 2006, 2004

Yarra Yering

Yarra Yering was established in 1969 after a long search for the perfect site by the late Dr Bailey Carrodus (a doctor of philosophy in plant physiology, not medicine, like so many of his confreres). He died in September 2008 leaving a legacy which deserves that much over-used epithet, unique. The labels for and the names of his two major red wines sound an immediate alert: the labels are hand-drawn, and feature laurel leaves in honour of his long-term partner Laurel, and the names, the enigmatic Dry Red No. 1 and Dry Red No. 2 (never did a back label besmirch a Yarra Yering wine), were all the information that customers were given. Particularly persistent enquiries would reveal that No. 1 was a Bordeaux blend, with cabernet sauvignon the dominant variety, and No. 2, a shiraz-dominant wine, with some viognier interplanted (the first such in Australia) and the possibility of other unspecified varieties, perhaps including a splash of mourvedre. The pinot noir itself was conventionally named, as was the chardonnay and viognier.

For several decades he alone made the wine, eschewing any vintage help (other than Laurel's). To achieve this, he had constructed square fermentation vessels, with stainless steel lining a half-tonne box looking rather like a tea chest, which could then be tipped into a basket press with a capacity of half a tonne, and thence to barrel. To the end he denied ever having to add acid to the magnificently deeply coloured red wines, and likewise refused to have analysis done, except when it was needed for export approval and, when the law changed, to state the alcohol on the label. The vines are dry-grown, and all the vineyard operations are carried out by hand.

In the 1990s he purchased two adjacent properties, one already planted and fronting Maddens Lane, which gave rise to Underhill Shiraz, and the other, on the opposite side of the vineyard, a vacant block which he contour-planted to the Portuguese port varieties, fulfilling a long-held ambition to make a vintage port-style wine, which he labelled Portsorts (since changed to Potsorts). The same vineyard block also produces a table wine blend, primarily touriga naçional, but also tinta cão, tinta amarela, alvarelhao, roriz and sousão; it is labelled Dry Red Wine No. 3.

The white wines defy conventional analysis and counter the trend towards finer and more elegant chardonnay made in other parts of the Yarra Valley, but Dry Red No. 1 and Dry Red No. 2 (and, not infrequently, Underhill Shiraz) are in many ways the Yarra Valley's answer to Wendouree. They are magnificent wines of great complexity, depth and texture, and very long-lived.

Most of the wine is sold to faithful recipients of the annual mailing list and visitors to the cellar door, but Yarra Yering has the habit of popping up in the most unexpected places around the world, usually top-end restaurants. In June 2009 Yarra Yering was purchased by Ed Peter, with the purchase of Warramate following in early 2011. Ed Peter's first Australian investment was in Kaesler Wines. He made it clear he did not intend to depart from the practices and principles of Bailey Carrodus, and also that Warramate was to be run as a separate winery producing the same wines as heretofore.

Yeringberg

Est 1863
Maroondah Highway, Coldstream, Vic 3770
Open By appt
Getting there 1 hour's drive from Melbourne CBD
Contact (03) 9739 1453; info@yeringberg.com; www.yeringberg.com
Region Yarra Valley
Lat 37°42'S
Elev 50–350m
E° Days 1253
Harvest 1 March–25 April

Estate vineyards 3.66ha
Varieties planted Viognier (1), chardonnay (0.53), cabernet sauvignon (0.53), shiraz (0.42), pinot noir (0.39), marsanne (0.26), roussanne (0.17), cabernet franc (0.12), merlot (0.11), petit verdot (0.06), malbec (0.05)
Dozens produced 1500 No increase planned.
Exports To China through Pran Cellar Australia (ph) 86 21 5178 0108; tina@cellaraustralia.com and to Hong Kong through Kedington Wines (Far East) Co. Ltd (ph) 852 2898 9323; info@kedwines.com. Also to the US.
Winemaker Guill and Sandra de Pury

Key wines

Yeringberg

How it is made: Simply named, but in fact a cabernet sauvignon-dominant blend including lesser amounts of cabernet franc, merlot, malbec and petit verdot, each separately hand-picked (and sorted) in the vineyard, and sorted again in the winery. The grapes are destemmed and crushed within 30 minutes of being picked, then fermented with cultured yeast in small open fermenters, hand-plunged, and basket-pressed after 9 days into French oak barriques (30–40% new) for 20–22 months, racked four times. SO_2, but no tannins or enzymes added; fined with egg white if needed. 450 dozen made.

How it tastes: Typically only 13% alc/vol, with bright colour, then a quite lovely display of black and redcurrant fruit supported by silky tannins and integrated, high-quality French oak. Cellar to 30 years from vintage.

Best vintages: 2012, 2010, 2008, 2005, 2004

Shiraz

How it is made: Made from 3 clones, each picked separately; vineyard and winery sorting as for the cabernet blend. About 25% whole bunches are included in the fermenters, and 2–3% viognier is crushed with the shiraz. Matured in French oak hogsheads (25% new, vintage dependent) for 18–19 months, racked 3 times, only fined if necessary. 450 dozen made.

How it tastes: Superbly elegant, medium-bodied wine with a fusion of red and black fruits, licorice, multi spices and hallmark silky tannins. Cellar to 30 years from vintage.

Best vintages: 2013, 2012, 2010, 2008, 2006

Yeringberg

Yeringberg was established in 1863 by Baron Guillaume de Pury, one of the foremost members of the influential and wealthy Swiss families who were responsible for the establishment of the Yarra Valley wine industry. In 1862 he purchased part of the vast Yering vineyard from Paul de Castella, and named it Yeringberg, in recognition of the fact that much of it was located on a large hill which looked out over the main bulk of Yering. It was on top of this hill that the first winery was built, and the house. The property has never passed out of the hands of the family, the present owners being Guillaume de Pury, grandson of the founder, and his wife, Katherine.

Much of the production of Yeringberg was destined for export: by the late 1860s almost 30ha of vineyard were established, and this area was subsequently expanded. The first winery has long since gone, but the one erected in 1885 still stands in near-new condition. The striking two-storey wooden building with a stone basement was a showpiece of technological design in its day. The grapes were carried to the top storey in a hydraulic lift and then crushed into railway trucks which ran along the top storey on a miniature railway line. From here on the winery operated entirely on gravity. Fermentation and pressing took place on the first floor, maturation in the basement.

The original vineyard was planted to shiraz, pinot noir, marsanne, trebbiano, verdelho, pinot gris, pinot blanc and gouais. It was for the marsanne that Yeringberg was most famous. François de Castella commented that, 'Yeringberg has produced some of the finest white wines ever grown in the southern hemisphere.' A few bottles of the wine made in the last decade of the 19th century and the first two decades of the 20th were part of a small museum stock at the winery and, tasted by me and others at various times between 1985 and 2000, all had exceptional freshness and youth.

When in 1969 Guill de Pury (as he prefers to be known) was persuaded by friends to re-establish a tiny portion of the vineyard on the exact spot planted by his grandfather 100 years earlier, the first grape chosen was marsanne. The varieties also included shiraz, which has had a unique history: planted by Frederick de Pury in the 1860s; removed after the 1921 vintage; planted by Guill de Pury in 1970 and pulled out after the 1981 vintage; and replanted by David (and Guill) de Pury in 1999. The 1980 and 1981 vintages were and are superb wines, and the wheel of fortune has turned sufficiently for shiraz to once again form part of the patchwork quilt of the 3ha vineyard.

Since none of the estate plantings exceeds 0.5ha, the quantity of each wine is of course limited. An 8ha block was planted at the behest of Accolade, with the grapes automatically going to Accolade. Ultimately, full operating ownership will revert to de Pury ownership, and children Sandra de Pury (winemaker) and David de Pury (viticulturist) stand to inherit one of the finest vineyards in the Yarra Valley. The wines are primarily sold by mail order (no cellar door sales) and through limited fine wine retail and restaurant venues in Sydney and Melbourne.

Yering Station

Est 1988
38 Melba Highway, Yarra Glen, Vic 3775
Open 7 days 10–5
Getting there 55 minutes' drive from Melbourne CBD
Contact (03) 9730 0100; info@yering.com; www.yering.com
Region Yarra Valley
Lat 37°42'S
Elev 50–350m
E° Days 1253
Harvest 1 March–25 April

Estate vineyards 67ha
Varieties planted Pinot noir (30), chardonnay (18), shiraz (14), cabernet sauvignon (5)
Leased or contracted vineyards 39ha
Varieties planted Chardonnay (14), shiraz (14), pinot noir (10), cabernet sauvignon (1)
Dozens produced 70 000 No increase planned.
Exports To China through The Wine Republic (ph) 010 5869 7050; info@thewinerepublic.com and to Hong Kong through Northeast Wines & Spirits Ltd (ph) 852 2873 5733; www.northeast.com.hk. Also to all major markets.
Winemaker Willy Lunn, Darren Rathbone

Key wines

Pinot Noir
How it is made: The hand-picked bunches are destemmed but not crushed, and the whole berries are chilled for a 6-day pre-fermentation cold-soak, with daily punch downs and occasional rack-and-return; at the end of fermentation the wine is pressed into 500-litre French oak puncheons (30% new), and aged for 12 months. The wine is given gentle crossflow-filtration prior to bottling. 2500 dozen made.

How it tastes: The bouquet has the fragrance of cool-grown pinot noir, the fresh, light- to medium-bodied palate with red cherry and wild strawberry fruit flavours, the French oak well integrated and balanced. The finish has the finesse and length essential for all good-quality pinot noirs. Cellar to 8 years from vintage.

Best vintages: 2012, 2010, 2008, 2006, 2005

Shiraz Viognier
How it is made: Like the pinot noir, utilises cultured yeast added after the destemmed, whole berry fruit has had a 5-day cold-soak; the 5% viognier is co-fermented, and the wine pressed to 225-litre French oak barriques (35% new) for 18 months' maturation. Crossflow-filtration prior to bottling puts a final polish on one of the most enjoyable and consistent of the Yering Station wines.

How it tastes: It has vibrant red and black cherry and plum fruit, fine tannins and gently cedary oak. Cellar to 20 years from vintage.

Best vintages: 2012, 2010, 2008, 2006, 2005

Yering Station

The establishment date of this Yarra Valley landmark could be said to be 1838, when the Scottish-born Ryrie brothers travelled south from New South Wales over the Great Dividing Range with their cattle, and took up a 17 500ha grazing licence, marking their arrival (in 1837) by planting the first grapevines the following year in what was to become Victoria. The next possible date could be 1850, when Paul, the first member of the Swiss de Castella family, purchased the land, in due course extending the vineyard with cuttings imported from Château Lafite in 1854, and building a large winery, with equipment purchased at the 1859 Bordeaux Exhibition in Paris. That year also saw the construction of the red sandstock brick building that houses today's cellar door for Yering Station.

The de Castella family was to head much of the viticultural history of Victoria until 1940, 20 years after the last vines had been removed, the region 'falling to the cow', in the words of François de Castella. The next establishment date to be used is 1988, when a small vineyard was planted; the wines were contract-made at St Huberts from 1991 to 1996.

In 1996, the adjacent Chateau Yering property was offered for sale by auction, together (in the first instance) with Yering Station, but with the option to simply buy Chateau Yering (and its magnificent house). That option was exercised, and the Rathbone family purchased the Yering Station portion. Design work immediately began with a leading Melbourne architect given the brief to establish a landmark tourist destination as well as a large modern winery. There are also conference facilities in the building.

By the end of 1996 up to 100 workmen were on site, continuing to work through the normally quiet mid-December to mid-January period, and the winery was ready for the 1997 vintage the following February. It was a remarkable achievement, and the large restaurant, with panoramic views up the Yarra Valley to the mountains behind (often the deep blue colour which so fascinated the Swiss vignerons a century earlier) provides some of the finest food to be found in the many excellent winery restaurants dotted across the landscape.

The winery was designed to accommodate the sparkling Yarrabank wines, a joint venture between the Champagne house Devaux and the Rathbone family, as well as the 70 000 dozen bottles of Yering Station wines. Making use of the gentle hillside location of the development, the winery is partly situated underneath the building visitors see on approach, and can be accessed by stairs leading down from the conference/office section of the building.

The business has been fortunate to have the services of two exceptional wine-makers: Tom Carson from 1997 to 2008, and since then Willy Lunn. Lunn spent 15 years (beginning in 1984) at Petaluma under guru Brian Croser, then two years at Shaw + Smith, followed by several years working in Oregon at the Croser family winery, which continued the sparkling wine experience he had gained at Petaluma.

Yering Station's principal focus is on pinot noir, shiraz viognier and chardonnay (all three made in both varietal and Reserve mode), but also makes excellent barrel-fermented rose; MRV, a marsanne, roussanne and viognier blend; and high-quality cabernet sauvignon.

Regional List

State	Region	Subregion	Winery
NSW	Canberra District		Clonakilla
	Hunter Valley		Brokenwood
			Lake's Folly
			McWilliam's Mount Pleasant
			Meerea Park
			Thomas Wines
			Tyrrell's
	Riverina		McWilliam's
QLD	Granite Belt		Boireann Winery
SA	Adelaide Hills		Ashton Hills
			Geoff Weaver Wines
			Petaluma
			Shaw + Smith
	Barossa Valley		Charles Melton
			Grant Burge
			Hentley Farm Wines
			Penfolds
			Peter Lehmann
			Rockford
			Seppeltsfield
			Torbreck Vintners
			Turkey Flat
			Wolf Blass
	Clare Valley		Grosset
			Kilikanoon
			Wendouree
	Coonawarra		Balnaves of Coonawarra
			Majella
			Wynns Coonawarra Estate
	Eden Valley		Henschke
			Pewsey Vale
			Yalumba
	McLaren Vale		d'Arenberg
			Hardys
			Wirra Wirra
	South Australia (Piccadilly Valley)		Tapanappa
TAS	East Coast Tasmania		Freycinet
	Northern Tasmania		Bay of Fires/House of Arras
			Tamar Ridge
	Southern Tasmania		Domaine A
			Stefano Lubiana
VIC	Beechworth		Giaconda
	Geelong		Bannockburn Vineyards
			By Farr/Farr Rising
			Scotchmans Hill
	Gippsland		Bass Phillip
	Glenrowan		Baileys of Glenrowan
	Grampians		Best's Wines
			Mount Langi Ghiran Vineyards
			Seppelt

State	Region	Subregion	Winery
VIC	*Heathcote*		Jasper Hill
	Henty		Crawford River Wines
	King Valley		Brown Brothers
	Macedon Ranges		Bindi Wine Growers Curly Flat
	Mornington Peninsula		Main Ridge Estate Moorooduc Estate Paringa Estate Port Phillip Estate and Kooyong Stonier Wines Yabby Lake Vineyard
	Nagambie Lakes		Tahbilk
	Pyrenees		Dalwhinnie Summerfield
	Rutherglen		All Saints Estate Campbells Chambers Rosewood Morris Stanton & Killeen Wines
	Sunbury		Craiglee
	Upper Goulburn		Delatite
	Yarra Valley		Coldstream Hills De Bortoli Wines (Yarra Valley) Domaine Chandon Mount Mary Oakridge Wines Seville Estate TarraWarra Estate Yarra Yering Yeringberg Yering Station
WA	*Geographe*		Capel Vale
	Great Southern		Forest Hill Vineyard
		Denmark	Burch Family Wines
		Frankland River	Alkoomi Frankland Estate
		Mount Barker	West Cape Howe Wines
		Porongurup	Castle Rock Estate Duke's Vineyard
	Margaret River		Brookland Valley Burch Family Wines Cape Mentelle Cullen Wines Devil's Lair Leeuwin Estate Moss Wood Vasse Felix Voyager Estate Woodlands
	Pemberton		Bellarmine Wines
	Swan Valley		Houghton

Published in 2014 by Hardie Grant Books

Hardie Grant Books (Australia)
Ground Floor, Building 1
658 Church Street
Richmond, Victoria 3121
www.hardiegrant.com.au

Hardie Grant Books (UK)
Dudley House, North Suite
34–35 Southampton Street
London WC2E 7HF
www.hardiegrant.co.uk

A Cataloguing-in-Publication entry is available from the catalogue of the National Library
of Australia at www.nla.gov.au
James Halliday's Top 100 Australian Wineries
ISBN 9781742708171

Cover design & photograph by Phil Campbell Design
Typeset in 10/11.5pt Utopia by Cannon Typesetting
Printed in Australia by Griffin Press

The paper this book is printed on is certified against the
Forest Stewardship Council® Standards. Griffin Press holds
FSC chain of custody certification SGS-COC-005088. FSC
promotes environmentally responsible, socially beneficial
and economically viable management of the world's forests.